The Legitimation of a Revolution

The Legitimation of a Revolution
The Yugoslav Case

Bogdan Denis Denitch

New Haven and London, Yale University Press, 1976

Library of Congress catalog card number: 75-18170
International standard book number: 0-300-01906-8

Designed by John O. C. McCrillis and set in Baskerville type.
Printed in the United States of America by
The Colonial Press Inc., Clinton, Massachusetts.

Published in Great Britain, Europe, and Africa by Yale University Press, Ltd., London.
Distributed in Latin America by Kaiman & Polon, Inc., New York City; in Australasia by Book & Film Services, Artarmon, N.S.W., Australia; in Japan by John Weatherhill, Inc., Tokyo.

Contents

List of Tables and Figures   vii

Acknowledgments   xi

1 A New Socialist Model   1

2 Relevance of the Yugoslav Experience:
Conflicts and Challenges   17

3 Conquest and Consolidation   29

4 Uprooting the Traditional Order   55

5 The League of Communists and Social Mobility   82

6 The Institutionalization of Multinationalism   105

7 The New Political Culture   149

8 The Question of Legitimacy   185

Appendix: Yugoslav Opinion Makers and
Their Social Role   207

Bibliography   233

Index   247

List of Tables and Figures

TABLES

1. Job Aspirations of Village Youth, Croatia, 1970   66
2. Religious Affiliations in Prewar and Postwar Yugoslavia   70
3. Attitudes toward Church Socialization of the Young, by Educational Level   71
4. Religious Identification and Practice of Students and Their Parents   72
5. Social Background of Students in Yugoslavia   77
6. Students of Working-Class Origin and Women Students, by Faculties   78
7. Seniority among 1958 Membership of the League of Communists   84
8. LCY Seniority and the First Job Taken after 1944 (Opinion Makers)   86
9. LCY Seniority and Role in NOB (Opinion Makers)   88
10. Representation of Various Strata in the League of Communists (1968)   91
11. Shifts in Social Composition of the League of Communists   94
12. League of Communists Membership Rate among Employed Persons   96
13. New LCY Members since 1968, by Occupation   99
14. Serbs in Higher Administration, 1939   106
15. Rate of Serbian Occupation of Major Ministries, 1918–41   107
16. Composition of Federal Presidency by Republic and Nationality   108
17. Nationality Breakdown by Republic, 1971   109
18. Breakdown of Top Administrative Bodies by Republic   110
19. National Composition of Federal Organs of Administration in 1969   111
20. Republic Origin of Functionaries Appointed by the Federal Assembly in 1968   111
21. Officer Corps of the Yugoslav Peoples' Army by Nationality, 1971   114

22. National Composition of LCY Membership, 1968 and 1971   121
23. Federal Legislative and Executive Activity in Yugoslavia, 1953–68   133
24. Occupational Background of Parliamentary Deputies in Socialist Yugoslavia   134
25. Educational Background of Parliamentary Deputies   135
26. Yugoslav Parliamentary Deputies by Age, 1953–69   135
27. Annual Growth Rate of Social Product Per Capita for Various Countries, 1952–66   140
28. Growth of Social Product in Yugoslavia, by Republic, 1952–68   141
29. Population Growth in Yugoslavia, by Republic   142
30. Relative Per Capita Income, by Republic, 1952–68   143
31. Illiteracy Rates in Yugoslavia, by Republic, 1970   144
32. Employment Structure by Republic, 1968   145
33. Social Composition of Workers' Councils, 1970   161
34. Self-Management and Socialism   163
35. Self-Management and Socialism, by League Membership   163
36. Self-Management and Socialism, by Age   163
37. The Power Structure within Enterprises   164
38. Degree of Dissatisfaction Elimination of Workers' Council Would Cause   165
39. The Meaning of Self-Management   167
40. Beneficiaries of Self-Management   167
41. Attitudes toward Self-Management among Six Sub-groups of Yugoslav Society, 1969   169
42. Comparative Analysis of the Efficiency of Economic Systems in Yugoslavia, 1911–67   170
43. Ownership of Fixed Capital in Economic Organizations, 1955–69   171
44. Attitudes toward Existing Income Differences (Slovenia, 1971)   172
45. Desired Income Differences, by Educational Level (Slovenia, 1971)   173
46. Verbal Egalitarianism by Educational Level (Slovenia, 1971)   174
47. Typology of Regime Authority   198
48. Income Distribution in Yugoslavia, by Republic, 1971   202

49. How Should the Younger Generations Be Educated
    about Nationality?   204
50. Summary of Responses to National Identity Question, in
    Croatia   205
A1 Occupations of Fathers of Public Opinion Makers   211
A2 Educational Background of Opinion Makers and Their
    Fathers   212
A3 Educational Background of Opinion Makers, by Group   213
A4 University Training Completed by Opinion Makers   214
A5 Membership in the League of Communists   216
A6 Employment Background of Opinion Makers   218
A7 Policy Opinions of Opinion Leaders   228

FIGURES

1. Percentage of Different Persons Mentioned by Each
   Group as Generally Influential According to the Sector of
   the Person Mentioned   222
2. Percentage of Different Persons Mentioned by Each
   Group as Generally Influential in Own Field According
   to the Sector of the Person Mentioned   223

Acknowledgments

In this study of the consolidation and legitimation of a revolution in a single country, I have had more help than can properly be acknowledged. It is, I hope, only the first in a series of such studies that will expand the debate on revolutions to underdeveloped areas. I have found invaluable for my purpose discussions with Yugoslav colleagues, particularly Rudi Supek, Mihailo Markovic, and Mladen Zvonarevic. Wolfgang Leonhard's persistent interest in developments in Yugoslavia and his encouragement have been of immense importance, as has that of Serge Mallet and Jean Pronteau. Juan Linz and Joseph LaPalombara have pressed me to complete this case study as a preliminary to further comparative work on social change and social revolutions.

Throughout the writing of the book, I have received unstinting aid and advice from my thesis sponsor and colleague, Allen Barton. The interaction with other colleagues at the Bureau of Applied Social Research has helped produce whatever methodological solidity the study has. Colleagues in the Research Institute on International Affairs, particularly Seweryn Bialer, Charles Gati, and Zbigniew Brzezinski, have added valuable insights. Charles Kadushin of Teachers College has been generous with the data he has developed in his studies of networks, and the administrator of the International Study of Opinion Makers, Selma Lenihan, has been indispensable. My research assistant, Vladimir Gligorov, has been enormously helpful in discussing the individual chapters. Needless to say, the errors and weaknesses of the book are all mine and are in no sense the responsibility of those who have generously aided.

This study could not have been attempted without the financial support of the Carnegie Foundation, the Ford Foundation, and the International Research and Exchange Board (IREX).

The Legitimation of a Revolution

1

A New Socialist Model

This is a detailed study of the development of the social and political bases of legitimacy of the revolutionary regime in Yugoslavia. I hope it raises more questions than it answers about the general body of writing and theory on social change and social revolution. Although a number of implications of general relevance for other revolutionary regimes are developed in chapter 2, the aims of the study are deliberately limited by my concentration on the single case of Yugoslavia. One of the reasons for this is my explicit bias, which holds that theories about model building and revolutionary transformations have all too often been at the expense of content and that a more productive way to approach the development of theory about social transformation is by intense, detailed studies of specific revolutions. This is all the more the case since we often lack sufficiently detailed information about given social revolutions to be able to develop broad generalizations. We know too little, for example, about the attitudes and beliefs of the peasant soldiers during the Chinese revolution, about the organizational methods utilized by the Bolsheviks in linking up diverse publics to which they had appealed, or, for that matter, about the degree of legitimacy and social support the old order had. It is too easy to conclude that, because the old social order was overthrown, it had lost legitimacy. In both the Chinese and Yugoslav cases, this is, in my opinion, true. However, it is an open question whether, in the absence of a foreign invasion and the physical destruction of the old social order by the foreign occupier, the Communist parties of Yugoslavia and China could have carried out the tasks they had set for themselves.

The Yugoslav case presents a particularly interesting problem because, by and large, it is a case where these tasks were primarily undertaken by native Communist forces which, having consolidated political power by the end of the Second World War, had to undertake at least two new campaigns to redefine the basis of their political legitimacy. The first, of course, was the result of the break with the Soviet bloc, which forced the Yugoslav Communists to develop their own national ideological variant of communism, in counter-position not only to the bloc but to the entire course of their own history, and to all of the political instincts developed in the party over the formative years. The second and, in my opinion, even more profound break occurred over a longer period—beginning roughly in 1958 and continuing into the present—when the Yugoslav Communists addressed themselves to the task of developing mass-based participatory institutions as a substitute for the existing models of social and political institutions under both capitalism and state socialism.[1]

Thus, the Yugoslav revolution can be considered in three stages: the stage of consolidation of power, characterized by a bitter guerrilla war which contained within it a war of liberation and a civil war; a stage during which the Yugoslav experience was probably most analogous to that of the Chinese Communists in the equivalent period: the stage of struggling for national independence and developing a specific socialist identity; and, finally, the stage of developing a social and political system based on the institution of workers' self-management.

In examining the consolidation and institutionalization of this revolution, we enter into an area relatively neglected by political sociologists as compared to historians and political scientists. The changes that occurred in Yugoslavia represented a sharp discontinuity with past social organizations and institutions and were revolutionary rather than incremental. It is my argument that it was precisely the mass mobilization of previously uninvolved strata during the first stage that made possible the successful completion of the second and the probable success of the third. This mobilization took place during the process of struggling for state power when the Yugoslav Communists developed a mass party, which emerged from

1. A poignant description of the difficulties in breaking with the bloc and their own past can be found in Vladimir Dedijer's *The Battle Stalin Lost* (New York: Universal Library, 1972), particularly pp. 141–51, where he describes the telegram sent from the party's Fifth Congress, ending with, "Long live our great friend, Josif Visarionovich Stalin!" Also see Milovan Djilas, *Conversations with Stalin* (New York: Praeger, 1958).

the civil war in 1945 with over 140,000 members.[2] Broad, active strata emerged during the revolution whose further development became linked with the continuous rule of the party and the institutions of postrevolutionary Yugoslavia.

Having alluded earlier to the similarities between the Chinese and Yugoslav cases, I also acknowledge that the differences are as salient. However, a central unifying factor linking these two great revolutions is the fact that they were fundamentally carried out by indigenous communist elites pursuing a strategy with only partial support from Moscow and that both had developed indigenous forms of mass mobilization diverging from the Russian pattern. It is therefore probably no accident that these are the first two great variants of national communism and that both, I would assert, are left-wing variants, that is, variants of national communism that regard themselves as more orthodox than Moscow. The end results are of course different. Yugoslavia, despite recent attempts to tighten up the party structure and crack down on both ethnic nationalists and liberal intellectuals, has produced what is by all accounts and by all measures known to me the least repressive and most open society run by a communist party.

Yugoslavia is open in a number of ways. To begin with, its frontiers are open to the extent that three and a half million Yugoslavs traveled abroad for tourism in 1972, and millions of foreign tourists have vacationed in Yugoslavia in recent years. Yugoslav film, television, and radio broadcast Western European and American plays and entertainment to the practical exclusion of contributions from Eastern Europe and the Soviet Union. The Yugoslav press is so much more open than the press of the other countries ruled by communist parties that it is in a different category and suffers from different problems. For example, in a study of the relative freedom of the press in selected countries conducted in 1966 by the Freedom and Information Center of the University of Missouri, the Yugoslav press was categorized as a "transitional system," between a partially controlled and a free press, a category in which it alone of the presses of communist countries is found. Precensorship has long been abolished in Yugoslavia, which is not to

---

2. Josip Broz Tito, *Report to the Fifth Congress CPY* (Belgrade: Komunist, 1948); also Alexander Rankovic's report to the same congress, available in English.

say that prosecutors do not from time to time move to prohibit an article or a book, and that attempts are not made to censor occasional movies. The debate on economic questions, social issues, problems of stratification, distributive justice, and the like is remarkably open to both party and nonparty contributors, and most critics of the Yugoslav system can easily find data in Yugoslav publications to buttress their arguments.

In this openness of Yugoslavia lies one of the problems of analyzing the changes in the Yugoslav regime. Most Western scholars operate within a framework shaped by early communist studies, particularly those of the Soviet Union, where the absence of open debate led to inferential reasoning; thus cleavages on issues have often been inferred from miniscule changes in formal party structure and leadership. The tendency therefore has been to assume that what one sees or reads in a communist country is only the tip of an iceberg reflecting far deeper cleavages and conflicts. Most American observers of Yugoslavia have stressed cleavages and conflicts that are presumed to be deeper than the ones expressed in the press, and the central questions raised almost invariably are: "What are the forces leading to the dissolution of a Yugoslav regime or system?" and "What is the fate of Yugoslavia likely to be after the death of Marshal Tito?" My approach is different in that I ask the opposite questions: "What are the forces leading to the consolidation and continued stability of the regime?" and "What are the forces that seek and need a Yugoslav socialist system?"

This leads us to an examination of the strata on which the social power of the present Yugoslav regime rests. I believe the key to the future development of Yugoslavia lies in the growing modernizing sector whose interests do *not* require a reversal of the social and political change that followed the revolution. When the institutions and groups involved are examined, the picture that emerges gives some clearer ideas about the prospects of continuity for the Yugoslav social and political systems.

First, beginning with social classes, it is clear that the peasantry, although it formed the bulk of the Partisan army in World War II [3] and benefited from the social changes launched by the revolution, is by and large outside of the political system today, neither hostile nor

3. See the figures for 1945 Communist Party membership in chapter 4.

particularly supportive. However, one should immediately add that this peasantry, rapidly diminishing in social weight and bereft of political power, is tied to the modern sector by the fact that it represented the point of departure in the enormous social mobility that occurred after the war, and therefore many if not most peasant families are linked through relatives and acquaintances to industrial workers and intelligentsia.[4] In any case, the peasants at this point are politically and socially neutralized and do not form a potential base for an opposition movement. Their fate apparently is to continue to diminish in numbers and to remain culturally disadvantaged compared with the urban population.

The Yugoslav industrial working class, particularly that larger section which has moved into industry from a rural background, represents the basic clientele of the current regime. No matter how specific policies may work out at a given moment, the regime has enabled them to make an enormous leap forward in social status, has permitted their entry into a modern life style,[5] and, in terms of its norms and symbols, acts in their direct interests. As the third stage of the Yugoslav revolution develops, this growing and vital class will assume more weight and, in my opinion, will increasingly play a stabilizing role in Yugoslav society as a whole. With its great social and geographic mobility, this stratum is uprooted from its traditional particularist background and therefore is least responsive to separatist ethnic nationalism and least likely to be hostile either to the institutions of self-management or to the social system as a whole. It is, further, a group whose social weight has been growing in recent years and which has not yet begun to utilize fully the existing opportunities for participation in the system. The leap from the village to urban existence for most Yugoslavs occurs through the factory, and it is the factory or the enterprise that forms the main locus of political and social interaction.

Turning to the intelligentsia, two broad groups can be identified: the technical intelligentsia and the so-called humanistic intelligentsia. The first group is generally the product of postwar Yugoslav

4. Borislav Dirukovic, "Ucese seljaka komunista," *Sociologija Sela* 8, nos. 27–28 (1970).

5. Bette Denich, "Social Environment and Economic Niches," in Proceedings of the Sixty-Ninth Annual Meeting, American Anthropological Association, 1970 (mimeo.).

society and particularly of the vast expansion of the educational system. It has benefited directly from the social mobility of the postrevolutionary years, and, while at times critical of the specific aspects of the economic, social, and political system, it is rooted precisely in those institutions which are central to modern Yugoslav society and generally reflects the values of the new Yugoslav political culture.[6] The technical intelligentsia thus represents one of the bases of support of the present regime, although its support is often modified by specific status demands which are potentially threatened by the institutions of workers' self-management.

The second group, a more complex one, historically played a major role in the burgeoning nationalism of the previously repressed nationalities of Eastern Europe. It is a heterogeneous group within which at least two subgroups can be identified. The first consists of the gatekeepers of traditional culture, who are the products of the faculties of philosophy and philology and have been the major carriers of linguistic and traditionalist nationalism in Yugoslavia. This group in general denies the legitimacy of the current regime because, among other reasons, it has not recruited leadership from strata traditionally prepared for such roles. The new leadership does not have the cultural and linguistic skills and training associated with the traditional elite.

The second subgroup within the humanistic intelligentsia centers around intellectuals loosely defined as Marxist humanists, who, while perceived as critics by the regime, in fact support it even while criticizing the specifics of day-to-day rule.[7]

In summary, the intelligentsia is split into opponents, partial supporters, and supporters playing the role of a loyal opposition. Regarding the first of these, the opponents, one more point should be made here. The opposition of the traditionalist intelligentsia is, of course, antiregime and anticommunist in its essence, but it is formulated primarily in ethnic nationalist terms. Although the carriers of that nationalism, being manipulators of symbols, often assume more weight in debate and in the media, both domestic and foreign, than their social weight would indicate, I believe that traditional nationalism has only sporadic and very limited support. I should also note that this schematic outline of Yugoslav social strata

6. Rudi Supek, *Humanisticka inteligencija i politika* (Zagreb: Razlog, 1971), pp. 63–86.
7. Ibid.

leaves out the remnants of the old educated middle classes, which can in general be treated as a part of the traditionalist intelligentsia. This group is in any case gradually vanishing through attrition.

A word about the institutions of the Yugoslav polity is now appropriate. In prewar Yugoslavia the basic institutional framework was provided by the civil service, the army, and the police, whose role was legitimated by the churches, particularly the Serbian Orthodox church, and the myth of national liberation. No party was genuinely Yugoslavia-wide, and therefore the party structure represented a coalition of national and regional parties and notables. The parties thus acted more as a channel for particularist demands than as a unifying cement. Today the army remains as a major Yugoslavia-wide institution, although formally far less active in the day-to-day politics of the state. Basically it acts as an institution through the organization of the League of Communists of the Armed Forces (LCAF), which is sometimes described as the seventh party in Yugoslavia.[8] In addition to the army, which, in terms of its ethnic composition and the classes from which it recruits its officer corps, is far more of a Yugoslav institution than was the prewar army, as my figures will show, there is of course the pivot of the Yugoslav system, the League of Communists of Yugoslavia (LCY). The league,[9] at least in the provincial cities and industrial centers, can be said, practically speaking, to include the most politically active sector of the population. It now numbers over a million, and although there is some tendency to regionalism it is still basically a unifying force representing the interests of the most modern and still numerically increasing sectors of Yugoslav society—the urban working class, the technical and general intelligentsia, and the modern administrative strata.

8. Yugoslavia is organized as a federation, with six republics and two autonomous provinces. Each of the six republics has its own party organization, although the LCAF is larger than the parties of two of the republics.

The six republics (Serbia, Croatia, Montenegro, Slovenia, Macedonia, and Bosnia-Herzegovina) are basically national homes of the constituent ethnic groups, with the exception of Bosnia-Herzegovina, where no single ethnic group has a majority. The two autonomous provinces associated with the republic of Serbia have large ethnic minorities: in Kosovo Albanians form the majority of the local population, and in Vojvodina, where there is a Serbian majority, there are large Hungarian, Croatian, and Slovak minorities.

9. Here and throughout the text, "league" refers to the LCY and not to the LCAF.

A third institution, the importance of which must diminish in time but which is still present on the political scene, is the organization of the Veterans of the War of Liberation (SUBNOR), a statewide organization deeply committed to maintaining the institutions for which its members fought. The trade unions, also active on a statewide level, become more important with the growth of the industrial working class and the increasing autonomy of the economy.

Absent from the present Yugoslav scene is anything resembling the massive, unified, centralized civil service of prewar Yugoslavia. The federal civil service is increasingly subordinated to the Federal Assembly, and both are based more and more on the constituent republics and provinces. The institutions that do cut across republics—the army, the league, the veterans, and trade unions—are all at least formally nongoverning institutions. On the other hand, the administrative and economic institutions that govern the day-to-day lives of most Yugoslavs are regional, local, or, in the case of the self-managing institutions, enterprisewide. Thus, on the institutional level we have crosscutting institutions with separate methods of aggregating power and with specifically defined, although sometimes overlapping, roles.

The Socialist Alliance can be best understood as the equivalent of a primary system in a single-party electoral structure. The many interest groups—women, youth, students, professionals, and so on—formally defined as social-political organizations within it are important only on specific issues.[10]

This thumbnail sketch of the bases of social power of the present Yugoslav system would be abstract if I excluded from it the unifying role of the Yugoslav revolutionary elite, which has dominated all of the institutions of Yugoslav society from 1945 to the present. This elite comprises those who participated in the war of national liberation and successfully adapted to the postwar tasks. In my usage it consists of a group not much larger than approximately 1,200 people operating on the federal and republic levels. A substantial part of it on the federal level is included in the universe of Yugoslav

---

10. Interest groups have considerable latent influence and sometimes act as catalysts; examples include student organizations in 1968 and Matica Hrvatska in Zagreb in 1969–70.

opinion makers discussed in the Appendix. Only recently have replacements for that elite begun to enter the political stage on the federal level. The effectiveness with which the revolutionary leadership has managed to socialize and form its replacements, of course, is a central question affecting the future of Yugoslav society. While social changes occurring since the revolution have called into action forces that will provide for long-range stability of the system, the gestation period necessary for the system to "take" required a conscious statewide leadership capable of normalizing and institutionalizing its role for the immediate future. This role of the leadership becomes easier as time goes on, and as the traditional value system fades into the past, and a new political culture develops to provide the basis for the legitimacy of Yugoslav society. The tasks confronting the new generation of leaders in Yugoslavia will be less difficult than those already successfully completed by the present revolutionary elite. However, they are at the same time more complex tasks because modern industrial society lends itself far less to charismatic, heroic leadership. Above all, the task of permitting the self-managing cells of society to assume increasing responsibility requires precisely that element of permissiveness and self-denial of control which the old leadership did not need to have.

In addressing itself to the third stage of the Yugoslav revolution, the Yugoslav leadership may well find that the organizational and political skills most suited to the struggle for power have now become dysfunctional. The problem at this stage is to breathe life into the existing formal structures, and to permit the development of Yugoslav institutions within the framework of the official ideology of the system. This in turn means that the Yugoslav political elite will have to engage consciously in the most difficult task of all, the liquidation of some of its own organizational power. All indicators available, including the voluminous social research, opinion studies, and community studies, convince me that the legitimacy of the social order is accepted by sufficiently wide strata so that rough-and-ready guerrilla techniques not only are no longer necessary but at this stage block the natural development of a healthy participatory and democratic society.

THE YUGOSLAV VARIANT OF COMMUNISM

In the case of Yugoslavia, one of the problems of approaching analysis of the system as a whole is that external observers all too often attempt to force it into a continuum of East European one-party states from which it differs drastically. Thus, for example, the question often raised by both friendly and hostile critics is: "In what sense can Yugoslavia still be called a 'communist' system?" In other words, is what we have presently in Yugoslavia the legitimation of a revolutionary regime or the adaptation of a communist elite to a point where the system is either regressing back to capitalism or evolving into a polity more analogous to those of countries ruled by social democratic parties? Paul Sweezy, for one, has argued that Yugoslavia is a case of a peaceful transition to capitalism. This argument, in my opinion, has no merit whatsoever. It is tenable only if one insists on a definition of socialism that follows the Soviet model and places a major emphasis on centralized control of the economy and society and on direct planning from the center without a market mechanism. Indeed, if that is socialism, Yugoslavia has moved a long way from it. However, when one examines the outputs of the Yugoslav system, the growing tendency toward egalitarianism in Yugoslav self-management, the campaigns against privilege which are simply not possible in any of the other East European countries, and the latent and real social power wielded by the workers through the instruments of self-management, one can conclude, even without considering the weakness of the private sector, that Yugoslavia is probably closer to a model of what Lenin called a workers' state and Marx and Engels referred to as the dictatorship of the proletariat, than any of the regimes calling themselves communist.

The private sector of the Yugoslav economy, of which much is made, employs fewer workers than does the same sector in either East Germany or Poland, and for that matter the limits on agricultural holdings in Yugoslavia are one-quarter of the maximum permitted in Poland. Therefore, much of the argument about the drift of Yugoslavia away from socialism focuses on something else entirely. The real focus of this critique is on the Yugoslav rejection of a developmental model that sacrifices consumption for an indefinite period to the development of heavy industry. Even here it is difficult to grasp what the critics of the present Yugoslav system have in mind. Surely the continual and gross failures of the Soviet agricultural policy and the repeated downward revisions of their five-year plans would at least give pause to critics of the Yugoslav system who argue the superiority of a highly centralized economic model.

The hostility of the orthodox Marxist critics of the Yugoslav system toward an emphasis on the popular desire for consumer goods has two roots: one is the idea that ordinary Yugoslav workers, technicians, and peasants should not be permitted to corrupt themselves with the goods associated with modern life styles in advanced Western Countries. This argument is most often made by persons who have never deprived themselves of any such goods. The second point is of course more salient, and is often made by Yugoslav critics of the status quo. In a society where private ownership of the means of production or private investment is excluded, the only way additional income can be spent *is* on consumer goods. Therefore, the Yugoslav middle classes and other groups that have salaries larger than those of the workers engage in a kind of conspicuous consumption that is primarily explained not only by the novelty of prosperity in that country but also by the simple fact that there is nothing else such money can be spent on. While this prevents the aggregation of wealth into potentially system-challenging channels, it does create social tensions and leads to repeated campaigns against social differences—differences which are, I would argue, more apparent than real.

Two key concepts are used throughout this book: modernization and legitimation. There is a rich literature surrounding both, and were this to have been a study of theories of legitimacy and theories of modernization, considerable time would have been spent on developing them. For my present purposes—the development of a case study—modernization is a series of closely linked phenomena associated with industrialization and democratization. I regard socialism, and particularly its participatory forms as developed in the self-managing system, as a radical form of democratization in its classic sense, that is, democracy as the rule of the people. To be more precise, I do not equate democratization and participation with pluralist definitions which stress mostly the *processes* of decision making rather than their outcomes. Industrialization has certain measurable cross-system consequences mainly associated with an increasing division of labor, the development of specialized bodies of experts, and the growth of an economy capable of producing surpluses potentially sufficient to end poverty and want.

Modernization also implies the break-up of the traditional society, particularly familial, patriarchal structures, and their increasing replacement by routinized, impersonal bodies where the function is distinct from the occupant of the post. Through the development of participatory forms, the Yugoslavs have clearly added a dimension that implies far greater participation on the policy-formation level than has been customary in either socialist or capitalist societies.

Legitimacy can be approached from a number of different directions, and I have chosen to use Richard Rose's middle-range dynamic model,[11] described in more detail in chapter 8, because it can be easily operationalized and is transsystemic. The process of legitimation in Yugoslavia involved changes in the social structure and in the values and norms on which the traditional order was based. The major focus of my book, therefore, is on the creation and acceptance of a new political culture and the creation of a functioning legal and economic social system based on it. The legitimacy of the system itself is measured by indicators of support and compliance, particularly among the strategically important strata on which the system rests. The Yugoslav regime is currently based on a combination of relatively high support and compliance, increasing all the time, above all within the growing industrial working class and technical intelligentsia. This is in turn underpinned by crosscutting institutions such as the League of Communists, the trade unions, the army, and the network of self-managing bodies organized along branches of industry. A special feature of this regime is the increased differentiation of institutions, creating a type of institutionalized pluralism within a framework in which both routinized bureaucracy and charismatic leaders and bodies function. My general appraisal of the Yugoslav system is therefore that it shows a high degree of legitimacy based on a predominantly socialist political culture which accepts the basic values and norms of the system, and a sufficiently institutionalized political regime which can

11. Richard Rose, "Dynamic Tendencies in Authority of Regimes," *World Politics* 21, no. 4 (July 1969).

effectively realize its intentions, with a highly participatory structure in the economy which successively socializes and mobilizes newly urbanized strata. The challenges to this legitimacy are seen as dispersed and fragmented along ethnic lines, and resting on strata which are becoming less important to the Yugoslav economy and society.

The Yugoslav system is thus a variant of communist systems where the original revolutionary and socialist transformation of the old social order has been carried out and institutionalized in a working modern dynamic society. The old class system has been shattered beyond all repair, and the latent and growing power of the self-managing institutions argues against the jelling of the bureaucracy and the new middle class into a new ruling stratum.

There are a number of useful studies of social revolutions directly relevant to my case. Among the more useful is Ross Johnson's *Transformation of Communist Ideology*,[12] which provides an indispensable blow-by-blow description of the genesis of Titoism as a distinctive variation of socialism. What comes through Johnson's work clearly is the fact of the imposition of workers' self-management and other specific variants of Yugoslav socialism from the top down. If there is a weakness in this work, it is in good part a result of the time span chosen. That is, the book does not begin to address itself to the effect of the structural changes on the social and economic base of the society and the consequent and necessary effect on the party leadership at the top. Half of the process is described but the more significant and intriguing half, the one that would explain what happened after self-managing institutions began to assume a social weight of their own, is not discussed. This is, of course, not a valid criticism, since that was not the book Johnson intended to write.

Chalmers Johnson, in his earlier *Peasant Nationalism and Communist Power*, explicitly addresses himself to the Yugoslav case and compares it with that of China, focusing on the period of the seizure of power.[13] His basic thesis is that peasant nationalism has formed the base for the Communists' rise to power in both China and Yugoslavia. In defining nationalism, he focuses on the processes of social mobiliza-

12. Ross Johnson, *Transformation of Communist Ideology: The Yugoslav Case, 1943–1953* (Cambridge: MIT Press, 1972).

13. Chalmers Johnson, *Peasant Nationalism and Communist Power: The Emergence of Communist China* (Stanford: Stanford University Press, 1962).

tion, by which he refers to the transformation of a people into a nation, and the development of a national myth which constitutes the justification of the legitimacy of the movement. In both China and Yugoslavia, the second followed the first. The process of social mobilization was greatly accelerated by the uprooting of the peasantry as a result of the invasions and the wars, and by the process discussed in my third chapter, where violence itself acted as a mobilizer of the peasants, pushing them increasingly into the resistance. This in turn helped transform the parochialism of the peasants into a national consciousness[14] and helped discredit the legitimacy of the old order, since the Communists were more actively ready to resist.

The second process, however, the development of a national patriotic myth, is a crucial one in the case of the two countries. It rests on the argument that the ideology advanced by the Communists in the process of resistance was primarily one of national liberation, and that this ideological element acted as the funnel through which the communist ideology of the cadre was legitimized. This in turn explains why in both cases the break with Moscow and the ideological transition of those parties to national communism reinforced the national liberationist ideology developed during the process of resistance. Here Johnson uses a fine interplay between base and superstructure within the concept of legitimacy and mass movement. On one hand, it was the original communist ideology that led to the decisions to resist the invader, but, once this process had begun, the new constituency and its expansion provided a base of mass support and legitimized guerrilla warfare and its main objectives, which, in turn, legitimized the Communist aims through a continual insistence on independence. However, again, while Johnson's argument is relevant insofar as he discusses the prospects of national communist groups coming to power by means of a war of national independence, it suggests no explanation of the consequent divergent developments of the two participatory forms developed in China and Yugoslavia. The mass line of the Chinese party seems designed far more to emphasize continual attempts at mobilization than the self-management approach of the Yugoslavs, which on the

14. During the resistance *Yugoslav* nationalism was emphasized by the Partisans with considerable success among their supporters.

contrary provides for institutionalized participation over long periods of time and is therefore primarily a form of socialization and
institution building.

A more general framework in which the development of a debate
arising out of the Yugoslav experience can be placed is provided by
Barrington Moore, both in his *Terror and Progress in the USSR* and in
his major study of revolutionary transformation, *The Origins of
Dictatorship and Democracy.*[15] Moore's work presents what is, to my
mind, a most fruitful introduction of Marxist categories into the
literature of social change and social transformation in the United
States. It deals, however, with the pre-Leninist and pre-Trotskyist
versions of that theory, which apply primarily to major polities and
are taken to emphasize the primacy of economic and social
development.

In the Yugoslav case, while the framework Moore provides of
course sets the limits of possible changes, the range of possible
changes seems to have been stretched out of all recognition. I am not
even sure that in an individual case, such as the Yugoslav revolution,
one must seek generally applicable patterns when it is so clear that
the particular adaptation the Yugoslav Communist leaders opted for
in 1950–52 was so very much ad hoc and full of improvisations.
What one can say, perhaps, is that the long-range changes in
Yugoslav society and structure are primarily affected by the
objective limits set by the level of development of the economy and
society. However, the short range has by now consisted of several
decades of experimentation and seems to have significantly altered
the options available to the future leadership of that country. That
is, in the case of Yugoslavia, any attempt to move back to a
centralized model, although such a centralized model was definitely
within the realm of the possible in the developmental period, would
now be met with major resistance and would probably involve a
level of repression that is outside the present rules of the game.

Therefore, to use Trotsky's concept of combined and uneven
development, the Yugoslav variant, for whatever reasons, has
become a new historical alternative and, as such, it now defines the
possibilities for other regimes in other situations without reference to

15. Barrington Moore, *Terror and Progress in the USSR* (Cambridge: Harvard
University Press, 1954), and *The Origins of Dictatorship and Democracy* (Boston: Beacon
Press, 1970).

the specific ideologies of the revolutionary elite in those countries. More simply put, there is a new body of historical experience about revolutionary transformation now made available to potential clients.

2

Relevance of the Yugoslav Experience:
Conflicts and Challenges

Yugoslavia has often been described as an almost ideal laboratory for political sociologists. It is relevant to those primarily interested in studying historical problems, for the case of the prerevolutionary Yugoslav state and later socialist Yugoslavia offers almost endless parallels to scholars concerned with nation building and development, and it is equally relevant to those primarily concerned with contemporary society. It is therefore unfortunate that Yugoslav scholars themselves have, by and large, not used comparative methods in their studies on pre- and postrevolutionary Yugoslavia.

Prerevolutionary historians and ethnologists in the areas that now comprise Yugoslavia developed principally under the influence of various strains of romantic nationalism opposed to the older legitimist schools. Both major schools tended to stress the uniqueness of the national mission of the particular nation rather than universal factors relevant to other polities. Thus, much of prerevolutionary ethnography suffered from the intense chauvinism or organic nationalism of the late nineteenth century. A good example is the work of the Serbian ethnographer Jovan Cvijic,[1] whose studies coincided chronologically with the growing aspirations of Serbian ruling circles to become dominant in the Balkans. His repeated stress of the unique "state-building" characteristics and special mission of the Dinaric mountaineers coincided with the social mythology of the military and political cliques dominating Serbia and Montenegro.

Yugoslav historians, and indeed most national historians, tended to place enormous stress on that particular period in the history of their own nation which coincided with its greatest geographic

---

1. Jovan Cvijic was an enormously prolific ethnographer and social geographer. His major work, *Balkansko poluostrvo*, was reissued in 1969 in Belgrade. The rest of his work is available in seventeen volumes issued by the Academy of Science of Belgrade.

expansion. Thus, much of nineteenth-century history was simply used to create a basis for legitimist claims for territorial expansion and dominance. This was as true of the historians working in the independent states of Serbia and Montenegro as it was of the South Slav historians in the Austro-Hungarian Empire. The latter developed a school of history primarily as a counterthesis to the claims of the Hungarians and Austrians and attempted to create, sometimes by outright forgery, a historico-legal claim of national continuity within expanded frontiers for their particular nation.[2]

Not only was much of the intelligentsia of the Yugoslav lands dominated by often rival nationalist sentiments and claims, but major institutions, such as the church, lent themselves directly to the underpinning of such claims. It would be almost impossible to isolate the Serbo-Croatian conflicts under the Austro-Hungarian monarchy, and even in modern Yugoslavia, from the respective roles of the Catholic and Orthodox churches. And, as is well known, the genesis of Bosnian Moslem Slav identity is found in Islam.

Thus, one of the first tasks for a comparative sociologist or political scientist is to cut through the underbrush of nationalist propaganda, disguised as scholarly work, and to address himself to the question of what forces existed both within and outside of Yugoslav society that *did* lead to the establishment of a Yugoslav state in 1918 and its reestablishment in 1945. With the worldwide decline of colonialism, a number of new nations have developed in a framework where their frontiers include diverse peoples and rival religious establishments, and the Yugoslav experience is therefore of general interest. Since two separate attempts to establish the basis for a Yugoslav state have taken place—one under the national bourgeoisies between 1918 and 1941, and one following the Yugoslav revolution of 1941–45—we can make a comparison of two alternate approaches to state-building. This advantage for comparative study is further augmented by the fact that the Yugoslav revolution went through relatively clearly differentiated stages of successes and failures.

The level of economic and social development in Yugoslavia today

2. See I. Racki, *Povijest hrvata* (Zagreb: Jugoslovenska Akademija Nauka, 1901); Grga Novak, *Hrvatska povijest* (Zagreb: Nedelne Informativne Novine, 1908), etc. A solid postwar treatment is found in Edvard Kardelj, *Slovenicko nacijonalno pitanje,* available in many editions (e.g., Ljubljana: Cancar, 1953). Also see Pavle Ilic, *Srpski narod i njegov jezik* (Belgrade: Srpska Knjizevna Zadruga, 1971).

is uneven, ranging from that characteristic of Central Europe to that of Central Asia; therefore the impact of conscious policies on such factors as social mobility, education, natality, and urbanization can be examined against a variety of backgrounds. This also means that Yugoslavia is posed as a possible model both for countries in the middle range of development and for countries designated as underdeveloped.

Historically, and up to the present time, the most significant single cleavage in Yugoslav society as a whole has been urban-rural. This problem, central to all developing societies, takes a particularly sharp form in Yugoslavia. One can almost talk of "two nations," roughly equal in size but grossly unequal in income, influence, and power. Not only is the peasantry, as noted in chapter 1, still practically excluded from the most dynamic sectors of Yugoslav society and its institutions but it is subjected to a number of conscious and unconscious pressures which clearly place it in an inferior position within the society as a whole.[3] To begin with, the very structure of representation is biased against the peasant. Even the system of representation on the commune councils is such that the socialist sector is guaranteed half of the seats, while there is no specific organization for the articulation of peasant interests as a whole, analogous to the trade unions. To be sure, representation is biased in the same way against the unemployed, housewives, and those in the private sector, but the very fact that the peasantry can be placed alongside that triad is of course unacceptable to the peasants, who have contributed heavily to the economic development of the country as a whole. Culturally the peasants are subjected to pressure from the mass media, which define the only desirable existence as urban and modern. The effect is naturally that the young and the ambitious are under continuous pressure to abandon the villages, which is unfortunate because a sufficiently rapid expansion of urban housing and employment does not exist.

On the other hand, it is also true that the peasantry has been more or less left to its own devices and is no longer subject to various campaigns formerly directed against private peasant property and village life. This is a two-edged proposition, since it also means that

3. "Selo i poljoprivreda u drustveno-ekonomskom razvoju Jugoslavije," special edition of *Sociologija Sela* 8, nos. 29–30 (1970).

the sociopolitical organizations that could link the peasantry to the modern sector, such as the League of Communists of Yugoslavia, tend to atrophy in the villages, having little to do that relates to the day-to-day problems of their constituencies. One could argue that a relatively underdeveloped society cannot simultaneously undertake the tasks of creating an advanced urban industrial sector and achieving countrywide modernization. The fact does remain, however, that the Yugoslav social revolution is an urban, industrial phenomenon today.

Another major problem for Yugoslav society is the need to replace an entire revolutionary generation in such a way that political continuity is ensured.[4] This is a problem central to many societies that have undergone a social revolution but it is found in a particularly concentrated form in Yugoslavia, for two reasons: first, the relative homogeneity of the generation of war and revolution leaders means that those in power will tend to retire at more or less the same time; second, their replacements will come from strata that have not had any analogous experience. The age homogeneity of the leadership group is a product of the brutal demands of guerrilla activity during the war, which placed an accent on youth, thus creating a cadre, mostly formed in 1941–45, which was uniformly young when it came to power. The fact that the membership of the Yugoslav Communist Party in June 1945 was 140,000, although only 3,000 members of the prewar party survived the war, means that the central formative experience for much of the present leadership on all levels of society was the revolution rather than the experience of work in the prewar illegal Stalinized Communist Party. This background, which over the years has become an ascribed quality,[5] is not duplicable by the replacements. Following the more routinized path of education, career, and political service, the second-generation leaders tend to develop within the framework of republics and localities rather than within a statewide arena, and they have neither the homogeneity nor the internal solidarity of the previous generation. Therefore, the absence of the crosscutting function of a relatively unified revolutionary cadre may become a serious problem in the future.

4. See the discussion of age cohorts in chapter 5.
5. This status, while historically acquired, has become ascriptive in that it is not an acquirable quality for younger age groups in the system.

This problem is further accentuated by the absence of statewide educational institutions, which means that the development of the new intelligentsia takes place primarily within the individual republics. The effect of decentralization in this respect is to reinforce the localist rather than the universal character of the new leadership since, as noted above, political careers are also generally limited by the frontiers of a single republic. The experiences of other multinational polities point out the serious problem posed by the development of a fragmented state leadership within a society where power aggregation tends to take place increasingly on geographic lines.

Another aspect of the Yugoslav experience that invites comparative studies is the problem of multinationality. The relatively naive optimism of both the liberal state-builders of the nineteenth century and the early workers' parties is challenged by recent developments. Their belief that localism, particularism, and nationalism were phenomena associated with traditional societies which would increasingly diminish as modernization and industrialization proceeded is contradicted by the growing localism and particularism in industrial Europe itself. The vitality of nationalism can be seen in the Catalan-Castilian dispute in Spain, the Wallon-Flemish dispute in Belgium, Slovak-Czech tensions in Czechoslovakia, recent French-English disputes in Canada, and the widening demand for regional autonomy even in relatively homogeneous states such as France, Italy, and England.

The search for national and local roots is, I believe, a general reaction to the increasing impersonalization and atomization of modern industrial society. The quest for identity apparently requires more intimate and personal symbols than those of the nation-state itself, and often the only symbols on hand are the traditional ones.[6] A personal sense of identity can also be provided by participation in mass political and social movements; however, this is less true when movements become the establishment. For that reason, ethnic nationalism as a phenomenon will not decline even in relatively stable developed societies, and attempts to resolve the need for

6. See the special edition of *Praxis*, no. 34 (1971), entitled "Trenutak Jugosloveskog socijalizma"; and Predrag Vranicki, "Socijalizam i nacijonalno pitanje," *Praxis* 5, no. 4 (1968). A solid, up-to-date treatment of the national question is in Stipe Suvar's *Nacije i medjunacijonalni odnosi* (Zagreb: Nase Teme, 1970).

national or ethnic identity within those polities will become of ever-widening interest. In this respect, the Yugoslav experience suggests solutions that make it almost an alternative model for the advanced societies.

The Yugoslav approach could be defined as a counterthesis to the generally accepted Jacobin model of organization of the modern nation-state. This model assumes the identification of the interests of the citizen with the state, defined as unitary, and assumes that the primary problem of representation is to assure some kind of equitable interest aggregation primarily on a geographic basis. It regards other factors such as ethnic nationality, profession, and workplace as fundamentally illegitimate or archaic ways of fragmenting representation since they contradict the concept of state interest. Conflict within such a national society exists and is legitimate but it is generally narrowly political within a framework where the parties usually compete for statewide mandates, or it is outside of the formal political framework where interest representation is organized along economic or professional lines.

The Yugoslav approach, which not only accepts the legitimacy of multinationality but institutionalizes it in the organization of the state itself, and which provides for a multiplicity of representation to the various chambers of the legislature, is an alternative approach geared to the fact that a modern citizen has a number of reference groups, any one of which at a given time can become the most significant. Thus, a citizen can be (1) a member of a given nation, (2) an adherent of a political party, (3) a member of an economic organization or profession, and so on, and any of these identities may become more critical for representation of his needs and demands than the others. In modern industrial society, probably one of the least important bases for representation is geographic proximity.

The recent conflict in Yugoslavia over the future of its underdeveloped areas is a problem common to most societies, even the very advanced. It is a constant theme in Britain, France, and, above all, countries like Italy, where wide gaps exist between the relative shares of different regions in the gross national product. In this context, the Yugoslav approach of consensus, where republic delegations are forced to hammer out agreements, rather than power aggregation on the statewide scale as the mechanism for the solution of such conflicts is at least unique.[7] It should thus be of great interest to the many political scientists who believe that the mechanical aggregation of majorities is becoming less effective as a means of dealing with such problems. For example, the problems created by the demands of minorities such as the blacks in the United States, while resolved in the formal political arena, are not resolvable by simple nose counts. Similarly the demands for cultural identity made by the French in Quebec are not resolvable by an all-Canadian vote.

The wide interest, particularly in Western Europe, in the subject of Yugoslav workers' councils and self-management is well-known. Some kinds of participatory approaches are now being proposed by trade unions and economic and social reformers for a widely divergent set of economic and political organizations. Thus, for example, the introduction of some elements of self-management has been proposed for industry that remains under private ownership, and consultation has been generally proposed as one of the more effective mechanisms for channeling class and economic conflict. An obvious contrast exists between the view that self-management is primarily an instrument for increasing efficiency and *enterprise* loyalty, and the view that it is an instrument of class rule by the workers. In the case of Yugoslavia, the class themes are immensely complicated by the natural tendency of a given economic unit toward a market-induced egoism. The income differences between workers in branches of the same industry, even when the skill level is kept constant, are at times greater than those within the same enterprise. Recent policies have sought to reduce such differences. The problem posed by the need to balance class consciousness and needs, projected in the general social and political arena, versus the fragmenting effect of a compartmentalization cutting across class lines, can be studied in Yugoslavia in a way not duplicable in any other society.

The development of workers' self-management within the framework of a market economy has also generated a set of real and

7. The practice in the legislature and in the organization of the cabinet utilizes consensus *(dogovaranje)*, and a republic cannot be outvoted. This is why the collective Federal Presidency, also composed of republic delegations, has latent legislative power to break potential logjams; it can decide by majority vote. This mechanism of the Presidency has not been used to date.

potential social conflicts. These can be roughly divided between those occurring *within* the workplace and those between the workplace and institutions and forces outside of it. Within the workplace, two contradictory goals exist: maximization of production and social organization of work—efficiency versus humaneness. A workers' council is simultaneously a town meeting and the apex of an increasingly complex organizational pyramid. An obvious conflict exists between the attempts by technocratically oriented managerial strata to stress efficiency and productivity and the natural resistance of the workers to any attempts to increase the pace of work or to alienate them from direct control over the process of production. Increased availability of consumer goods and luxuries has created pressures from the professional strata for greater income differentials. Hiring university graduates from the outside rather than systematically upgrading workers for professional jobs, perhaps by sending them to universities, widens the gap between the "experts" and blue-collar workers. The tendency for some enterprises to merge makes the problem of representation within self-management ever more complex.

Conflicts between the enterprise and outside forces are also systemic. The more obvious problems are those posed by the narrow self-interests of an enterprise—the scandalous pollution of rivers and parts of the seacoast, the production of goods whose social value is dubious, irresponsible pricing, the tendency to regard the enterprise as a form of collective private property, and the like. On the other hand, there are attempts from the "outside" to interfere with the normal prerogatives of self-management in hiring and firing, demands for favors, and the desire of poorer communities to tax the more successful enterprises for the sake of general development. A number of studies show that Yugoslav workers do have a higher level of participation and control than is the case in either the centralized socialist models or under capitalism. However, self-management cannot be treated in isolation from the rest of the society, and the study of conflicts within and outside the boundaries of given enterprises will obviously have to relate to more general themes.[8]

8. Chapter 7 goes into more detail about Yugoslav self-management. Recent Yugoslav sources on conflict and self-management include *Drustveni konflikti i socialisticki razvoj Jugoslavije*, vols. 1–3 (Belgrade: Filozofski Fakultet, 1972). See also the special edition of *Sociologija*, no. 1 (1972), in English and French; and *Participation and*

In the absence of interest-aggregating institutions that cut horizontally across the geographic and institutional divisions based on the republics, there is an almost automatic tendency to emphasize localism. The problem is perhaps that too many decisions that in other societies have required conscious intervention by parties and trade unions are left to the automatic workings of the market and economy. The tendency to seek particularist roots in a modern industrial society would seem to me to lead almost inevitably to a revival of ethnic nationalism in its various forms unless conflict lines are developed which cut across national divisions, or unless major emphasis is placed on lines of positive Yugoslav-wide identification.

The problem seems not uncommon in other societies. For example, one line of cleavage within the Left in the United States in recent years has been the sexual one, sharpened by the creation of a women's liberation movement. However, intersecting that particular cleavage are at least two others that may be more important at a given moment: the racial cleavage and, of course, the class cleavage. Without these crosscutting lines the role of the women's movement would be to split the black and trade union organizations along sex lines. By analogy, it seems to me that constructive social conflicts within a complex polity such as Yugoslavia assure that intersecting cleavages on a number of lines will curb the tendency toward vertical aggregation of power within geographic units. *In that case, the cleavage lines act to bind the society together since they permit alternate aggregations on different issues.* For example, this would permit the aggregation of interests in all republics on the issue of economic development, underdeveloped areas thus banding together across formal republic lines. On the issue of the social demands of the working class, a natural vehicle already exists in the trade unions, but for them to supply this indispensable cement they would have to act, at least on some questions, increasingly on a statewide level. This explains the recent political offensive of the LCY and the growing stress on social and class themes. The present emphases on class solidarity and on the uniqueness of the Yugoslav model of socialism as a humane and just social order are obvious attempts to strengthen positive lines of identification that surmount particularism.

Self-Management, vols. 1–6, Papers of the First International Conference on Participation and Self-Management (Zagreb: Institut za Drustvena Iztrazivanja, 1974).

Another conflict in Yugoslav society is posed by the rapid development of institutions of higher learning since World War II.[9] This has created a situation where relatively underdeveloped Yugoslavia is among the first countries in the world in the proportion of university students in the appropriate age group. Since there is no quota system to limit the flow of students into faculties with poor employment prospects, an unemployed university-educated or partially educated intelligentsia has been created. There are several problems here. The society as a whole pays for an expensive, often socially not particularly valuable, education, primarily for the children of the better-off strata. The traditional value placed on nonmanual work means that partially educated students have a set of false aspirations which the society cannot fulfill, since hopefully the number of white-collar and bureaucratic jobs will not expand indefinitely. Further, the pace of development of higher education has had two negative consequences: on one hand, it has led to a neglect of secondary and vocational education, since these are downgraded; on the other hand, it has been an entering wedge for middle-class values and world views, which spread to a whole stratum of youth who will inevitably be discontented with what their society can reasonably provide for them. This encourages on the part of the students demands for status that run directly contrary to the egalitarian values of the revolution and even to the egalitarian rhetoric they often use to frame their own discontent. Only the most energetic intervention by Yugoslav social and political institutions can, I believe, reverse this continuing trend which devalues manual labor and makes the aspiration for a white-collar or professional job almost universal.

Another set of problems confronting Yugoslavia is posed by the reversal of some of the specific social gains of the revolution as society routinizes and becomes relatively depoliticized. Interesting indices could be devised to gauge this, such as a measurement of the relative role and participation of women in prewar Yugoslavia, during the revolution, in the period immediately after the revolution, and in more recent years. What apparently occurred was a vast opening-up

9. Miodrag Milenkovic, "Razvoj visokoskolskog sistema u Jugoslaviji," *Ideje* 1, no. 2 (Belgrade, 1971); and Vera Janina-Lagneau, *Education, egalité, et socialisme* (Paris: Anthropos, 1968). In English, *Innovation in Higher Education: Reforms in Yugoslavia* (Zagreb: Organization for Economic Cooperation and Development, 1970).

of opportunities and personal horizons during the course of the national liberation struggle and in the years immediately following. The patterns of traditional authority in the villages and towns were shattered, but as society again became "normal" some traditional values tended to reassert themselves. Thus, the range of opportunities open to a young woman today is more limited than that available right after the war.

Generational cleavages are reinforced by the unselective, wholesale use of West European societal models of behavior, which are pushed by the mass media, particularly the popular journals and television. This is an area where the absence of conscious intervention by the political leadership, combined with growing apoliticization, has probably led to the greatest erosion of socialist values. In the near future Yugoslav social scientists will certainly have to concern themselves with the question to what extent the socialization of a whole new generation reflects the effects of commercialized European culture rather than the values of a socialist revolution. My feeling is that the patterns of consumption among the more prosperous, the advertising campaigns with their endless stress on luxury goods, and the flood of West European and American entertainment have created role models that are in almost complete contradiction to the values of any socialist or egalitarian society.[10] This in turn leads to a revival of political campaign processes on the part of the League of Communists.

Reviewing briefly the main conflict lines in Yugoslav society as a whole, we can see that the issues raised have a general application to three types of societies: (1) developing societies primarily concerned with the problem of state building and maintenance of national independence; (2) socialist societies facing the problems arising out of decentralization and democratization; and (3) advanced industrial societies dealing with the problems of anomie and depersonalization produced by industrial development. What is immediately evident here is that current conflicts in Yugoslavia simultaneously include those one would expect to find in underdeveloped societies and those that are only now being approached in the most developed ones. In this lies what is perhaps the basic contradiction in

10. Rudi Supek, *Humanisticka inteligencija i politika* (Zagreb: Razlog, 1971), ch. 4, pp. 87–108. Also Vojin Rus, "Kulturna politika," *Nase Teme*, no. 11 (November 1972).

present-day Yugoslav society: the contradiction between the mundane possibilities of a relatively underdeveloped, small, independent nation-state, and its heroic aspirations to solve the complex problems of multinationality, industrial democracy, egalitarianism, and social mobility in a way that has not yet been attempted anywhere in the world. Therefore, the success or failure of the Yugoslav social experiments has a twofold relevance: it is relevant to all societies seeking a path of independent development and modernization; at the same time, it is an attempt, perhaps too ambitious given the existing objective social and economic possibilities, to solve the problems facing socialism in advanced industrial societies.

But this is the situation in Yugoslavia at the present time. The rest of the book deals with the years leading up to the revolution, the period of consolidation of power, and the institutionalization of the revolutionary regime, so let us take a look backward.

3

Conquest and Consolidation

The main thrust of Yugoslav history between the world wars has been described by an American political scientist as follows:

> Yugoslavia's inter-war history thus closed with her major ethnic communities unreconciled, her citizens' civil liberties violated, her economic unification and development stunted, and her agrarian-demographic problems only partially alleviated at the price of economic and political dependence on Germany. The brutality and cynicism of successive regimes had long ago estranged the best of the intelligentsia, while sheer incompetence and primitive exploitation had quite alienated the peasants and workers. But it was only after the German army had, in April 1941, exposed the structural brittleness of the superficially impressive state apparatus that the country's pent up ethnic and social rages exploded into civil and revolutionary war.[1]

The quotation summarizes well the total loss of legitimacy and of the ability and power to rule effectively of the pre–World War II Yugoslav regime. The tragedy was aggravated by the fact that in April of 1941 no contenders for power, no alternate regime, appeared in sight. The prewar parties had already in good measure discredited themselves by the experience of the interwar years.[2] This was as true of the governing parties as it was of the opposition. The major parties found themselves frozen in postures of opposition ethnic politics, and no Yugoslav-wide social or political force appeared to have either a real or potential social weight sufficient to reorganize a postwar Yugoslav state.

1. Joseph Rothschild, *East Central Europe between the Two World Wars* (Seattle: University of Washington Press, 1974).
2. Ibid. Also Wayne S. Vucinich, "Interwar Yugoslavia," in *Contemporary Yugoslavia*, ed. Wayne Vucinich (Berkeley: University of California Press, 1969).

The Yugoslav Communist Party, at the close of this period—which preceded the guerrilla war and resistance—certainly did not appear to be a serious contender for power. Many of its approximately 12,000 members were known to the police, and their ability to operate effectively under the conditions of Axis occupation was further reduced by the fact that the prewar Yugoslav police turned over its Communist files to the occupying forces intact. In addition to regular members, the party had an even larger youth movement, the SKOJ, numbering some 20,000, and a shifting body of sympathizers considerably demoralized by the Hitler-Stalin Pact, which was still in effect at the time of the German invasion of Yugoslavia.[3]

To be sure, the Communist Party had enjoyed wider support at the time the Yugoslav state was founded; it reached a peak in the November 1920 elections to the Constituent National Assembly, when some 198,000 votes were cast to elect 58 CPY deputies. Party membership at that time was over 65,000. However, in the years that followed, partially because of police repression and partially through its own tactical and strategic errors, the party was reduced, so that in 1932 there were fewer than 1,000 members. In 1937, under the leadership of Josip Broz Tito,[4] it began rebuilding its cadres. Thus, even to sections of its own cadre, the party certainly did not appear capable of challenging the remnants of the old social order, leading a war of liberation, and reconstituting a federal Yugoslav state after the war.

How the party accomplished these tasks is one of the themes of this book, and in this context it is important to examine some of the effects of violence on social change in Yugoslavia.[5] This chapter

3. The best Yugoslav source on the history of the party and league is Pero Moraca et al., eds., *Istorija SKJ* (Belgrade: Prosveta, 1965). A flawed émigré history of the CPY is available in English: Ivan Avakumovich, *History of the Communist Party of Yugoslavia*, 2 vols. (Aberdeen: Aberdeen University Press, 1964). See also Vladimir Dedijer, *Tito* (New York: Simon & Schuster, 1953).

4. Dedijer, pp. 100–32; Avakumovich, pp. 122–73.

5. While the materials on the general topic of violence and social change are voluminous and still growing, most useful for my purposes were: Harry Eckstein, ed., *Internal War* (New York: Macmillan, 1964); Gil C. Alroy, *Involvement of Peasants in Internal Wars*, Center of International Studies, Princeton University, research monograph 24 (Princton, 1966); Chalmers Johnson, "Civilian Loyalties and Guerrilla Conflicts," *World Politics* 14, no. 4 (July 1962); Chalmers Johnson, *Revolutions in the Social System* (Stanford: Stanford University Press, 1964); Alexander Dallin and

primarily discusses the Partisan War of 1941–45 [6] which had as its
aims resistance against the foreign occupier, and a basic social
transformation of the prewar political and social order. In order to
place the effect of the Partisan War in a meaningful context, some
historical background is essential, for it is part of my argument that a
historical background of prolonged guerrilla warfare and national
wars of liberation created a situation in which the use of armed
struggle by the Yugoslav Communists for political and social ends
was not considered illegitimate, even by their opponents. That is, it
was not the Communists' violence and armed struggle that were
considered illegitimate. Opposition to the Communists was based on
different grounds and was offered by forces that had proved no less
ready to use force for political ends.

The historical legitimacy of armed struggle, absent in most other
peasant societies, and the existence of an armed peasantry in the
mountainous areas of the country where the Partisans built their
strongholds created conditions particularly favorable to the rapid
build-up of their forces from small guerrilla bands to a guerrilla
army capable of consolidating state power. In this respect, the
Yugoslav Communists came to power under circumstances unique in
Europe, with the possible exception of Albania. This uniqueness

George Breslauer, *Political Terror in Communist Systems* (Stanford: Stanford University
Press, 1970); Martin Oppenheimer, *The Urban Guerrilla* (Chicago: Quadrangle, 1969);
Henry Bienen, *Violence and Social Change* (Chicago: University of Chicago Press, 1968);
Barrington Moore, *Terror and Progress in the USSR* (Cambridge: Harvard University
Press, 1954).

For more general background on Yugoslav history, with particular emphasis on the
Partisan War, I suggest the following: Robert Lee Wolff, *The Balkans in Our Time* (New
York: Norton, 1956); Charles Jelavic, ed., *The Balkans in Transition* (Berkeley:
University of California Press, 1963); Jozo Tomasevich, *Peasants, Politics, and Economic
Change in Yugoslavia* (Stanford: Stanford University Press, 1956); Vucinic, *Contemporary
Yugoslavia*; Stephen Clissold, *Whirlwind: The Rise of Marshal Tito to Power* (New York:
Cresset, 1949), and *A Short History of Yugoslavia* (Cambridge: Cambridge University
Press, 1966); Vladimir Dedijer, *Tito.* Two recent works are Jozo Tomasevich's *War and
Revolution in Yugoslavia: The Chetniks* (Stanford: Stanford University Press, 1975), and
Vladimir Dedijer et al., *History of Yugoslavia* (New York: McGraw-Hill, 1974).

6. A discussion of the Yugoslav political cultures can be found in my article
"Political Cultures and Social Mobility," in "Proceedings of the World Congress of
the International Sociological Association," Varna, 1970 (mimeo.). The more general
reference, of course, is Gabriel A. Almond and Sidney Verba, *The Civic Culture*
(Princteon: Princeton University Press, 1963).

helped develop other specificities not at all self-evident immediately after World War II. For instance, a system that bases its legitimacy on successful armed revolution, made possible by a peasantry both willing and able to engage in prolonged warfare, has built-in limits as to how far it can antagonize its base. In addition, it can make a convincing case to any potential invaders that an invasion would, at the very least, be a costly venture—a fact that did a great deal to make possible the break with Yugoslavia from the Soviet-run bloc and its continued independence.

THE TRADITION OF VIOLENCE
IN THE YUGOSLAV LANDS

Violence has played a major role in the Yugoslav lands for a long time. The effect of violence on the country's political cultures varied, as did the intensity of violence and the degree of popular participation in it. A rough analysis locates the centers of this violence, which often took the form of social banditry[7] and endless guerrilla skirmishes, in four major areas: (1) the military frontier of the Austrian Empire, a *cordon sanitaire* separating civil Croatia[8] and Vojvodina from the Turkish Empire; (2) Montenegro, a confederation of warring clans claiming independence; (3) Serbia proper, which aspired to become the Piedmont of Yugoslavia;[9] and (4) the lands that had remained under more or less effective Turkish control up to 1912.

Widespread communal violence was limited mainly to the lands directly or indirectly under Turkish occupation, and to the immediately adjacent territories, whose social structure had to be adapted to the needs of almost perpetual skirmishes and war. Turkish warfare during the conquest of the South Slav lands in the fourteenth and fifteenth centuries destroyed the fragile social structure of the medieval Balkan Slavic states. The Turks waged a religious war on the states, wiped out or absorbed the local nobility, and initially

---

7. This concept is discussed at length in Eric Hobsbawn's *Social Bandits and Primitive Rebels* (Glencoe, Ill.: Free Press, 1959).

8. Up to 1884 much of Croatia was organized as a military frontier; the rest of the country was known as "civil" Croatia.

9. The image of the Piedmont, that is, the analogy with the national liberation and integration of Italy, was consciously used by political elites in Serbia during the latter part of the nineteenth century.

created relative stability for the peasantry. As the Turkish Empire expanded, it tended to be preceded by continual raids whose function was to weaken the social structure of the target areas, making their eventual absorption into the empire easier. In reaction to these raids, a counterforce was developed, primarily an armed peasantry whose family structure began to regress to the earlier clan organizations to meet the requirements of self-defense. The clans, or extended families, held land in common, usually received in return for military service, in the border areas. This military service was either on the side of the Ottomans, who encouraged raids into Hungarian, Austrian, or Venetian territory, or on the side of the Austrians and Venetians, who needed a defense guard.[10]

Thus there developed over a wide belt in Yugoslavia in the seventeenth and eighteenth centuries a Cossack-type culture, where the peasantry was free, armed, and organized along quasi-military lines. This is reflected in the oral traditions and culture of the peasantry from those areas even today. While warring destroyed the nascent literacy of the notables, it gave rise to a cycle of epic, warlike, oral poetry, analogous to the sagas of the Norsemen. The impact of these epics on the contemporary mores in wide areas of Yugoslavia is unparalleled in Europe.[11] During World War I, anthropologists in Serbia found that, while over half of the army recruits were illiterate, two-thirds of them knew at least some of the oral epics by heart.[12] The figures for Montenegro would have been, in all probability, more striking, since there the clan structure retained some cohesiveness up to World War II, while illiteracy was even higher. These epics, sung by both Orthodox and Catholic mountaineers and frontiersmen, formed a common core of oral heritage for Serbs and Croats. Moslem Slavs had their own ballads; the heroes differ but in most other respects they are similar to those of their Christian fellow South Slavs. The message of the epics, some of which take over two hours to recite, is one of continual, relentless

10. See Gunther Rothenberg, *The Military Border in Croatia, 1522–1741* (Urbana: University of Illinois Press, 1960) for a description of the social structure of the borderlands.

11. The best collection of the ballads in English is Albert Lord and Milman Parry, *Serbo-Croatian Heroic Ballads* (Cambridge: Harvard University Press, 1953).

12. Mary Edith Durham, *Through the Lands of the Serbs* (London: E. Arnold, 1904), pp. 83–88.

resistance and war; the sole manly virtues stressed are personal courage and cunning in combat.

As the modern Serbian state developed during the nineteenth century, this tradition of violence was emphasized and organized along more modern lines. The social atmosphere prevalent throughout the Serbian Revolution of 1804–15 must have been something like that of Montenegro at the beginning of this century, as portrayed by the English anthropologist Mary Edith Durham. She described a population where the men over fifteen were armed, where the proudest boast was having taken an enemy's head in combat, where extended blood feuds lasted for decades, and where the economy was pastoral, supplemented by looting. Both the military and civil leaders of the Serbian revolt were veterans of many skirmishes with the Turks. Some had been typical Balkan bandits of the legendary mold *(hayduks, uskoks)*, that is, bandits, who, at least in theory, robbed the "rich" (primarily the Turkish overlords) and had considerable support from the local peasantry. Even the few priests in the leadership bore arms and led bands in combat.[13]

The Serbian Revolution was both a war of independence and a *Jacquerie*. The foreign oppressor was also the feudal landlord. Elimination of Turkish rule thus involved a social revolution in the countryside, and one result of the wars of independence was that the peasantry obtained legal title to the land it worked. A further consequence was the creation of a society without a gentry[14]— a society in which the bulk of the population was freeholding peasants, carrying arms as a matter of right, and where social mobility occurred primarily through entrance into the small standing army, the police, or the government bureaucracy. This meant that success was directly associated with entry into the governing caste, and there was high social mobility, since there was no source of recruitment into its ruling establishment except the peasantry. The high social mobility characteristic of this society did not of course imply that the resulting structure was not exploitative or inegalitar-

13. Ibid., pp. 32–58.

14. For a discussion of the special role of the gentry in Eastern Europe, see Robert Lord, "The Polish Crisis of the Eighteenth Century," and Henry Marczali, "The Ruling Class of Hungary," both in *Man, State, and Society in East European History*, ed. Stephen Fischer-Galati (New York: Praeger, 1970).

ian. It was merely the Balkan version of a society open to the talented and ambitious.

After the establishment of an initially autonomous, later independent, Serbian principality, the history of the unification of the Yugoslav lands reads like a chronicle of wars. The wars of 1848, 1875, 1878, and 1888 culminated in the Balkan War of 1912, which eliminated the last vestiges of Turkish rule in Macedonia, while the War of 1913 settled the question of the division of Macedonia among the victors. The periods between the wars were marked by intermittent guerrilla warfare in Bosnia (1849–74) and Macedonia (1898–1910). Such opposition to the Moslem overlords was undertaken by the local peasantry, often reinforced by young intelligentsia from Serbia and Montenegro. These guerrillas acted primarily under the influence of romantic nationalism of a Jacobin type, but a brief guerrilla period was also good preparation for any future political or army career. The fact that, at least in nationalist terms, these wars were successful, particularly for the Serbs and Montenegrins, helped increase the acceptance of warfare and violent armed resistance as the most effective way of achieving national ends.[15]

The Balkan wars were followed within a year by World War I. From the viewpoint of the pan-Yugoslavs, World War I was a war of liberation fought against the Austro-Hungarian Empire, in which more than half of the Yugoslav population lived. It is useful to remember that the formal reason for the outbreak of World War I was the assassination of the Austrian archduke Ferdinand in Sarajevo by young Bosnian radical nationalists who had received at least moral encouragement, if not arms, from that section of the young Serbian officer group which had been most intimately associated with the guerrilla warfare in Macedonia.[16]

World War I resulted in the unification of the Yugoslav lands for the first time in history, at an enormous human cost, in good part paid by the Serbs and Montenegrins. Estimates were that some 20 percent of the population of those two kingdoms perished during the war, and that the army casualty rates were approximately 40

15. The first two chapters of Vladimir Dedijer's *Sarajevo* (New York: Random House, 1968) are an excellent discussion of the effect of the successful Balkan Wars on the politics of the nationalist groups in the Yugoslav lands.

16. This is convincingly argued by Joachim Remak in his book on the assassination, *Sarajevo: The Story of a Political Murder* (New York: Criterion, 1959).

percent dead and wounded.[17] In the organization of the new state, however, the relevant factor was that the army regarded itself as a victor—the unifier, and therefore the creator of the new state. Although Serbia and Montenegro were occupied throughout much of World War I by the Austrians and Bulgarians, large sections of the countryside were dominated by guerrilla bands.

The unification of Yugoslavia brought together into a single nation-state peoples with a highly developed and successful warlike tradition, and territories previously part of Austro-Hungary, where people had lived under an orderly, if bureaucratic, civil government for centuries. It united a Serbo-Montenegrin establishment that regarded itself as being in the direct tradition of Jacobin nation-building (the nation being understood as the nation in arms), with territories that had a far higher level of economic and social development, a more developed bourgeoisie, and a political elite who had developed their skills under Austro-Hungarian parliamentari-anism with its stress on localism, particularism, and legality. It merged into one polity a basically civil society and two kingdoms whose social and political processes had been dominated by the need to prepare for and wage war.

The mix created in the newly unified country was explosive. The internal stresses inherent in the merging of widely different political cultures, a heritage of unsolved social questions, and the attempts to establish a centralized Yugoslav state rapidly provoked an opposi-tion, the extreme wings of which turned to terrorism. The Croatian ultranationalists, the Ustasi,[18] and the Macedonian IMRO (Internal Macedonian Revolutionary Organization) received financial aid and refuge from Italy, Hungary, and Bulgaria. The early communist movement had a terrorist wing soon eliminated by the police. The first minister of interior was assassinated by a young communist intellectual in 1921; the leader of the Croatian peasant party, Stepan Radic, and five of his fellow deputies were shot in parliament in 1928; and in 1934 King Alexander was assassinated in Marseilles by Macedonian and Croatian terrorists. Throughout the entire interwar period, the more conservative veterans of the guerrilla

17. See Tomasevich, *Peasants, Politics, and Economic Change*, pp. 226–29.
18. The Ustasi were Croatian fascists led by Dr. Ante Pavelic. Up to 1941 they were financed by Mussolini's Italy. After April 1941 Pavelic became the head of the Croat quisling state.

warfare in Macedonia and of World War I maintained a paramilitary organization called the Chetniks.

Of course, political life in interwar Yugoslavia was a good bit more complex than this sketch implies. However, political violence was widespread to the point where it could almost be viewed as the normal situation. In addition, this violence was general and was used by the government and its paramilitary supporters as well as by the opposition. To be sure, the readiness to resort to violence was not equal in all parts of the country. Slovenia, for example, remained relatively peaceful, with violence limited to some strikes and bloody repression by the gendarmerie. However, most of the rest of the country witnessed intermittent political violence by the government and its opponents during the interwar period.

WORLD WAR II: OCCUPATION AND RESISTANCE

When this fragile Yugoslavia, rent by internal dissension, found itself in the path of the Axis advance, it collapsed within ten days after the German invasion of April 6, 1941, despite the military tradition of the Serbs and Montenegrins who dominated the armed forces. Serious long-range consequences for later developments were implicit in the collapse of the army, its surrender in the field, and the escape of the government into exile in London. The demoralizing impact of this came home somewhat later, but the obvious contrast between the bitter and successful resistance during World War I and the shoddy performance of the army and government at the outset of World War II went a long way toward destroying whatever legitimacy the political order still had. For a people whose entire recent history had been deeply influenced by a tradition of successful wars of national liberation, the failure of the army to offer a creditable resistance destroyed one of the major pillars of the pre–World War II social order. One of the justifications for maintaining a unified Yugoslavia had been that the more developed regions of Croatia and Slovenia would acquire, in exchange for their taxes and loss of autonomy, at least the defense establishment indispensable for a nation-state in the modern world. The lack of major social advances in Serbia and Montenegro and the lack of sufficient investments for development had also been justified by the financial needs of the army.[19]

19. Ibid., pp. 628–29, 693–95.

The wartime occupation of Yugoslavia was characterized by extreme repression and brutality. The country was dismembered, various slices going to Hungary, Bulgaria, Italian-ruled Albania, Italy, and Germany, while the remaining parts were organized into three quasi states: Montenegro was given limited autonomy within the framework of the Italian Empire; Serbia was initially subjected to a form of administration similar to that of occupied Poland, that is, more or less direct occupation; and a much-enlarged Croatia was established as a German-Italian satellite and ally. Within two months of the establishment of the new order, government massacres began in Croatia. These massacres had two basic causes: the fact that the new Croatian state was now in the hands of the fascist Ustasi, and the fact that close to half of its population was Serbian. The openly stated aim of the government was to convert a third of these Serbs, expel a third, and eliminate the remainder.[20] Since much of the Serbian population lived in mountainous areas and had a long-developed warrior tradition, armed resistance broke out almost immediately, placing much of the country in the hands of guerrilla bands. Unfortunately, and predictably, some of the guerrilla bands also engaged in reprisals against their Croat and Moslem neighbors.[21]

In the summer of 1941, following the invasion by the Soviet Union, massive revolts developed in wide areas. From the very beginning of organized military resistance to the Axis occupier and their local supporters, two rival forces emerged: (1) the communist-led Partisans; and (2) the forces based in part on the remnants of the old army, mostly Serbian, under the command of Colonel (later General) Draza Mihailovic, and popularly known as the Chetniks.

20. Apart from differences in historical development, the major difference between the Serbs and the Croats is that the former are Orthodox and the latter Catholic. Conversion, therefore, implied a change in national identification. This had been the case under the Turks, where conversion to Islam meant denationalization and entry into the ruling nation. A fuller discussion of the political cultures of Yugoslavia and the role of religions can be found in my essays "Political Cultures and Social Mobility in Yugoslavia," already cited, and "Religion and Social Change in Yugoslavia," which was read at the International Symposium on Religion and Atheism in Communist Societies, Ottawa, Canada, 1971.

21. There are many sources on the wartime massacres; the most accessible is George W. Hoffman and Fred Warner Neal, *Yugoslavia and the New Communism* (New York: Twentieth Century Fund, 1962), pp. 41, 70, and 73.

Mihailovic was recognized by the Yugoslav Royal Government in London as the head of all resistance in the country and was named minister of the armed forces in successive London cabinets. The Chetniks resisted the occupier in the name of the old social order and the Royal Government in exile in London. They stressed their continuity with the Serbian national tradition and regarded themselves mainly as engaging in a defensive holding action until the time when the Allies could land. Thus they avoided, even in the early stages of war, a direct confrontation with major Italian and German units and generally limited themselves to a defense of the more mountainous and inaccessible areas. In contrast, the Partisans, under the leadership of the Communist Party, regarded themselves from the beginning as an all-Yugoslav force, which was fighting for a new social order as well as against the occupier. In the early days of resistance, the peasant guerrilla bands tended to join whichever force was on their terrain. However, after a few abortive attempts at cooperation, the Chetniks and the Communists found themselves locked in a bitter civil war which increasingly drove the nationalist Chetniks into first accommodation and later tacit and then open collaboration with the Italians and Germans. After all, both groups were concerned with the postwar social and political order, and the fact that the Partisan army established its own civil government wherever it liberated territory was regarded by the nationalists as an attack on the legal government of Yugoslavia.[22]

The country thus found itself engaged in both a civil war and a war against foreign occupiers. The human losses were staggering. Out of a population of some 16 million, the Yugoslavs lost 1.9 million, of which 1.1 million deaths were directly attributed to the war and to massacres. Most of the losses were probably the result of the civil war rather than of direct enemy action. The Partisans alone by the end of the war claimed 350,000 dead and 400,000 wounded.[23] The losses to the civilian population were, naturally, unevenly distributed. Some of the areas that had featured prominently in the resistance suffered terribly. However, when estimating the costs of the revolutionary war, it should be recognized that for many people there were no real alternatives to resistance. For example, Communists and their known sympathizers were hunted men in any case;

22. Ibid., p. 70.
23. Ibid., pp. 41 and 86–88.

their chances of survival by going underground in the cities proved worse than when they joined the armed resistance in the mountains. It was in the cities that the occupier and the quislings were most powerful and consolidated power most effectively. The case of the Jews was similar, and the few Jewish intellectuals and students who survived the war were in the Partisan units. For that matter, Serbs in the Ustasi ruled parts of the country and could often survive the massacres only by resisting—a fact later recognized by the Germans themselves, who put a stop to major massacres after the first year of occupation. By this time, however, the peasants in active resistance would accept no guarantees by Axis forces that a no-reprisals policy would be followed if they did surrender.

For many, therefore, armed resistance appeared to be the safest course, if anyone was to survive at all. This still begs the question as to why the resistance proved as effective as it did. Surely the existence of a population that knew how to use arms and had a tradition of defending itself, even against a "legitimate" government, did much to facilitate the task of the Partisans.

The Partisan leadership was all too aware of the fact that many of the peasants in their ranks had not joined out of ideological conviction as much as out of fear of massacres and reprisals by the occupier. In a number of areas, the Partisans attacked individual soldiers and police posts that had no direct military value, fully understanding that the result would be a punitive expedition, driving the population of the area into flight and the men into the hills where they wound up joining forces with the Partisans. This ruthlessness of the Partisans in the early period forced a transition from the traditional pattern of village defense against outside threats to the village itself, to the formation of units large enough to hold liberated territory and resist large enemy units.

While the existing tradition almost guaranteed resistance, an additional factor was needed in order to transform this highly localist tradition of defense into a war of national liberation. In the nineteenth century that additional factor had been provided by the expansionist nationalists. During World War II, when the costs of resistance were so much higher, this organizational impulse required the kind of highly centralized and ruthlessly nonlocalist force that could be provided only by the Communists, because the cost of resistance at that scale was jeopardizing the fabric of social order itself. Given the novel ruthlessness of the enemy, resistance now meant total mobilization, breaking down the authority patterns of old over young, men over women, solid peasants over the "shiftless," and so on. So fundamental a shake-up of village order hardly promised that a return to "normalcy" would be possible after the war. But if this made the traditionalists in the villages uneasy, the Communists were also very conscious of the dual effect of a war of liberation on the social structure and social stability of the villages. The difference is that they regarded the shake-up of the village social order as a welcome and desirable side effect of the struggle against the occupier and for state power.

THE EFFECTS OF THE REVOLUTIONARY WAR ON POSTWAR YUGOSLAVIA

The Yugoslav Communists came to power in a way that sharply differentiated their power base from that of the other Eastern European states. They are not on a continuum with the East European states, where Communism was brought in by the victorious Soviet armies or, in the case of Czechoslovakia, where the political preconditions for the takeover were made possible by the Soviet victory. Rather, Yugoslavia is more analogous to countries in which the accession to power was the result of a victorious civil war, and in this respect it has more in common with North Vietnam, China, Cuba, and Albania. When one enumerates the countries where a communist party has come to power primarily through its own efforts, it becomes evident that what they all have in common is that they are *independent* communist regimes whose social and political policies are the result of the conscious political direction of the national leadership. They also share the fact that the class foe was by and large wiped out before power was consolidated (except in Cuba), and that the revolutionary government began with a countryside that was already basically transformed.

The Yugoslav Communists came to power with a number of unanticipated by-products of victory. The first was a large body of experienced Partisan fighters who greatly outnumbered the prewar underground party. The Communist Party had entered the civil war with some 12,000 members, of whom not more than 3,000 were alive by the end. However, by the end of the war, in June 1945, there were

140,000 party members.[24] The new cadres seasoned by wartime experience had developed a self-confidence alien to the apparatniks of most East European communist parties. The exigencies of civil war and guerrilla warfare put a premium on initiative, since, no matter how centralized the formal structure of party and partisan leadership was, circumstances constantly arose calling for local decisions. The local party leaders were also forced to mobilize far broader strata than they had been able to reach in the prewar period, in order to make the essential step from guerrilla bands to an army of liberation. This in turn meant, again through no conscious planning and indeed against the formal ideological prejudices of the party, that the bulk of the army was peasant. Even the Proletarian Brigades of the Partisan army were often composed of students, unemployed intellectuals, workers, and peasants. Thus, the cadre developed during the war was a composite of prewar underground party and youth leaders, a relatively small number of workers, a vast majority of peasant origin. One characteristic of this type of a cadre that still has a marked effect on the structure of the political leadership of the country is the unusually large role of younger persons. A less desirable consequence is the relative age-homogeneity of those presently in power. The brutal necessities of guerrilla warfare had placed a premium on youth.

The second unanticipated consequence of the war was that a very large number of peasants had become uprooted from their villages and could not easily return to traditional village existence. In the first place, many of the villages had been physically destroyed. Also, the victorious Partisan veterans had a claim on the new social order. Thus, many of the peasants entered the cities via the Partisan army or were resettled in the richer lowlands as a reward for their wartime performance. This relocation of peasants was facilitated by the fact that over 700,000 persons were expelled or emigrated from Yugoslavia as a result of the civil war;[25] much of this population was composed of the German minority that had lived in the prosperous northern plains, the wealthier peasants who had allied themselves with the anti-Communists, and prewar government notables. The

24. See my essay "Mobility and Recruitment of Yugoslav Leadership: The Role of the League of Communists," in "Proceedings of the World Congress of the International Political Science Association," Munich, 1970 (mimeo.).

25. See Hoffman and Neal, *Yugoslavia and the New Communism*, pp. 28, 31, and 41.

movement of mountaineers into the plains created a substantial population whose economic and social betterment depended on the new social order.

A further consequence of the large-scale uprooting of the peasantry was the facilitation of the entry of peasants into industry. The government did not need to use repressive measures to get peasants from the countryside into the cities in the early stages of industrialization, and the later stages created a new dynamic—networks developed connecting the villagers to the cities where they now had relatives. Increasingly, propaganda for the new modern life style was carried back to the villages by newly urbanized peasants returning to visit their families.

Another major consequence was the greater self-confidence of the party and its supporters, based on their defeat of their internal enemies in open warfare. This sharply differentiated the Yugoslav party from the other East European parties. Most of the latter took power in societies that had not undergone a civil war, and where the remnants of the old parties and hostile classes were still present. Thus, in the other East European countries, repeated purges characterized the first decade of the new regime, building up a widespread store of resentment. In the case of the Yugoslavs, the entry of the communist regime to power by and large concluded the purge rather than marking its beginning. As a consequence, the Yugoslav party was able to make much broader concessions to popular sentiment, and, after a relatively short abortive attempt at collectivization, it worked out a modus vivendi with the new peasantry which has lasted to this day.[26] The fact that the party did not have to "war" on its own peasantry in turn meant that greater energies were freed for the modern sector and that the new regime gained wider acceptance. In effect, the compromise was that the party left the villages more or less alone and concentrated on developing a dynamic, modern sector in the cities to act as a magnet on the countryside. The self-confidence developed by the Yugoslav leadership goes a long way to explain its successful resistance against the rest of the Eastern European bloc when the Stalin-Tito break took place. The Yugoslav leadership did not feel that it owed its

26. Ibid., pp. 133, 136, 171–72. The peasants have retained most of the land, over 85 percent of which is in private peasant plots.

victory to external forces, and it believed that it could draw upon broad layers of the population if resistance again became necessary.[27]

The ruling establishment recruited from the victorious guerrilla army also effected a very rapid change in the status of women in Yugoslav society. It is difficult to estimate how much of this was the consequence of party ideology and how much can be ascribed to the effect of massive armed resistance. However, women served in Partisan units in substantial numbers both as fighters and as auxiliaries, and this had an irreversible effect on the villages in which they operated, and on the postwar makeup of the elite. Part of the Partisan strategy in villages had been to place great value on the participation of women and the young. This policy was in part dictated by wartime strategic needs but the effect has been long lasting. One must remember that the Partisans were strongest, for obvious reasons, in the most primitive and backward parts of the country. The mountains, which had been the archetypal stronghold of patriarchal values, were the major recruiting ground for the elite Partisan units. Thus, the war shattered a whole set of preconceptions in the backward mountain areas, although it had less of an effect in the plains. The women who entered the Partisan units and, through them, the party, were not ready to go back to traditional patriarchal households. Nor were the young Partisan veterans willing to accept the authority of the village elders. They both joined the migration into the cities and the upward movement into the ruling establishment.

While the broad outlines of Yugoslav social policy toward women have remained unchanged since then, the social position of women has regressed somewhat. Among the present elite, women occupy top posts in the political structure far more often than in the economic structure. Also, in the higher party bodies women constitute a larger proportion than in the lower party bodies,[28] that is to say, the

---

27. During the Czechoslovak crisis, the Yugoslav army distributed arms in the villages and factories. Reservists are expected to keep arms in their homes. Arms registration laws are very liberal and private ownership of pistols, shotguns and rifles is widespread. (Personal observation.)

28. This is also reflected in the political institutions. Thus, there are 18 women in the 183-member upper chamber of the Federal Assembly, while the figures in the individual republic chambers are 21 out of 399 in Bosnia, 9 out of 254 in Montenegro, and 21 out of 333 in Macedonia, ranging up to a high of 25 out of 285 (still under 10

Partisan generation of women has maintained its position, but their gains have not carried over into younger age groups to the same extent.

The needs of civil war, combined with a war against a foreign occupier, dictated a type of resistance that utilized all available human power and could not permit itself to be limited by traditional ascriptions of roles to women. The period of postwar rebuilding was also a period of mobilization, and part of the party cadre was composed of women wartime leaders. As the society normalized and the pressures on the peasant society to make extraordinary efforts were removed, however, the traditional patterns tended to reassert themselves, though this was less true in the cities and in modern industry.

The formal structure is egalitarian. There are masses of women professionals, doctors, engineers, dentists, and politicians. It is worth noting, however, that, even where the legal demands of the traditional women's movements have been achieved, the social pressure of tradition is reflected in a decreasing number of women in political life. Normalization also means privatization and depoliticization of broad layers of the population; therefore, it is primarily in the public arena, subject to the direct influence of the League of Communists, that formal equality continues to assert itself.

A former Partisan colonel, a woman, pointed out to me that, when it was most difficult to serve in the armed forces, namely, during the guerrilla war, women were considered capable of doing so, but that in the peacetime forces the tendency has been to retire women officers as soon as possible. A lesson may be found in this: in traditional societies the social upheavals created by civil wars may do more to advance women's equality than formal reforms; however, subsequent "normalization" and stabilization will roll back at least some of the gains.

The destructiveness of the civil war had two side effects that proved to be important in the development of the new Yugoslavia. The first was the traumatic effect of the wartime communal massacres and civil war, the very massiveness of which repressed expression of local ethnic nationalism for at least two decades. The

---

percent) in the case of Slovenia. In the lowest-level institutions, i.e., the commune committees, women account for 2,821 out of 40,791. *Statistical Yearbook* (Belgrade: Savezni Zavod za Statistiku, 1970), pp. 63–64.

consequences of nationalism run rampant were only too evident. The Yugoslav Communist Party thus benefited from the moral discrediting of the prewar leaders, whose politics had been held to have led directly or indirectly to the fratricidal Serb-Croat-Moslem massacres. A genuine revulsion toward the immediate past, particularly among the young, made it unnecessary for party propaganda to create one.

Second, the physical destructiveness of the war—which had left much of the country in shambles, over a quarter of the population homeless, and industrial capacity reduced to less than 30 percent of what it had been in 1941[29]—meant that the major task of rebuilding could be used as a cement for new loyalties. My impression is that very little compulsion needed to be used in the formation of the work brigades right after the war. The desperate need to rebuild was self-evident.

Indirect consequences of the civil war are still present. One is the extremely high emphasis placed on education, both regular and adult, as an instrument for effecting social mobility. This can be traced to the immediate postwar need to train professionals, administrators, and bureaucrats quickly for a new social order where most of their predecessors either had been eliminated or were politically unacceptable.[30] The fact that the Communist regime was also a mobilizing, modernizing regime meant that the need for cadres was in any case greater than the supply of prewar educated strata.

The rapid social mobility of the former Partisan fighters has proved both an asset and a problem. The asset is the dynamism that characterizes the society, and the feeling that all positions are open to men of talent and energy, regardless of social origin or previous training; the feeling is widespread that training can come later in one's career if one misses the normal opportunities open to the members of the middle classes in the cities. There is thus a breakdown of the mystique that formerly identified middle-class

29. Tomasevich, *Peasants, Politics, and Economic Change*, pp. 297–98; Hoffman and Neal, *Yugoslavia and the New Communism*, pp. 86–88.

30. The very rapid mobility of the early postwar elite is discussed in Lenard Cohen's "Social Background and Recruitment of Yugoslav Political Elites, 1918–1949," in *Opinion-Making Elites in Yugoslavia*, ed. Allen H. Barton, Bogdan Denitch, and Charles Kadushin (New York: Praeger, Special Series, 1973).

culture and background with technical competence. It has become clear that many of the new factory directors and local leaders, people with a minimal formal education, perform as adequately as the old elite with its cultural monopoly.

The problem is, however, that the high mobility rate could not be maintained after the society began to normalize. After a massive university system was developed in response to the immediate postwar needs, the growth in the number of graduates began to exceed the capacities of the society to absorb them in positions for which they considered themselves suited. This problem is made more acute by the age structure of the Partisan cadre. Most of the Partisan leaders were in their early twenties during the war, which means that the age group occupying the leadership posts is not about to retire in the immediate future. These are men and women ranging from 45 to 55, in their prime of life, who have held leading posts for a generation. No expansion of a normal sort can create sufficient posts for the younger, well-trained, educated generation produced by the postwar universities.[31] Consequently, the seeds of a real generational conflict exist. In addition to this conflict, as noted in chapter 2, a large proportion of the wartime generation of leaders will probably retire at about the same time, making continuity of leadership a potential problem. This difficulty is aggravated by the intense solidarity of the Partisan veterans and their feeling that their generation had been tempered by a major social revolution and a bitter civil war. They do not see their successors, who are probably technically more competent, as having that additional quality which is created only by an intense common struggle against overwhelming odds. They joined an illegal, hunted party waging a war in the mountains; their would-be successors joined a ruling establishment.

This fundamentally ascriptive quality or, rather, this quality that has *become* ascriptive over the years, is not duplicable. Considerable bitterness exists among the young because they have no functional equivalent of the Partisan experience to test them, and to assure to the able, the lucky, and the courageous rapid passage into the elite. It is, after all, not their fault that they were born after 1931. These younger generations must try to advance under conditions where "pull" and connections are increasingly replaced by the bureau-

31. See Denitch, "Mobility and Recruitment of Yugoslav Leadership."

cratic norms of a modern industrial society. Achievement measured
by conventional schooling and routinized loyalty is now expected.

As we have seen, the historic relationship of violence to the social
structure in Yugoslavia created a structure in wider areas of the
country, particularly those that had been within or on the borders of
the Turkish Empire, that was almost unique in contemporary
Europe. In these areas, which have been subject to prolonged
violence, the adaptation of the family structure to the necessities of
war and the expansion of kinship networks for the purposes of
self-defense lasted into the twentieth century. There emerged a
peasantry with a tradition of armed self-defense and de facto, later
de jure, ownership of the land it worked. In turn, this meant that,
when a modern nation-state was first established in those parts of
Yugoslavia in the early nineteenth century, the state apparatus
tended to be recruited from those who had played a role in the wars
of national independence or had been guerrilla leaders. The political
elite was thus inseparably linked to the tradition of war. The middle
classes developed relatively late and had little influence. The first
two modern factories built in Serbia in the nineteenth century were a
cannon foundry and a munitions factory, both owned by the state
rather than by members of the bourgeoisie, which was then almost
nonexistent. Out of a rough-hewn egalitarianism, imprinted with a
pattern of almost continual violence, there emerged a relatively
repressive, inegalitarian regime with the police, the military, and the
bureaucracy as major exploiting strata.

The tradition of militarism and the national liberation struggles
began to atrophy after World War I, only to be reawakened under
the severe challenge of the Nazi occupation and the policy of
extermination pursued against segments of the population. This
Nazi-sponsored violence, far better organized, could not be resisted
effectively by traditional means. The policy of massive reprisals in
areas that showed resistance at the beginning of the Partisan War
made the costs of resistance too great for locally based traditional
elites who wanted to resist in the name of the old social order. In any
case, the latter believed that the ultimate fate of Yugoslavia would
be determined by the results of the war in general, and not by the
struggle of the Yugoslav resistance. Thus, the traditional nationalists
soon ceased resisting the occupiers and devoted most of their

attention to their real postwar rivals, the Partisan army and the Communist Party that led it.

For the Communists, however, the extreme social dislocation caused by the resistance proved to be an asset. The very brutality of the occupying forces acted as a recruiting agent in some areas. When villages were destroyed, their younger and more energetic inhabitants readily joined the Partisan guerrilla bands when possible. After a while, when resistance had reached a certain level, it became evident to the Nazis that reprisals no longer were effective. The Germans themselves concluded that the reprisals, precisely because they gave no alternative to the peasant population, were an ineffective way to fight the Partisans. By this time, however, the Partisans had built up a substantial core of guerrilla fighters and had begun receiving massive military aid from abroad. In a way that reminds one hauntingly of another guerrilla war, the raising of the ante on violence destroyed the moderates and the traditional notables as a political force in the field, leaving as contenders only those who were able to cope with the violence in an organized way without paying much attention to the local effect of that violence on particular villages or areas.

The violence of the civil war destroyed the fabric of the traditional village society and upset its internal balance to the point where the traditional parties ceased to be able to draw support from it. In guerrilla warfare, it is the vigorous and the young, rather than the experienced and the old, who are at a premium. Thus, a generational revolution occurred in the villages, paralleling the Communist consolidation of power. It was striking that right after the Communists' consolidation of power, most of the party's leadership in the villages was composed of persons who normally would have been considered far too young for such responsibilities. The mean age of the party cadre in one area studied was twenty-one.[32] The effect on the village authority structures of having young, uprooted peasants placed in positions of authority was enormous. It was also in the villages that the change in the role of women in the immediate postrevolutionary period was the greatest. The party policy of recruiting the young and of challenging the traditional authority of

32. Bette Denich, "Social Mobility in a Yugoslav Town" (Ph.D. diss., University of California, Berkeley, 1969). Chapter 2 discusses the party cadre in the postwar years.

the family and clan had the indirect effect of speeding up the entry of women into modern society.

Since the guerrilla war also had the characteristics of a civil war, most of the potential enemies of the Communist Party had been eliminated by the end of the war. The party's consolidation of power, therefore, was followed by a decrease of terror and violence, reversing the pattern common to the rest of Eastern Europe. This is not to say that the Yugoslavs purged fewer members of the prewar elite and political parties, but rather that they had eliminated them in the context of a civil war that had forced most of them into a tacit alliance with the enemy occupier. Thus, Yugoslavia was remarkable even in the period of its most rigid monolithicism for the relative absence of purges.

The function of such purges is, after all, not irrational. Terrorism directed against non–party members acts to disarm potential opposition, impress the society with the all-powerful nature of party rule, and increase the ability of the party to mobilize manpower for modernization. Above all, it acts, or attempts to act, to break down the traditional ties of solidarity that could operate as a defense against the pressures of the party and the state. Terror against party members themselves maintains the aura of continual mobilization and the state of tension inside the party necessary to prevent the formation of cliques which, after all, do require an element of mutual trust.

In Yugoslavia, terror against party members was utilized only in the period immediately after the Tito-Stalin break, when it had a completely different function. It was not a fevered fantasy of the prosecutors but the hard reality that part of the party apparatus was penetrated by Russian agents and Russian supporters; this explains the purges in Yugoslavia in 1948–51. But even during that period this "terrorism" was remarkable for its lack of killings.[33] Most of the party members who were purged and jailed as pro-Russian were released within two or three years. By East European standards, that hardly rates as terrorism. Furthermore, terrorism against the population as a whole was at no time systematically utilized, and even the

---

33. Figures on political executions are all but impossible to get. It is the consensus of most Western scholars that the number of deaths was very small. The total number arrested and jailed, however, was over 150,000.

policy of confiscation of estates and factories was carried out, at least nominally, within the framework of wartime measures, that is, the estates and factories of wartime collaborators were confiscated. Since, with very few exceptions, the prewar bourgeoisie had collaborated with the Nazis, the social displacement of this entire class occurred primarily under the guise of patriotism rather than as a confiscatory policy of the party. To be sure, the few noncollaborators had their property seized not long after. Still, the confiscation was by and large perceived as a measure resulting from the civil war. Members of the former middle and upper classes who remained in the country were treated more leniently than elsewhere in Eastern Europe, partly because those who had most compromised themselves had retreated with the Germans in 1945.

In short, the Communist Party perceived, quite accurately, that it had relatively few internal enemies and that these few, shattered by defeat, were dispersed throughout the population, which was either friendly or neutral.

One feature that characterized the coming to power of the other East European regimes is the fact that they were forced into a sharp conflict with the peasantry. Since in most of these countries peasants formed the majority of the population, this naturally reinforced the need for a relatively high degree of repressiveness. By contrast, the Yugoslavs, having come to power precisely on a peasant base, avoided this problem. Except for a brief attempt, abortive and unsystematic, to collectivize in 1951, party policy toward the villagers has been laissez-faire. Eighty-five percent of the land is in private peasant hands. The 15 percent that is not was mostly confiscated from the German minority and the rich, not from the peasants. The regime's agrarian maximum of 10 hectares did not mean a reduction of the holdings for the majority of the peasants; on the contrary, the land reform increased the holdings of most peasants. Where the party did interfere, it did so indirectly, by destroying the authority patterns, by pushing ahead youths and women, and even more by creating a modern sector which increasingly drained the villages of the vital, the ambitious, and the young. The party policy toward the peasantry is based on the assumption that they will gradually move into the industrial sector as it continues to expand and that the ones who remain in the villages will become efficient small producers, increasingly part of the new modern social order.

This is the meaning behind the policy of pushing consumer goods, since the rising demand for available consumer goods proves to be more effective than terror in inducing the villagers to adapt their production methods to the market. And I believe that one of the reasons for the policy toward the peasants is the party leadership's very vivid recollection of the capacities of the peasantry when pushed too far.

An argument can be made that the decentralization of the administration and the economy found in Yugoslavia, unique among East European countries, can also be traced to the civil war. The fact that the party cadres had proved themselves in the extreme test of the civil war and the further test of a break with the Soviet bloc meant that the national party leadership had more confidence in the local leaders than would have been the case with a party built on persons who had joined a ruling establishment. Also the conditions of guerrilla warfare had imposed a type of decentralization which put a premium on local initiative and innovation within broad, centrally determined, political and strategic guidelines. This created a very different type of cadre from those developed by the more regular bureaucratic paths of advancement in the other East European communist parties. Not only did the top leadership have more reason to place confidence in local leaders, and consequently less fear of a loss of authority, but the local leaders were accustomed to handling authority without referring all problems to the center. A guerrilla army is painfully aware of the fact that it requires support from its base and environment. A party formed in the process of guerrilla warfare is, in my opinion, far less likely to engage in policies that antagonize the mass of the population than a party coming to power either by a coup d'état or with the help of foreign allies. The degree of liberalization and expanding freedom in Yugoslavia can therefore be linked to the fact that the state is run by a party most of whose leadership was formed in a prolonged period of mass resistance.[34]

34. This was not the case in Cuba, of course, where the revolutionary war was far less massive in terms of the number of people involved and more limited geographically, but it was the case in North Vietnam. Both of those polities are now far more repressive than the Yugoslav one. However, I would argue that the Vietnamese case is

The experience of the civil war provided sufficient impetus for a whole generation. That generation's career is coming to an end. The newer breed of political leaders is increasingly recruited from among those who are too young to have played a role in the civil war. The resistance mystique is also probably wearing off among the population as a whole. Attempts by the League of Communists to keep it alive seem to have limited effectiveness. The society is thus becoming more normal in one way. However, it is the early mobilization stage in communist takeovers that is historically the most painful, and in that phase, now past, the path to power of the Yugoslav Communist Party played a decisive role in creating what is today by far the most decentralized and least repressive of the communist-ruled polities.

The interesting question to consider is, what would be a functional equivalent to a guerrilla war. After all, if it is the fact that it came to power as a result of the guerrilla war that makes the Yugoslav party so liberal, we might conclude that a precondition for establishment of a liberal communist regime is that it come to power following a civil war. In my opinion, the functional equivalent in modern industrial societies is a party that builds up its cadres over a prolonged period of class conflict and becomes a mass party before coming to power—specifically, something like the case of Italy, where the party is not just a bureaucratic apparatus or a clique of revolutionary conspirators but a mass party with innumerable linkages to its supporters. It also has a leadership that has proved itself over the years, a mass base it cannot afford to antagonize, and an independence from its sister parties in Eastern Europe, all of which suggests that such a party coming to power would probably be neither capable nor desirous of establishing a repressive regime over the mass of the population. Thus, ironically, it would seem that Italian reformism and its Yugoslav counterpart—the mass party and massive guerrilla warfare—both create polities in which the linkage between the party and its mass base is firm and where the party cannot set itself up against the society it rules.

This tentative conclusion is, of course, profoundly pessimistic about the prospects for stable, popular, modernizing regimes in

---

explained by the fact that the civil war had not yet been concluded, whereas Castro's regime came to power through something more analogous to a putsch than to a prolonged war involving masses of peasants.

underdeveloped countries. Most of the "new" nations are ruled by elites that came to power neither through mobilizing the population for a massive armed struggle nor through the creation of a mass party with a stable base and leadership. Therefore, an intimate linkage between the rulers and the ruled is generally absent. This creates fragile polities, where little stands to prevent the military or any other minority from seizing power, and where little pressure exists to satisfy the needs of broad social strata. Most "revolutionary" groups in such countries are small, elitist cliques whose guerrilla bands show remarkably little ability to mobilize any kind of mass support. Where this is not the case, as in Tunisia, Algeria, and the Portuguese African colonies, I believe that stable polities capable of meeting the tasks of modernization and state-building, with relatively little repression, will tend to emerge.

4

Uprooting the Traditional Order

The previous chapter discussed the effects of violence and the combined civil war and war of liberation on social change in Yugoslavia. I turn at this point to the systematic destruction of the institutional basis of the old social order which occurred during the period immediately after the war. The institutional underpinnings of the prewar social order varied from region to region. However, the nexus of the superficially imposing Yugoslav state apparatus before the war was the expanded civil service bureaucracy and the armed forces, primarily Serbian, supported by the private ownership of industry and commerce and, to a lesser extent, the large landlords.[1]

The ideological legitimation of the old system had three basic roots, religious, national (ethnic), and social. Religion in the Yugoslav lands often coincided with nationality and the Serbian Orthodox Church accepted the legitimacy of the pre–World War II Yugoslav state as a successor to the previous Serbian and Montenegrin kingdoms. The Catholic hierarchy had a more ambivalent attitude, as did the Moslem religious establishment. However, all three regarded themselves as barriers to drastic social change and, above all, as barriers to a communist-led social revolution. The Second World War had badly shaken the hold of the religious establishments on broad masses of the people, in part because of the collaboration of some churches with the occupiers, but above all because the forces mobilized to carry out the social revolution were aggressively atheist and took steps to destroy the economic holdings of the churches, as one of their first postwar measures.

The rapid process of modernization and urbanization after the war uprooted vast numbers of peasants and placed them in an

1. The best discussion of pre–World War II Yugoslavia is found in Jozo Tomasevich's *Peasants, Politics, and Economic Change in Yugoslavia* (Stanford: Stanford University Press, 1956). See also Wayne S. Vucinic, ed., *Contemporary Yugoslavia* (Berkeley: University of California Press, 1969), ch. 1, pp. 3–58.

environment where the churches had little if any effect on their lives. Religious observance in Yugoslavia is increasingly limited to the old and to the rural sector, and the fragmentation of the religious communities has made impossible the creation of a counterweight analogous to the role the Catholic church played in Poland and, to a lesser extent, in Hungary. Further, the churches are additionally imperiled even in their current weakened state by the fact that traditionalist and nationalist forces in Yugoslavia often seek to use religious tradition and organizations as a base for their operation. In any case, there being no national Yugoslav church, the churches are regionally based. They tend to be increasingly disregarded by the modern intelligentsia and workers in most regions.[2]

The old civil service, having placed itself in good part at the disposal of the occupiers, was demolished by the victory of the Partisans. Postwar social mobility filled bureaucratic slots with persons who owed their advancement to the victory of the social revolution and who in most cases came from newly activated strata. The old social base of the prewar civil service was narrow, and, while that civil service was modernizing and shared a general ideology of progress as defined by Compte, it proved to be, by and large, both inefficient and enormously expensive.[3] The notables in the villages had been generally compromised during the civil war and were in any case replaced by the new National Committees of Liberation, which deliberately included women, the young, and the poor. These National Committees of Liberation formed the core of the new state power, even during the war, and evolved into the present organs of communal self-government. A number of the functions previously filled by civil servants are now filled by elected bodies of citizens.[4]

As for the old military establishment, the Royal Army lost whatever legitimacy it had because of its miserable performance

2. The most recent work on religion in Yugoslavia is summarized in the special edition of *Nase Teme*, no. 12 (December 1972); in particular see Srdjan Vrcan's "Vjera i politika," pp. 2004–19.

3. Tomasevich, esp. ch. 13, pp. 233–61.

4. For a good normative but somewhat dated description of the Yugoslav system, see George W. Hoffman and Fred Warner Neal, *Yugoslavia and the New Communism* (New York: Twentieth Century Fund, 1962). Yugoslav sources are too numerous to cite but perhaps the best is Dusan Bilandjic's *Borba za samoupravni socijalizam u Jugoslaviji, 1945–1969* (Zagreb: RAD, 1969).

during the German invasion of 1941. A new officer corps was formed out of Partisan cadre and very few of the prewar officers were coopted into the new structure. The army party organization has effectively socialized the new officer corps into the values of the party, and the army should be considered, insofar as it acts politically at all, as one section of the party organization. Since the officer corps is recruited from poorer regions and strata, it tends to be intensely loyal to the new regime.

The economic measures undertaken by the revolutionary regime in Yugoslavia immediately after World War II were more drastic than those undertaken in other East European countries, since the civil war had in good part eliminated the prewar bourgeoisie in addition to providing the formal justification for the first wave of nationalization. Land reform in Yugoslavia set a maximum land-holding lower than that of Poland and prevented any prosperous class of peasants from developing in the countryside. Nevertheless, as noted in chapter 3, the reform increased the holdings of the majority of the peasants. Subsequent rural depopulation through industrialization and urbanization has created a situation where this maximum may well be increased, although the development of anything resembling a kulak class is unlikely since the most generous proposals would still limit holdings to a maximum of twenty hectares of arable land (the present limit is ten hectares).

The basic policy that has been tacitly worked out by the new regime and the peasantry is a compromise: "live and let live." In practice this means the division of Yugoslav society into two segments: (1) a modern, industrialized, urban sector which participates in the new institutions of Yugoslav socialism, and (2) the rural sector, which until the last few years was left to stagnate but remained basically independent of the sociopolitical institutions of the regime. The enormous and convincing emphasis on the virtues of urban life and modernization in Yugoslavia has meant that the most energetic, potentially mobile, and ambitious peasants abandon the countryside, making the village population increasingly older and predominantly female.

The private sector in the Yugoslav economy is not only tiny but it is a new sector based primarily on artisans and small restaurant owners and is not a lineal descendant of the prewar owning classes. It represents fundamentally a thin layer of petit bourgeoisie, which exchanges its relative material prosperity for a pariahlike political status. It has almost no social and political weight and occasionally becomes the target of campaigns against increasing social differences. The number of persons employed in the private sector has declined slightly in the period 1966–70 and now comprises around 5 percent of the total nonagricultural work force.[5]

Fundamental to the destruction of the old social order was the elimination of the cultural near-monopoly of the middle and upper classes. The vast, unprecedented expansion of the system of higher education in Yugoslavia has broken up the previous monopoly by offering higher education to strata previously excluded. The expansion of university education involved not merely a quantitative increase in the number of students in institutions of higher learning but above all a qualitative change in the structure of university education, emphasizing technological and economic faculties at the expense of the more traditional faculties of law and philosophy. This created a new middle stratum which bases its status on the expertise necessary to an expanding modern economy rather than on the traditional role of the gatekeepers of a national culture. This new layer, whose expansion will continue in the foreseeable future, is reinforced by the increasing education of the working class and a homogenization of urban culture, both of which attack the old values of particularism and traditionalism. Mass media are becoming more responsive to the needs of the new middle stratum and the urban working class at the expense of specific national cultural heritages, creating a Yugoslav-wide culture which in turn is increasingly integrated into European and world culture. Thus the urban citizens of Yugoslavia relate increasingly to musical and other cultural forms of the industrialized Western world, breaking their link with the traditional village culture.

In this situation, the League of Communists, as the carrier of the values of modernization in the society, finds itself reflecting more and more the values and life styles of a growing sector of the population which has rejected the traditionalist view of progress as a zero-sum game, that is, the idea that progress can only occur at the expense of other strata, or that individual success can occur only at the expense of other individuals. It has turned to the notion of "expanding

5. *Statisticki godisnjak Jugoslavije, 1972* (Belgrade: Savezni Zavod za Statistiku, 1972).

goods" as a basis of social advancement and progress; in other words, growing sectors of the Yugoslav population accept as normal an expanding economy with widening opportunities for the able and ambitious. So long as the party remains associated in the minds of the newly urbanized strata with economic and social progress in which they share, its legitimacy is assured. Memories of the old social order for most Yugoslavs refer to their rural past and an absence of progress.

Part of the resentment of the traditional middle classes and intelligentsia toward the new social order is a reflection of the fact that a real social revolution took place. A social, as distinct from a political, revolution necessarily means that whole social strata have moved into roles that were not traditionally ascribed to them and wield political and social power in violation of the traditional norms. Thus, a theme found among the older literati and intelligentsia who speak for the remnants of the former social order is peculiarly reminiscent of some of the themes found in the nineteenth-century novels in Britain and France which reflected the resentment of the older gentry toward the new industrial and mercantile bourgeoisie. The new rulers are perceived as having no roots, no culture, and thus no proper equipment in terms of education and background to qualify them for their new status. Clearly, this judgment is objectively false, since it can be shown that the educational attainments of the new Yugoslav opinion-making elite are in no way inferior to those of the traditional occupants of such roles (see the Appendix). On the contrary, university education is now the major road to social advancement, and what is in fact objectionable to such critics is the absence of traditional class criteria for recruitment to higher posts. Simply put, the characteristics of the new elites in terms of accent, cultural habits, and social background are those of socially mobile peasants and workers who have advanced through the twin roads of political activism and education. If this shift in the social composition and style of the new notables were not present, we would conclude that a political revolution had occurred without concomitant social upheaval.

THE DECLINE OF THE RURAL SECTOR

Central to the destruction of the social order of prewar Yugoslavia are the major demographic shifts that occurred after the revolution, changing Yugoslavia from a predominantly agricultural country to one entering the stage of middle development. However, before we begin to analyze this process, a cursory glance at the historical background would be useful.

Patterns of land ownership and the status of peasants varied considerably in the lands which were joined to make up post-Versailles Yugoslavia. Basically, one can divide the Yugoslav lands into three rough categories: those that had been under Austro-Hungary (with the exception of Bosnia and Herzegovina), lands that had been occupied by the Turks up to the Balkan Wars, that is, Macedonia, southern Serbia, and Kosovo, and lands that had been within the framework of the independent prinipalities of Serbia and Montenegro. The division is rough, and a more detailed discussion can be found in Jozo Tomasevich's excellent *Peasants, Politics, and Economic Change in Yugoslavia*, and my own short essay on political cultures in Yugoslavia (see the Bibliography).

In the Austro-Hungarian lands, the serfs were liberated in 1848; this was not extended to Bosnia-Herzegovina, where the institutions of late Ottoman feudalism were maintained. Large-scale landlordism was present, with estates owned by both private landlords and the Catholic church, and the impoverished peasantry in most areas held landholdings below the minimum necessary to maintain the large families that were then the norm. Farms with holdings of 1,000 or more acres were scarce, amounting to only 0.05 percent of the total number of farms, but they controlled a disproportionate 22.4 percent of the total land. At the same time, farms less than 5 acres in size accounted for 44 percent of all farms but held only 8.4 percent of the land. There was a middle peasantry, with holdings of 5–20 acres, comprising 41 percent of the total land and 47 percent of all farm units, and a smaller number of substantial peasants with holdings of over 20 acres. In Vojvodina, in the same period, 32 percent of all farmland was in farms of over 1,000 acres, and a substantial proportion of the remainder was in the medium-sized households owned by the German minority in that region. Because of primogeniture, Slovenia had managed to maintain more substantial peasant households, 10 acres being the average, and had fewer large farms.

In the case of the Turkish-ruled provinces and Bosnia-Herzegovina, the majority of the peasants were serfs, owning no land or at the very most only the garden around the house; some 7,000

landlords, almost exclusively Moslem, had holdings worked by over
90,000 serf families in Bosnia, and the independent peasants were
also almost exclusively Moslem. The pattern was even more extreme
in Macedonia. There the serfs were legally freed by the beginning of
the century and could leave the land; subsequently they evolved into
sharecroppers who owed up to thirty days of labor a year to the
landlord in addition to between one-third and one-half of the crop.
Given tremendous land hunger and agricultural overpopulation,
there were always serf families to replace those that chose to leave.
On the other hand, it is true that, where the laws were enforced, the
landlord could not drive a serf family off the land so long as it met its
legal obligations.

The pattern in Serbia sharply diverged from that of the rest of the
Yugoslav lands. To begin with, since Serbia was the product of a
successful peasant uprising against Moslem landowners (1804–15),
the land relations reflected what were in the future to become
radical peasant demands. As early as 1840, the Civil Procedures Act
was enacted specifying an agrarian minimum and providing each
peasant household a minimum of land not alienable for debts.
Peasant indebtedness was endemic to all of the Balkan lands and this
was an early attempt to prevent the moneylenders and usurers from
altering the face of the countryside.

In 1873, a major new amendment to the Civil Procedures Act,
known as section 4A of article 471, was enacted. This act became the
model for which the peasant parties in other provinces strove. It
provided in much more specific detail for the protection of peasant
householders. The following property was protected from foreclosure
for private debts: (1) a house, stables, and a house-lot of up to "one
day's plowing," or 5,760 square meters; (2) a minimum of 3.4
hectares (8.5 acres) of cropland, vineyards, orchards, or forest
(including the house-lot) for every tax head (male adult) in the
household; (3) two oxen, two buffalos, or two draft horses, plus ten
sheep, five goats, and five pigs; (4) one plow, one cart, one hoe, one
ax, and so on; (5) enough food for the family and livestock to last
until the next harvest. This represented a minimum which could not
be alienated from the peasant and which he could not sell unless he
changed his trade or profession. That is, if there was any other heir
in the family who could take over the land, it would revert to him,
the idea being to ensure the minimum number of peasant households

considered socially necessary. Even with this radical peasant legislation, by World War I, 11 percent of all peasants were landless. However, in all of Serbia there were only six farms larger than 200 hectares, while 68.68 percent of all households held between 4 and 20 hectares of land. The majority of Serbian peasants were thus small and middle peasants, capable of subsisting on their own holdings.

The pattern in Montenegro was complicated by the fact that most of the land was owned by clans and extended families, and the major landowning problem was really the right to grazing land, which was settled by traditional law. There were no feudal holdings in Montenegro.

Post-World War I Yugoslav land reforms were strongly influenced by the Serbian law mentioned above, but they took considerable time to be enforced. Thus in Yugoslavia as a whole in 1931 the average size of a holding was 5.3 hectares, or less than 1 hectare per capita, while on the other hand 2.5 percent of the households owned 27 percent of all agricultural land, and 34 percent of the peasant households owned less than 2 hectares.

Postrevolutionary Yugoslavia thus inherited a highly stratified pattern of landholdings and a peasant population from the poorer and more mountainous regions that had major claims on the postrevolutionary regime. Nevertheless, two factors affected land policy in the period from 1945 to 1953. On the one hand, the substantial landholdings of the prewar German minority in Vojvodina and Slavonia—lands held by the church and by large private landholders—were confiscated in the immediate postwar years. This created a land fund of almost 3 hectares per household for potential distribution. On the other hand, the postwar Yugoslav government was the most orthodox of the communist regimes in Eastern Europe and was the first of the regimes to attempt to carry out collectivization. Collectivization policies were, in fact, most aggressively pursued right after the break with Moscow, when the Yugoslavs sought to prove their orthodoxy. Thus the land taken over by nationalization and from the German minority was turned over to agricultural cooperatives and state farms, rather than to the peasants, and all land over the new agrarian maximum of 10 hectares per household was also confiscated. This action was accompanied by strong pressures on individual peasants to enter into the coops. By 1952–53 peasant resistance and the resulting lower productivity brought about a change of policy and a dismemberment of many of the collectives. The present pattern was established by the mid-1950s; under it, 9.4 percent of all available agricultural land is in the coops, while close to 90 percent is in private hands. There are also state farms, particularly in Vojvodina. An examination of peasant land ownership in 1969 showed that approximately 39 percent of all households owned less than 2 hectares each, which amounted to 9.2 percent of the agricultural land area; a second group of some 35.6 percent owned from 2 to 5 hectares, accounting for 31 percent of all agricultural land, while the largest share of agricultural land, 59.7 percent, was held by 25.4 percent of the households. The legal maximum of 10 hectares is currently being redebated since population pressure on the land has been drastically diminishing. There are also proposals to enact a legal minimum which would abolish farms smaller than 1 hectare. However, most of the households owning less than 2 hectares appear to be worker-peasant households, that is, households in which at least one and sometimes more members of the family work in industry, and the farm is mainly used as a supplement. The future of private land ownership in Yugoslavia appears to lie with the group holding 5 to 10 hectares—an amount large enough to benefit from mechanization and capable of producing for the market—and recent government policies are facilitating this development.

Peasants in Yugoslavia are free to move and may sell their land. However, agricultural land cannot be owned by persons who are not working peasants, thus, agricultural land can be sold only to other peasants or to coops.

With this brief background in mind, we can now examine more closely the shift from agriculture to the middle-development stage. A glance at the figures will give us some conception of what this process must have meant for the individuals involved and for the social fabric of the villages and small towns. Expressed in percentages, the aggregate shift involved a decrease of the agricultural population, which was somewhat more than 75 percent of the total population in 1940, to 67.2 percent in 1948, 60.9 percent in 1953, 49.6 percent in 1961, 41.6 percent in 1969, and 36.6 percent in 1971.[6] Thus, a drop

6. Ibid., 1948, 1953, 1961, 1969, 1971.

of over 30 percent occurred in the short twenty-three years from 1948 to 1971. This shift took place within the living memory of the majority of present Yugoslavs and was accompanied by further disruptive processes in the countryside which seriously undermined the basis of traditional society.

To begin with, as the total agricultural population dropped, the percentage of households in the rural sectors that had *at least one member* working in the socialized industrial sector increased. To be specific, from 1960 to 1970 the percentage of rural households that had at least one member working in nonagricultural sectors increased from 40 to 45 percent, and in at least two republics—Slovenia and Macedonia—it is now over 50 percent.[7] That is to say, a substantial part of the families that have remained in the countryside are now linked with the modern urban sector. Simultaneous with this process, which now involves over a million and a half workers living in the rural sector, other processes have shifted the demographic composition of the countryside since, for reasons that are generally well known, the migrants from the countryside to the cities represented the most energetic work contingents. That is, the age groups from 20 to 30, and males in particular, were overrepresented in the shift that occurred. The magnitude of these changes can be expressed in some further gross statistics. Almost 3 million persons left the countryside between the end of the war and 1961, and by 1970 the total was over 4.5 million. This has not only left the traditional rural sector weakened numerically but has left the villages disproportionately populated by women, the old, and the very young.

This vast urban migration filled the cities and the smaller industrial centers with a population that forms the bulk of the present Yugoslav working class, and one whose ambitions and aspirations have been ripped loose from the traditional limits imposed by the village culture. It has also radically transformed the views of those remaining in the countryside. A study in 1970 by Mladen Zvonarevic of the aspirations of youths in the villages in one of the republics, Croatia, illustrates this point rather well. The study, undertaken in 1970, examined a sample of village youth from 15 to 25 years old and among other things asked a set of questions about

7. Ibid.

political perceptions and aspirations.[8] The first question was about the importance of self-management as a basis of socialism. If we compare the responses of the village youth to the population of the republic as a whole sampled in the same year,[9] we find that not only is there no notable difference between the responses of village youth and the population as a whole, but the same general variables affect all the responses, so that the percentage responding "self-management is the most important ingredient of socialism" ranges from 72 percent for the respondents who have completed any kind of secondary school to 27 percent for those who have four grades of elementary school or less. This indicates that, not surprisingly, one factor in political socialization is the educational system, and it suggests that education affects rural youth no less than their peers in the cities. As education spreads, therefore, the similarity between village and city youth will be reinforced. Further responses indicate that village youth do not differ markedly from city youth in other respects. For example, when asked about their attitude toward religion, the majority—57 percent of village youth and 60 percent of city youth—answered that religion is unnecessary to man. What makes this response all the more remarkable is that we are here comparing village youth with a control sample which, for this question, was limited to the city of Zagreb, a large, sophisticated urban center, and it shows that even in the most Catholic of republics, the prospects for the church do not look rosy. When responses are broken down by education we find the same pattern noted above: a positive attitude toward religion correlates negatively with educational attainment.

Some of the other relevant indicators are that only 24 percent of the village youth expressed a desire to continue living in the villages, clearly indicating that there is general support for the trend of deruralizing Yugoslavia. Responses to a question about job aspirations are shown in table 1. The trend is clear. The overwhelming majority not only want to leave the village but have job aspirations

8. Mladen Zvonarevic, *Seoska omladina u S.R. Hrvatskoj* (Zagreb: Institute of Social Research, 1971).

9. While the data in the section that follows are from only one republic, it must be emphasized that Croatia is the republic in which traditional and Catholic influence would be expected to be highest. Therefore this Croatian data can be assumed to understate my points, if anything.

Table 1

Job Aspirations of Village Youth, Croatia, 1970

Agriculture	23.7%
Industrial work	35.7
White-collar work	10.0
Education and services	
(secondary schooling)	12.0
University teaching or professions	6.1
No answer	12.5
Total	100.0%

SOURCE: *Javno mnenje stanovnistva S.R. hrvatske, 1972* (Zagreb: Institut za Drustvena Iztrazivanja, 1973).

that link them to the modern sector and which, given the relative flexibility and openness of the Yugoslav educational structure, are not overoptimistic or unattainable.

Another general point could be made about the fate of the rural sector which is suggestive as to the future developments of Yugoslavia. While the League of Communists has refrained from any social and political offensive in the villages since the abortive attempts to collectivize in the early 1950s, it does appear that the present modus vivendi between the peasantry and the new social order is shifting in favor of the socialist sector, even in agriculture. In the period between 1960 and 1970, the growth rate of agricultural productivity was 1.7 percent in the private sector, and 9 percent in the socialist sector. This trend, reflecting the growing consolidation of the state farms and cooperatives, and the ever increasing productivity resulting from further mechanization and rationalization of Yugoslav agriculture, makes the socialist sector even in this sphere increasingly dynamic.[10]

In terms of the total agricultural product for the same period, the socialist sector's share has grown from 12 percent in 1960 to just under 30 percent in 1969, with 66 percent of all wheat and 52 percent of all corn being produced by that sector. The trend has continued since then and can be expected to continue, given the

10. Dobrosav Tadic, "Changes in the Countryside, 1961–1969," *Yugoslav Survey* 10, no. 4 (November 1969).

increasing emphasis placed on agricultural productivity in Yugoslavia. This means that, even though there is no formal political pressure on the agricultural sector, a combination of internal disintegration—particularly the rising percentage of households partially dependent on the industrial sector—and the growing efficiency of the socialist sector permit me to make the following prognosis. The pace of abandonment of the private rural sector will, in all probability, increase, the only limit on it being the growth rate of the industrial and urban sector and its ability to absorb new migrants. In other words, even the present high rate of mobility is probably lower than that desired by the potentially mobile population still left in the rural sector.

One of the social problems of modern industrial Yugoslavia is that there has been no effective central planning—and none can be anticipated given the Yugoslav decentralization in this field—regarding the rate of urbanization, and the illegal or rather nonlegal construction of housing for new migrants on the outskirts of industrial cities is therefore a continuing problem.

In discussing the disintegration of the traditional sector in Yugoslav society, I should make clear that the economic pressures on the individual peasant household have eased considerably from the prewar period, although this was quite possibly not the result of conscious planning. Thus the continual trend toward parcelization of rural holdings, in the absence of primogeniture[11] (which bedeviled the peasantry all the way up to the outbreak of World War II), has apparently stopped: in 1930 there were 2,069,000 private agricultural holdings; in 1951, 2,591,000; in 1960, 2,618,000; and in 1969, 2,634,000. These figures show that in the postwar period the number of private agricultural holdings has not kept pace with population growth, and that, given the extent of urban migration, pressure on the land proper is easing. When we add to this the fact that the number of economically unviable households (roughly those with less than 2 hectares of land) has increased from 35.1 to 39 percent of all holdings, it is clear that the peasant-worker sector now developing in the countryside will further shift in the direction of industrial work, leaving behind a small rural population with viable holdings which can be integrated into the market economy as it in turn modernizes.

11. Except in Slovenia, where the trend toward parcelization was not as great a problem.

What I am saying here is that not only will the rural sector diminish in size but it will undergo an internal transformation, resulting in a modern peasantry linked to the modern market economy, utilizing the economic and social institutions of the modern society. This transformation, almost completed in Slovenia, generally furthers the process of the destruction of the traditional village culture.

The Neutralization of Religion

In the early postwar years, the Communist Party and the government showed considerable direct hostility toward organized religion. Because of the role the churches had played throughout the war, this anticlericalism aroused far less resistance than might have been expected. Part of the Moslem religious establishment was compromised during the war by its collaboration with the new fascist state of Croatia and by the role of the Mufti of Jerusalem in helping to recruit an entire SS division of Moslem Slavs. At least two major figures in the Catholic hierarchy, Archbishop Saric of Sarajevo and Archbishop Stepinac of Zagreb, collaborated with the new Croat state and the occupiers. The record of the lower hierarchy was not much better, and at least in parts of Bosnia and Herzegovina Franciscans were directly involved in massacres of the Orthodox peasantry. To be sure, a few Catholic priests aided the Partisans, but this was clearly against the orders of the hierarchy, except in Slovenia. The Orthodox hierarchy was less tainted by collaboration. Patriarch Gavrilo, imprisoned during the war, retained his position after the war. However, although some Orthodox priests supported the Partisans—one even becoming a member of the General Staff—they were suspected, with good reason, of monarchist and nationalist sentiment.

The repressive policies toward organized religion in the early postwar years failed to provoke substantial resistance since many non-Communists felt that the churches had clearly discredited themselves during the war and bore a substantial share of responsibility for the virulent nationalism and chauvinism that had led to fratricidal massacres. It is difficult to overestimate the revulsion aroused by the massacres and the civil war, even among the religious and particularly among the young. The churches thus found themselves after the war in a situation where they had lost a good deal of their legitimacy and where the old use of religion as a surrogate for national identity had begun to break down. This was most marked in the early postwar years in the situation of the Catholic church in Croatia. Its titular leader, Archbishop Stepinac of Zagreb, had been tried as a collaborator and was effectively removed from any participation in church affairs by being exiled to his native village after release from prison. Other figures had found themselves in exile or compromised to such an extent that the church in the early period had to adopt a very low profile. In contrast to the situation in Poland or Hungary, where the communist parties have had to deal with a church organization that has maintained its continuity and legitimacy as a national institution, the Catholic church in Yugoslavia had to compromise to exist. Despite the official Yugoslav policy of religious toleration, land reform expropriated church holdings, and the influence of the church among young, educated, and modern Yugoslavs has declined sharply until very recently.

I deal here with only the three major religious groups in Yugoslavia: Serbian and Macedonian Orthodox, Roman Catholic, and Moslem. There are, to be sure, over thirty registered religious communities;[12] however, the other ones are for the most part small and localized, and have no particular importance. Two existing communities have been drastically affected by the war and its consequences. The Jewish community was almost exterminated during the war and then further reduced by emigration. The Protestant community was based in part on the German minority in Vojvodina which was, by and large, deported after the war. The more recent Yugoslav censuses do not break down the population by religious affiliation. However, table 2 gives a comparison of the prewar and postwar breakdowns. The major changes revealed are the relative drop in membership of the Orthodox and Catholic churches and the growth of the nonreligious ("atheist") category to the third rank numerically. The Moslem community does not show a drop primarily because the birthrate is highest in the Moslem areas. However, one must be extremely careful not to identify those who declare themselves as being *members of a confession* with the *religious*. In

12. Branko Bosnjak, ed., *Religija i drustvo* (Zagreb: RAD, 1969). In English, the best available article is Radosav Perovic, "Religious Communities," *Yugoslav Survey* 10, no. 3 (August 1970).

Table 2

Religious Affiliations in Prewar and Postwar Yugoslavia

| | 1931 | | 1953 | |
	Number (in thousands)	Percent	Number (in thousands)	Percent
Orthodox	6,785	48.7	7,011	41.4
Roman Catholic	5,218	37.4	5,383	31.8
Protestant	231	1.7	148	0.9
Other Christian	68	0.5	71	0.4
Moslem	1,561	11.2	2,083	12.3
Jewish	68	0.5	—	—
Others and undeclared	2	—	156	0.9
Atheists	—	—	2,085	12.3
Total population	13,933	100	16,937	100

SOURCE: Hoffman and Neal, *Yugoslavia and the New Communism*, p. 33.

all cases, but particularly with the Orthodox, the former declaration is often to be taken as a declaration of nationality. Table 4 below shows that the majority of students who declare themselves as belonging to a particular faith are not practicing believers. This is less true of the population as a whole than of the Orthodox group alone, but it is a factor that should be kept in mind.

Another factor affecting the churches in Yugoslavia in the postwar period is the massive social change caused by the urbanization of the country. The peasantry was brought into a whole network of relationships and institutions where the church had little place. The process did not affect all areas equally, however. One has to turn to the political cultures of Yugoslavia to explain the different impacts made by a unitary policy on a range of religions and regions. Today the level of religious practice is, of course, lowest in the cities. However, there are certain areas such as Montenegro which, although quite undeveloped and rural, show consistently lower participation and identification with religion than the national average, while Slovenia, the most advanced republic, shows the lowest percentage of atheists. The reason for this is to be sought not only in historical factors but also in shifts in attitudes toward religion by the local political leadership in what is an increasingly decentralized state.

A 1967 study of Yugoslav public opinion, conducted by the Center for Public Opinion in Belgrade,[13] included a question about the attitude of the public toward the growing activity of the church in organizing social activities for the young. The exact wording of the question was: Do you approve or disapprove of the church's increased activity among the young? For the country as a whole, 25 percent approved, 48 percent disapproved, and 26 percent had no opinion. In terms of the republics, the rate of approval was highest in Slovenia (48 percent) and lowest in Montenegro (16 percent) and Kosovo (11 percent). Sixty-nine percent of the Montenegrins disapproved, against only 26 percent in Slovenia.

Some other breakdowns of this data, however, are probably more representative of present attitudes toward religion. For example, if we break down the respondents by age, we find that 18–25-year-olds were far less religious (21 percent positive) than those 65 and over (41 percent). In short, the church has been losing ground, at least among the young. This is also clear from a breakdown of the data by educational level. As table 3 shows, the effectiveness of education as

Table 3

Attitudes toward Church Socialization
of the Young, by Educational Level

	Approved	Disapproved	No opinion
Illiterate	37%	24%	38%
Completed:			
4 years of schooling	30	39	30
8 years of schooling	26	53	20
Skilled workers' school	16	66	17
Gymnasium	9	73	17
University or higher school	6	83	10

a means of antireligious socialization is considerable, and, based on that, the prognosis for growing church influence in Yugoslavia would be pessimistic. This is particularly the case since, as noted earlier, the number of people exposed to higher education is continually growing, especially among the young.

13. Ljiljana Bacevic, *Jugoslovensko javno mnenje o omladini i religiji* (Belgrade: Institut Drustvenih Nauka, 1969).

In the long run, social changes in Yugoslavia, as they create a fundamentally modern and mobile society, will probably continue to break down religious identifications. My own studies (in 1965) of the Yugoslav students, a group most sensitive to such changes, indicates that religion today serves primarily as a national or ethnic self-description. A few figures may be illustrative. My sample was composed of 2,528 students at the Universities of Belgrade, Zagreb, and Sarajevo. When asked about their religious identification, 1,017 (or close to 40 percent) stated that they did not believe in God. The other figures, given in table 4 are even more interesting. As a cursory glance at this table shows, the larger proportion of the students who identified themselves with a religion are not practitioners, and this also holds for their fathers. In the case of their mothers, except for the Orthodox, a considerably higher proportion practice their faith. Mothers in general show a higher level of religious observance, which is not surprising since they are less likely to be participating in the modern sector.

These figures also show that Catholicism has maintained itself to a higher extent than Orthodoxy. My sample was broken down geographically as follows: 1,268 students from Belgrade, 925 from Zagreb, and 335 from Sarajevo. Thus, although there were fewer Croats, or Catholics, in the sample, there were more than twice as many practicing Catholics than practicing orthodox Christians. The greatest drop-off is among the Moslems. This is, in my opinion, because Islam is not merely a religion but a way of life, the unity of

Table 4

Religious Identification and Practice of Students and Their Parents*

	Students			Fathers			Mothers		
Religion	No. pro-fessing	% prac-ticing	% not prac-ticing	No. pro-fessing	% prac-ticing	% not prac-ticing	No. pro-fessing	% prac-ticing	% not prac-ticing
Catholic	626	43	57	720	45	55	826	55	45
Orthodox	567	23	77 !	877	41	59	972	43	57
Moslem	113	16	84 !	179	41	59	203	62	38
	N = 1,511								

SOURCE: Seymour M. Lipset and Bogdan Denitch, "Codebook on Yugoslav Student Survey" (mimeo., 1965).

* As reported by students.

which is more fragile when faced with a fundamentally lay modern society.

In pointing to the factors in the social transformation of Yugoslavia that militate against organized religion, one must be careful not to overlook two opposing tendencies. The first is the enormous flexibility of modern Catholicism, particularly its radical wing. Articles on the subject of social Catholicism in Yugoslav journals and the work of the revolutionary priests in Latin America and worker priests in France have created a model of Catholicism that may well prove attractive to the young and even to the young intellectuals.

The other factor is the resurgence of traditionalist ethnic nationalism among some Croatian intellectuals, particularly literary intellectuals. The nationalism of this group has expressed itself not only in linguistic polemics, but also in an attempt to identify with the historic roots of Croatian identity, which is interpreted as fundamentally Catholic. During the nationalist "explosion" in 1969–71, in elections for a student pro-rector (assistant rector) at the University of Zagreb, the victor was a Catholic traditionalist nationalist, much to the distress of both establishment and nonestablishment Marxists. In my opinion, this is a reflection of the fact that religious groups can act as a focus for generalized discontent that is not otherwise expressed. It must be added that such successes represent a danger for the church. The Roman Catholic church has worked out a modus vivendi with the Yugoslav authorities and, although polemics are occasionally directed at the church press, it would be foolhardy for the church as an institution with a stake in the social order to identify itself with an opposition group.

However, it must be added that a number of church figures have taken a very positive attitude toward the two major contributions of Yugoslav socialism: decentralization and workers' self-management. Both of these are often defended in church publications as aspects of a humane and just social order, viewed as closer to the present teachings of the Roman Catholic church than the practices of either the capitalist or the communist world. Yugoslav Marxist spokesmen recognize this and in turn make a distinction between the various currents within the church.[14]

14. See Vrcan, "Vjera i politika," and Petar Segvic, "O Politickim tendencijama u Crkvi kod nas," *Nase Teme* 12 (December 1972).

As we have seen, in Yugoslavia the major denominations have, for historical reasons, often served as a focus of national identity. Thus, even today, after major social transformations, a large majority of the population identifies with particular religious groups. (This was recognized in the latest census, where the category "Moslem—as an ethnic group" exists for the Moslem Slavs of Bosnia-Herzegovina.

Indications from the existing studies are that atheism is a phenomenon most often found in the modern sector, that is, in the cities and among the social groups that have benefited most directly from the social changes resulting from the revolution. Religion and tolerance toward the social activities of religious groups are inversely related to education.

The present policy of the Yugoslav government is one of continued separation of church and state, and of religious toleration. While all religious groups continue to exist, the Roman Catholic church, being by far the best organized and most flexible, is the most active and has retained the greatest hold on its believers. It is not, however, a Yugoslav-wide church but is identified with only two of the Yugoslav nations and one major minority (Slovenes, Croats, and Hungarians, respectively).

Continued tension between the Catholic church and the League of Communists can be expected because of conflicting claims in the area of education, social policy, and family. This tension is mitigated, however, by the plurality of approaches now used by *both* organizations. The secularization of the political system removes the external pressure on the faithful; on the other hand, the development of a progressive current within the church makes cooperation and tolerance more likely.

Continuing social change in Yugoslavia—the expansion of secondary and higher education, the effects of urban existence, the waning of provincialism, and the slow decrease of the peasantry through the expansion of the industrial working class—indicate a continued decline of religion as a focus for social life and national identity. This trend, however, will probably level off at some point. At that time, when religion is truly a citizen's private affair, one can postulate several forms and levels of religious life. The traditional forms will continue, primarily among the old, rural, and passive sectors. In the modern sector, the Catholic church will probably remain the only genuine competitor to a form of Marxist humanism, and both will probably compete with indifference.[15]

HIGHER EDUCATION AS AN INSTRUMENT OF SOCIAL CHANGE

The revolutionary Yugoslav regime, while still in the mobilization phase that preceded the consolidation of state power, undertook major campaigns against illiteracy and attempted to extend education into the rural sector. Apart from the general desirability of education, education was and is viewed by the party as serving a major socializing function in destroying the old values and creating allegiance to the new values introduced by the revolution. The educational campaigns lasted through the period of reconstruction, at least up to 1952.

The spread of education in the countryside was popular since both prewar peasant movements and the modernizing bourgeoisie in the cities had placed a high value on education. However, the party's special emphasis in the early period on rural education was linked in part to the fact that a good portion of its rural cadres had come from the teachers' colleges and had been village schoolteachers. In the mid-1950s, as the mobilization phase was subjected to the processes of routinization in the society as a whole, the site of major educational innovations shifted to higher education.[16] On the elementary level, except for the traditional Moslem resistance to the education of women, the system appears to have a high degree of acceptance, to be decentralized down to the level of the communes, and to involve substantial participation by local citizens' bodies.[17]

In the secondary schools there is already rudimentary participation by the students themselves through a system of student delegates on the school boards. On this particular level, the revolutionary regime did not quite succeed in destroying the division of the secondary school system into elite schools, or gymnasia, and more

15. There has recently been a slight revival of Orthodoxy among a small group of Serbian nationalist intellectuals. However, while Serbian nationalism may be fairly common among the Orthodox clergy, Serbian nationalists have not tended to be religious, and Serbian nationalism has not tended to be religious. Serbian nationalism has modern and secular roots and can be described as Jacobin.

16. See *Innovation in Higher Education: Reforms in Yugoslavia* (Zagreb: Organization for Economic Cooperation and Development, 1970), esp. pp. 35–39.

17. Ibid., pp. 69–75.

specifically job-oriented secondary schools such as the medical, economic, and technical schools. Only in the case of the technical schools has a substantial shift in the character of instruction been successfully combined with a high acceptance by the universities of the graduates of the system.[18]

The reforms on the University level are more innovative and are the clearest where conscious attempts have been made to develop institutionalized channels for the education of the technical strata necessary to the system. As noted earlier, the university system went through a rapid expansion after the war so that the first graduating classes, in 1949–50, were three times the size of those in prewar Yugoslavia. By 1960, the expansion of higher education had reached such an extent that major institutional reforms were clearly needed. Numerically, students had increased from 11 out of 10,000 inhabitants in 1938–39 to 76 per 10,000 in 1960. A shift in the breakdown among the faculties took place, with increasing emphasis on the technological and engineering faculties and the development of the faculty of economics—as the general substitute for the role previously held by the law faculties—in recruiting administrative cadres for the state and economy.

Since the development of self-management, the universities have assumed greater autonomy and are themselves run by the equivalent of workers' councils. Reforms in 1968 introduced students into all levels of university administration. One-third of the faculty senate is elected by the students, one of the two pro-rectors must be a student, and student representatives sit on faculty committees and participate in all decisions except those involving salaries.

Some of the most important changes have been in the social composition of students, which can be seen in tables 5 and 6. The first of these gives very rough figures for the prewar and postwar makeup of the student body. What has to be kept in mind when one examines table 5 is the fact that the student population has been continually expanding: by 1970 there were 261,203 students, comprising approximately 1.3 percent of the entire population—a fourfold increase since 1950. This expansion, given the emphasis on the university as a major recruiting agency for socially and politically important jobs, has created a relatively open opportunity

18. Ibid., pp. 85–90.

Table 5

Social Background of Students in Yugoslavia

Father's Occupation	1938–39	1950–51	1960–61	1970–71
Worker	3%	12%	20%	21%
White-collar	50	51	41	39
Farmer	18	18	13	12
Private craftsman	15	7	3	3
Professional *	12	8	19	21
Unknown	2	4	4	4
	100%	100%	100%	100%

SOURCE: *Innovation in Higher Education*, p. 84.

* The total percentage of professionals in Yugoslavia has of course increased since 1938.

structure. Since 1952 no class quota system has been applied to the recruitment of students, and since the late fifties the Yugoslav universities have increasingly acted as independent centers of political socialization with minimal influence from the League of Communists.[19]

Though the data are somewhat fragmentary, table 6 illustrates two separate but related points. First, the percentage of students from working-class families in the technical faculties is higher than that of workers in the overall population, while it is lower in the "traditional" faculties. The percentage of women is very high in the medical sciences and in the faculties of arts and letters, natural science, and mathematics, which are the faculties that prepare high school teachers.

The breakdown of students of working-class origin is particularly interesting when one considers the great emphasis party theoreticians place on the technical intelligentsia as a crucial element in the present phase of Yugoslav development. Graduates of the engineering and technological faculties have more prestige and are better

19. This growing political autonomy of the universities has been under recent attack by the league leadership, especially in Belgrade and Ljubljana. However, even in the context of the attacks, the league demands are "moderate," viz., that the league organization within the universities assume more responsibility in personnel selection. As of 1974, the control was in the autonomous Senates of the faculties where the LCY seems to be in the minority.

Table 6

Students of Working-Class Origin and
Women Students, by Faculties

Faculty	Working-Class Students		Women Students[c]
	1959–60[a] (Zagreb)	1964–65[b] (Zagreb, Belgrade, Sarajevo)	1965–66 (All universities)
Civil engineering	26.2%	28%	18%
Mechanical engineering	25.8	28	17
Economics	24.7	25	33
Veterinary science	24.7	22	16
Forestry	21.5	18	15
Pharmacy	20.5	19	77
Electrical engineering	19.3	19	19
Natural sciences and mathematics	18.8	21	39
Technology	18.6	19	19
Agriculture	15.7	14	15
Dentistry	15.3	17	52
Medicine	15.2	15	43
Law	15.1	16	32
Arts and letters	14.3	15	57
Architecture	13.6	12	21

[a] Data from *Innovation in Higher Education*, p. 95.
[b] Data from Lipset and Denitch, "Codebook on Yugoslav Student Survey."
[c] Data from *Innovation in Higher Education*, p. 103.

paid than graduates of the traditional liberal arts faculties, and they have much better employment opportunities. Thus, these faculties come as close as any to being contemporary elite faculties.

In considering the high percentage of women in the medical faculties, particularly in the faculties of medicine and dentistry, one must remember that, in the various studies of occupational prestige carried out in 1967–68 by Eugene E. Hammel, doctors were close to the top of the prestige ladder, surpassed only by mechanical and civil engineers, and they were substantially higher than political workers, lawyers, and teachers.[20] For that matter, doctors are among the

20. Eugene A. Hammel, *The Pink Yo-yo: Social Prestige and Occupations in Yugoslavia*, Institute on Eastern Europe (Berkeley: University of California Press, 1969).

highest paid professionals in Yugoslavia today. Thus neither women nor the children of workers are shunted off to "second-rate" faculties.

Even with the recent growth of unemployment in Yugoslavia, only 3.3 percent of all Yugoslavs working abroad in 1970 had a university or higher school degree.[21] This is remarkable, given the fact that the Yugoslavs have an open frontier and no limit on emigration, and that university graduates—particularly from the technical and medical faculties—are easily employable abroad.

The role of higher education in uprooting the institutional and social bases of the old social order can be summarized as follows: the rapid expansion of opportunities for a university education has tended to demystify the role of university-educated intelligentsia and dilute it numerically. The increasing emphasis on technical and medical faculties has further undermined the strength of the traditionalist intelligentsia, and these faculties, having a higher percentage of working-class students and women, tend to produce cadres whose success is linked with the Yugoslav socialist regime.

In the period since the consolidation of power, the university has gone through three fairly clear stages: (1) initial expansion aimed at providing the necessary minimum of educated cadres for the administration of an increasingly complex modernizing state; (2) the shift in emphasis from law to economics and from arts and letters to technology, reflecting the needs of the Yugoslav society and of the economy, which moved from the stage of extensive development to the stage of intensive development in the late 1950s; and (3) the stage of structural reforms in the universities themselves, begun in the 1960s and being completed only now, which introduced the forms of self-management into what remains one of the most traditionalist structures in present-day Yugoslav society. The universities are traditional in the sense that, while they now provide massive education under criteria resembling those of American universities with open admissions policies, the university faculties as corporate bodies, as well as the students, have managed to develop a high degree of autonomy from the League of Communists and the state. This autonomy is a self-protective reaction to what had been a highly politicized society; the universities have tended to use their

21. Milije N. Kolic, "Some Basic Features of Yugoslav External Migration," *Yugoslav Survey* 13, no. 1 (February 1972).

traditions and the special knowledge and importance of the professo-
rial cadres as a barrier against arbitrary intervention by the political
leadership in the life of the university. This has created a reluctance
on the part of the university bodies to participate in the social and
economic reforms going on in the society as a whole.

The political socialization of university students occurs in a
framework more independent of the league than any other in
Yugoslavia. The student organizations have tended to be articulate,
active, and autonomous. Consequently, the various critical strands
present in the society in a more amorphous form have tended to find
concentrated expression in the universities. Thus, in the period from
1967 to 1969, the universities were dominated by something
resembling a New Left current, reaching its peak in the student
demonstrations of 1968 and 1969 which demanded greater egalitarianism, an attack on corruption, the introduction of self-management
into the political system, and a general return to more orthodox
Marxist values. This particular set of demonstrations was defused by
the adoption, at least nominally, of a number of the students'
demands and the cooptation of many of the student leaders into the
official structures. In 1970, in Croatia, on the other hand, the student
allies of the local Croatian leadership entered into a coalition with
traditionalist nationalist elements, leading to a general student strike
in Croatia which was followed by a crackdown from the league
center and a political offensive by the league against ethnic
nationalism and separatism.

No matter what the rhetoric or specific demands of the students
and the more articulate members of the faculties may be at any
given point, the Yugoslav universities are, in my opinion, profoundly
radical institutions at least in one sense: they are the socializers and
the formers of the technical intelligentsia and the meritocracy which
is crucially important to the present stage of Yugoslav development.
The emphasis on meritocracy undermines both the traditionalist
concept of legitimacy, since it implies that all posts should be open to
persons of talent and training irrespective of background or sex, and
the legitimacy of the postrevolutionary leadership, which stressed the
now ascriptive role of the wartime activist in the recruitment of
cadres to leading positions.

A further consequence follows. With widespread university education, the number of alternate candidates for important posts in

society will increase, and therefore competition for those posts will also increase. This competition either will be contained within the system, following institutionalized channels, or will lead to the creation of a discontented intelligentsia which considers itself illegitimately deprived of its proper role in society. The likelihood that this new intelligentsia will frame its demands in a manner hostile to the present Yugoslav system is small. What is far more likely is that a growing articulate, educated public—disproportionately represented in the party and the various political institutions of the society—will insist on a greater congruence between reality and those normative claims of the system relevant to their status needs, that is, "competence = training = education," and its performance. In other words, it will criticize the system within the framework of its own legitimacy.

5

The League of Communists and Social Mobility

A considerable body of literature already exists on the relationship of social mobility to economic change. American social scientists have examined that relationship in both advanced and underdeveloped societies. However, little empirical research has been done on societies in which a ruling communist party has been in power for a number of years. Such data as we do have, based primarily on research in Yugoslavia, Poland, and Czechoslovakia, treat the problem of mobility essentially in terms of economic change, neglecting for the most part the role of the party either as a conscious director of the social change involved or as a primary channel for mobility.[1]

Membership in the League of Communists of Yugoslavia is clearly related to participation in the social system and to social mobility, particularly to the first basic step for most Yugoslavs—the move from the rural, passive sector into the modern industrial sector—but the causal relationship is not obvious. It seems fairly clear that, in the immediate postwar period, league or party membership itself, particularly when combined with wartime achievements, directly affected both the opportunities for and the pace of individual advancement. This is the case in Yugoslavia because, as we have seen, the party came to power after a bitter war against a foreign occupier and its collaborators which assumed the aspect of a class and civil war as well. Much of the prewar establishment was eliminated since part of it was compromised by collaboration while

1. See Eugene A. Hammel, *The Pink Yo-yo: Social Prestige and Occupations in Yugoslavia* (Berkeley: University of California Press, 1969); Bette Denich, "Social Mobility in a Yugoslav Town" (Ph.D. diss., University of California, Berkeley, 1969); W. Wesclowski and K. Slomczynski, *Social Stratification in Polish Cities* (Belgrade: Institut Drustvenih Nauka, 1967).

others were regarded as at least potentially hostile. The low educational level of prewar Yugoslavia, on the other hand, offered a limited number of possible replacements for the entire social class displaced, and as a consequence tens of thousands of former peasants, workers, school dropouts, and provincial semi-intellectuals were suddenly assigned to the many major and minor roles that had to be filled in the society. The determination of the revolutionary government to industrialize and modernize only accentuated this process, since this required many more administrators than had been needed by prewar Yugoslavia. In recent years, however, more universalistic criteria have been used to fill the more socially desirable roles, and the primary acknowledged criterion has become higher education. The league has consciously recruited those who seem most promising according to nonascriptive criteria like ability or education, although this trend is partially checked by the ideological stress on expanding the proportion of workers in its membership.

However, the league, even though it renounces the role of direct shaper of day-to-day policy and defines itself primarily as the leading ideological guardian of an essentially self-managing society and economy, is a key factor in the social changes taking place in Yugoslavia, and its social composition reflects this fact. It is hard to imagine an active citizen who considers himself socially and politically involved in contemporary Yugoslavia who is not a member of the league. No doubt there are some, particularly in the rural sector or among dissident intellectuals, but they are the exception. The political public of Yugoslavia, or at least its most active part, is in the league.

In addition to its role as the major vehicle for active political participation in the system as a whole, the league functions as the representative of the new values of industrialization and moderniza- tion. It articulates a new value system counterposed to the tradi- tional rural values and life style, and for many it eases the transition to the new life style characteristic of modern society. To be sure, the value of modernization was accepted by some of the prewar Yugoslav elite, but what is noteworthy today is the fact that masses of workers and peasants now accept it, desire it, and demand a share in it. This modernization has affected the lives of countless peasants who formerly lived outside any but a subsistence economy; it alters the family structure and patterns of authority. It has undermined the old value systems based on religion and tradition.[2] Today there are some doubts about the effects of modernization on life style, but these are found mostly among religious traditionalists and nationalists or among intellectuals who themselves have long enjoyed the benefits of being in the modern sector and only question its desirability for the workers and peasants.

The Communist Party of Yugoslavia entered World War II with some 12,000 or more members, of whom, according to its own figures, only 3,000 survived. These figures were reported in 1948, and since that time many of the 3,000 survivors have no doubt died. Many others have surely retired or been pensioned off, especially since the wartime periods of imprisonment and battle are counted as double when retirement ages are figured. Thus, it would be safe to assume at least a 50 percent attrition rate: probably only 1,500 of the original 3,000 are still active politically. In any case, in 1968, members, both retired and active, who had joined the league in 1940 or earlier comprised only 0.3 percent of total LCY membership. Seniority among league members is shown in table 7. Four basic age groups logically emerge:

1. Those born before 1917, the prewar generation, who were at least 24 years old when the war broke out and thus could

Table 7

Seniority among 1958 Membership of the League of Communists

Date Joined	% of 1958 Members	
pre-1940	0.3	
1941–44	5.4	21.0
1945–48	15.3	
1949–52	13.8	
1953–57	13.5	
1958–62	20.9	
1963–67	15.8	
1968	15.0	

SOURCE: *Borba,* special suppl., January 24, 1970.

2. Wayne S. Vucinich, "Nationalism and Communism," in Vucinich, ed., *Contemporary Yugoslavia* (Berkeley: University of California Press, 1969); also Joel Halpern, "Modernization," in the same volume.

conceivably have participated in the work of the prewar, illegal Yugoslav Communist Party. This group could also have completed their professional training before the war and revolution. They were 51 years old or older at the time I interviewed them in 1968.

2. Those born between 1918 and 1923, the generation of war and revolution. Between 18 and 23 years old in 1941, these persons could have participated in the Partisan movement from its very first revolt. The party tended to keep its older and more experienced cadres (the "prewar generation") out of Partisan units and instead engaged in illegal work or political work; thus, the 18–23-year-olds had the greatest chance to use the war itself to win their spurs. They were between 45 and 50 years old at the time of interviewing.

3. Those born between 1924 and 1929, the generation of the consolidation of power. Members of this group, between 11 and 17 years old when the war broke out, could have participated in the Partisan war, particularly in the later stages. They played their key role in the consolidation of power at the end of the war and in the first grim years of reconstruction and development of new Yugoslavia, and most of them were tested during the bitter years of the Cominform split. They were 39 to 44 years old at the time I interviewed them, that is, generally the age of the secondary cadres.

4. Those born after 1930, the generation of self-management. Too young to have participated in the war, mostly too young to have been involved in the consolidation of power or affected by the Cominform split, members of this group have been primarily shaped and entirely educated in the postrevolutionary period. They are just beginning to show up in the leadership of the country.

The influence of party seniority on the career advancement of the league leaders is complex since, for one thing, it is clear that the "superseniority" of the previctory years is not duplicable for the younger two age groups, or for that matter for the even younger groups that are now being formed. We can, however, examine the relationship between seniority and the beginning of the postwar careers of a sample of opinion leaders studied in 1968 (see the Appendix, note 1), breaking them down by sectors. This is done in table 8, where the opinion leaders in the sample are divided into two groups: pre- and post-1944 LCY members. The first striking pattern in the table is the contrast between the proportion of political and nonpolitical jobs for the two groups; a large majority of pre-1944

Table 8

LCY Seniority and the First Job Taken after 1944 (Opinion Makers*)

Job	Pre-1944 Members (N = 261)		Post-1944 Members (N = 213)		Percent Difference
Political positions					
Party-LCY	70	(26.8%)	6	(2.8%)	− 24.0%
Other organizations	29	(11.1)	20	(9.4)	− 1.7
Government	62	(23.7)	29	(13.7)	− 10.0
Legislature	4	(1.5)	2	(0.9)	− 0.6
Defense (army, police)	37	(14.2)	16	(7.6)	− 6.6
Total	202	(77.4)	73	(34.2)	− 43.2
Nonpolitical positions					
Mass communications	29	(11.1)	55	(25.8)	+ 14.7
Culture, education	15	(5.7)	35	(16.5)	+ 10.8
Economy	15	(5.7)	50	(23.5)	+ 17.8
Total	59	(22.6)	140	(65.8)	+ 43.2

* See Appendix.

members initially took political jobs, while the majority of post-1944 joiners began their careers in nonpolitical jobs. This is at least in part a reflection of the different periods involved. The second striking difference is in the proportions of those who started out in party or league jobs in the two seniority groups. Over one-quarter (26.8 percent) of the opinion leaders who joined the league before 1944 found their first postvictory job in the league, while another 11.1 percent began working for other political organizations. By contrast, a far smaller number of those who joined after 1944 started out in any kind of political job, and of the political jobs, a very small number were in the league itself. This is a result, among other things, of the shift in the role of the league organization, which ceased to be the universal lubricant of the system. It also reflects in part the fact that a greater proportion of the later joiners come from the professional sectors.

SENIORITY IN THE PARTISAN WAR

Seniority in the league plays a major role in both the type and the pace of mobility. In Yugoslavia, party seniority cannot be treated separately from a second type of ascriptive status, which correlates very closely with league seniority, that is, status in the Partisan army and the war of liberation (NOB). This is a factor that will change in the future, but it still plays a major role in leadership mobility. For a number of reasons, which only illustrate the importance of acknowledged status as an NOB veteran with specific seniority and rank, it is difficult to get reliable statistical data for the participation of the population as a whole in the NOB. To begin with, a number of levels of participation are formally recognized:

1. Veterans of the original uprising (June 1941), those holding the "National Hero" medal, and major underground activists; there are around 24,000 in this group.
2. Participants who joined before September 9, 1943 (the fall of Italy); I estimate that no more than 300,000 of this group are living.
3. All other veterans, with the addition of those who have "helped"—a flexible term.

The first two groups have special benefits, particularly in pensions, employment, and housing.

The official Yugoslav statistics show 1,350,000 "resistance veterans." This figure, however, also includes all those drafted from the autumn 1944 to the end of the war, underground workers, those who have established claims to have "helped" (in some cases using pull), and a few simple fakes. (Every year there is some announcement of a scandal following the discovery of unjustified claims.)

For the present generation of leaders, who fall mainly in the first two groups, with some in the third, NOB status is of considerable importance. To date, a combination of the two types of seniority— party membership and war experience—has clearly been necessary for promotion into the categories the opinion leaders find themselves in, particularly for the political categories, but to some extent even in the professional categories.

In the case of those opinion leaders who are broadly representative of the party leadership, it becomes evident that membership in the league before 1944 was directly related to the role in the Partisan War, as might have been expected. Out of 263 persons who were members before 1944, only 1 did not participate at all (probably having spent the time in prison), and only 8 "helped," which could have meant anything from offering food to a passing Partisan unit to

Table 9

LCY Seniority and Role in NOB (Opinion Makers[a])

Rank in NOB	pre– 1941	LCY Member from: 1942– 44	1945– 48	1949 on	Non- member	Total	
Colonel or higher, or high political functionary	91	43	14	1	4[b]	153	374
Officer or commissar	19	63	16	2	2	102	(72.3% active
Soldier to lieutenant	12	27	57	15	9	119	partici- pants)
Role in War							
"Helped"	1	7	20	7	6	41	
Too young			7	43	9	59	143
Did not participate		1	18	13	11	43	27.7%)
Total	123	140	132	81	41	517	

[a] See Appendix.
[b] Includes 2 former members of LCY/CPY.

highly dangerous political work. Slightly more than half, 134, had either senior officer rank in the war (colonel or above) or were important wartime political workers, which generally meant administrators of liberated territory who also participated in Partisan units. Another 84 were officers or political commissars and 39 served in the ranks or were noncommissioned officers. All in all, 72.3 percent of these opinion leaders were active combatants, mostly of higher rank.

The group that joined after the war (1945–48) still has a majority of veterans, most of whom, however, served in the ranks. I would guess that many of them joined the party as a consequence of their war record. Interestingly enough, there is little difference among the opinion leaders between the war records of the league members who joined after 1948 and those of the nonmembers. The nonmembers have, if anything, a higher record of wartime activity although this is accounted for by the age of the more recent members of the league.

An examination of the wartime activity of the opinion leaders by the age groups identified above confirms the impression that participation in the war was as necessary as membership in the league for their mobility. In the prewar group, 82.1 percent were active participants, 52.8 percent holding the highest ranks; 10.6 percent helped and 7.3 percent (mostly intellectuals) did not participate. The age group born in 1918–23 shows even higher participation: 87.4 percent were active combatants (38.5 percent in the highest positions), 7.7 percent helped, and only 4.9 percent did not participate at all. The third group (born in 1924–29) is still relatively high in participation: 71.7 percent were combatants, but most of these were only soldiers and noncommissioned officers; 7.2 percent helped, and 21.1 percent did not participate, some because of their youth. The fourth group (born after 1930) naturally shows very little participation, although even among them 5.4 percent were active combatants and 3.6 percent helped.

The present leaders rank high on both types of seniority, and I would assume that, among opinion leaders in the first three age groups, only the exceptional technical expert will be found to be without such ascriptive status.[3] In the case of the fourth age group, clearly they cannot have been expected to build up Partisan War seniority. Some of the antagonism of the younger educated cadres toward the veterans is explained by the fact that the contributions of the latter cannot be duplicated and veterans are thus outside the arena of equal competition in terms of the society's present needs. This problem is more complicated than it seems, for, while it is reasonable to expect in the near future the retirement of those in the first age group who are now at least in their mid-fifties, those in the second and third groups are still relatively young. The older leaders often appear to the ambitious young to hold their posts only or primarily because of seniority.

THE SOCIAL COMPOSITION OF THE LEAGUE OF COMMUNISTS

Little reliable information exists about the social composition of the party in the prewar years. Impressionistic sources and the geographic distribution of the members indicate that the member-

3. The question whether seniority in the league and War of Liberation should be regarded as earned or ascriptive is interesting. However, I feel that, in competing for *present* functions in the system, seniority should be regarded as ascriptive. It is not in any case an earnable quality for those outside the appropriate age group.

ship was composed primarily of workers, small-town intelligentsia—
a very broad term in Yugoslavia in those days—and students.
University and high school students as well as students at teachers'
schools were very important not only because the youth organization
(SKOJ, Savez Kommunisticke Omladine Jugoslavije) was considerably larger than the party in 1941[4] but also because these students
tended to play a major role in the Partisan War. The pattern early
in the war was for party cadres to stay in the cities and continue
organizing illegal and underground activities, while the young, less
experienced members, or those party members who were known to
the occupiers and thus could not work in the cities, went into the
mountains. The needs of Partisan warfare gave a disproportionate
importance to the members of the party and the youth in small
towns and villages, compared to the members from major cities.
Although most of the present opinion leaders now live in the
Yugoslav capital, Belgrade, only 5.8 percent were born there.

Since the opinion leaders represent the very top of the social
hierarchy of the country, the remarkably low proportion recruited
from the prewar capital underlines the great social mobility and the
break in continuity with the prewar leading strata. This is confirmed
by data in Lenard Cohen's essay on the immediately postwar
political elite: 94 percent came from provincial areas (small towns or
villages) and 69 percent were of rural origin.[5]

The league's social and age composition is of course of major
interest to its leadership and they spend considerable effort studying
it and attempting to shape it. Reporting to the Presidium of the
league in December 1969, Mika Tripalo made the following
comment:

It has never been considered that *all* social strata should be
proportionally represented in the League of Communists. On
the contrary, one of the conditions for the achievement of the
leading ideo-political role in society consists in the fact that the

    4. The party had about 12,000 and SKOJ about 20,000 members in 1941. See
Tito's *Report to the Fifth Congress CPY* (Belgrade: Komunist, 1948); see also Ivan
Avakumovic, *History of the Communist Party of Yugoslavia*, 2 vols. (Aberdeen: Aberdeen
University Press, 1964), 1:185–86.
    5. Lenard Cohen, "Social Background and Recruitment of Yugoslav Political
Elites, 1918–1949," in *Opinion-Making Elites in Yugoslavia*, ed. Allen H. Barton, Bogdan
Denitch, and Charles Kadushin (New York: Praeger Special Series, 1973).

Table 10 Representation of Various Strata in the League of Communists (1968)

Stratum	No. in LCY	% of LCY Member-ship	No. in Yugoslav Population	% of Popula-tion	Strata in LCY	Index of Represen-tation	Rank Order
Workers	356,838	31.2	2,439,000	18.6	14.6	1.6	6
Administrative employees	139,529	12.2	900,000[a]	6.8	15.5	1.7	5
General intelligentsia	128,763	11.2	442,866	3.4	29.1	3.3	3
Pensioners	90,238	7.9	1,256,000[a]	9.2	7.2	0.8	7
Army and security[b]	90,014	7.4					
Security personnel only	30,600	2.1	83,730	0.6	36.5	3.5	3
Private farmers	84,329	7.4	4,420,000[a]	33.8	1.9	0.2	9
Managers ("leadership personnel")	82,941	7.2	107,732	0.8	77.2	9.0	1
Technical intelligentsia	49,900	4.4	112,340	0.8	44.4	5.5	2
Students (university and higher schools)	37,083	3.3	143,000	1.1	25.8	3.0	4
Housewives and "others"	33,528	2.9	2,700,000[a]	20.6	1.2	0.1	11
High school pupils[c]	32,250	2.8					
Unemployed	15,721	1.4	327,000	2.5	4.9	0.5	8
Private craftsmen	4,956	0.4	292,000[a]	2.2	1.2	0.2	9
Total	1,146,000	100%	13,139,000[d]	99.8%			

SOURCE: The figures for league membership and the breakdown are from the special supplement to *Borba*, January 24, 1970. Lenard Cohen helped prepare this table.

[a] Because of changes over time in the breakdowns in Yugoslav statistics, we had to estimate the figures either from *Statisticki godisnjak Jugoslavije, 1969*, or from English issues of *Ekonomist*.

[b] We do not have the statistics for the Yugoslav army, but we have figures for "security personnel."

[c] It is difficult to calculate the relative representation of high school pupils since it is not clear what base to use; only older high school students were recruited to the league.

[d] The total population of Yugoslavia in 1968 was 20,154,000. We used as a population base those who could have been members of the League of Communists, roughly, the population over 18 years of age.

League of Communists *should rely mainly on those social strata whose social and material interest is identical with the fulfillment of the program of socialist transformation* [my emphasis]. It would also be naive to believe that quantitative indicators of representation of some social strata in the League of Communists simultaneously show adequately their influence on policy making in the League of Communists. . . . The League of Communists has 356,834 workers—direct producers making up 31.1 percent of the total membership. . . . If one adds to the workers' percentage those of the intelligentsia directly involved in the realms of education, culture, and public health, as well as technical intelligentsia and students (without including administrative and management staff), then these groups make up over 60 percent of the total composition of the membership of LCY.[6]

Now let us examine the social composition of the league. Table 10 summarizes the social structure of the league as of January 1970.[7] In addition to a breakdown of the league membership by social strata, it gives the size of the given stratum in the population the league could recruit from, the percentage of the members of the strata who are members of the LCY, and a simple index of representation in the league as well as a rank order. The heavily overrepresented groups are the managers (of enterprises and institutions) by a factor of 9, followed by the technical intelligentsia (5.5), security personnel (3.5), general intelligentsia (3.3), and students (3.0). Grossly underrepresented are the unemployed (1.5), private farmers and private craftsmen (both 0.2), and housewives (0.1), representing some 59.1 percent of the population which could be in the league. Even if one were to exclude private craftsmen, who are presumably underrepresented for ideological reasons of their own as well as the league's, over half of the adult population is involved. To be sure, workers and administrative employees are also slightly overrepresented, but the key fact is that the groups that are heavily overrepresented, by a factor of 3 or more, comprise only 6.7 percent of the potential population. We could thus make the following simple breakdown:
    Group I (heavily overrepresented): 6.7 percent, consisting of the

6. *Borba*, special suppl., January 24, 1970.
7. The index is obtained by dividing the percentage of the given group in the league by its percentage in the population used as a base.

present and future cadres of the society, its experts and administrators, and the candidates for those roles.

Group II (slightly over- or underrepresented): 34.6 percent, strata working in the modern sector or those benefiting from the social advances of postrevolutionary Yugoslavia.

Group III (heavily underrepresented): 59.1 percent who are primarily outside of the modern sector, generally not covered by the social insurance system, and outside of the system of self-management. For that matter, these groups are also underrepresented in the political system as a whole since, being outside of the socialist sector, they vote for only one-half of the commune self-government and are thus underrepresented in the indirect elections further up the republic and federation ladders.

It is clear that the groups considered by the leadership to be essential for running and administering a modern society are well represented in the league. More to the point, two other factors bear on the whole question of the representativeness of the league. The league recruits the upwardly mobile and, in a society where access to the key instrument of mobility—education—is relatively open,[8] this means that there is continuous recruitment from the otherwise underrepresented groups, as individual members of those groups begin to move upward into the modern sector. For that matter, it is not simply a question of moving *upward* on the educational scale. A move by peasants or private craftsmen into the modern sector by entering the working class serves much the same function. A second factor at play here is the question of the social origin of the strata currently in the modern sector and especially of the heavily overrepresented strata (managers, technical and general intelligentsia, security personnel, and students). Among the opinion leaders group—men close to the very top of the present social and political pyramid—56.4 percent had fathers who were either workers or peasants and most of whom had only four years of education or less. The more striking evidence is in table 11, which shows that in 1946 the combined peasant and worker percentage of party membership

8. The study of Yugoslav students I conducted for S. M. Lipset showed that, in 1966, 49 percent of all students had fathers who lived in villages up to their twenty-fifth birthday and slightly over 65 percent had fathers who were workers or peasants. Lipset and Denitch,. "Codebook on Yugoslav Student Survey" (mimeo., Berkeley: University of California Institute of International Affairs, 1965).

Table 11

Shifts in Social Composition of the League of Communists

Year	Total Membership	Workers	White Collar	Peasants	Other
1946	253[a]	27.6%	10.3%	50.4%	11.7%
	(71[a])	(71[a])	(26)	(130)	(30)
1948	482	30.1	13.6	47.8	8.5
		(145)	(65)	(231)	(41)
1950	607	31.2	19.0	43.4	6.5
		(189)	(115)	(263)	(39)
1952	772	32.2	18.9	42.8	6.1
		(249)	(146)	(330)	(47)
1954	654	28.3	29.8	22.6	19.2
		(185)	(195)	(148)	(125)
1958	829	32.7	34.8	14.7	17.8
		(271)	(289)	(121)	(148)
1962	1,018	36.7	36.4	9.6	17.3
		(373)	(371)	(97)	(175)
1966	1,046	33.9	39.0	7.4	19.6
		(355)	(408)	(77)	(205)
1968	1,146	31.2	43.8[b]	7.4	18.7[c]
		(356)	(491)	(84)	(215)
1971	1,025	28.8	45.5	6.7	19.0
		(295)	(466)	(68)	(195)

SOURCE: 1946–68 figures: *SKJ u uslovima samoupravljanja* (Belgrade: Kultura, 1969); 1971 figures: "Report to Central Committee LCY," *NIN*, no. 1135 (October 1972).

[a] To the nearest thousand.
[b] Combined administrative officials, intelligentsia (all), security and army, managers.
[c] Pensioners, students, high school pupils, housewives and others, unemployed and private craftsmen.

was 78 percent, 50.4 percent being peasants. Clearly, much of the present cadre was recruited from these strata. This mobility, particularly in the recent past, has altered part of the story of the present social composition of the League of Communists, since groups I and II include many members who were previously in the third group.

The shift that has been taking place in the league over time is more difficult to follow since the older Yugoslav statistics gave only four classifications: workers, peasants, employees (meaning all white-collar occupations, including professions), and others (primarily housewives and pensioners). Still, the general movement can be followed, even granting the possibility that some of the categories shift somewhat in definition.

A cursory examination of table 11 shows that, except for the period between 1952 and 1954, the league has grown steadily. Its growth, however, while spectacular between 1946 and 1952, tapered off and now roughly keeps pace with population growth. A slight spurt did take place in 1968, reflecting a league drive in the face of the tensions surrounding the invasion of Czechoslovakia and the effort to recruit youth. What is remarkable is the steady shift in composition. Most spectacular, of course, is the relative and absolute drop of peasant membership, from 50.4 percent to 6.7 percent, or, in absolute numbers, from 330,000 in 1952 to 68,000 in 1972.

The drop in peasant membership in the league reflects four factors: (1) The party recruited peasants heavily during the war years when the very nature of Partisan warfare meant that much of the recruitment had to take place in the rural areas. Whatever the character of the Partisan movement in the early years of the war, toward the end the mass of the movement and the new army consisted of peasants (often uprooted ones). If anything, party figures understate this fact since, for ideological reasons, the party stressed recruitment of workers. Nevertheless, this recruitment offered an opportunity never to be met again for those of peasant origin to step on the escalator of social and political mobility in large numbers. The party continued recruiting in the villages in the immediate postwar period while the new social order was being consolidated, but, though the absolute number of peasants increased by a factor of two-and-a-half between 1946 and 1952, the number of workers increased by more than three times and the number of white-collar workers (and administrative personnel) increased sevenfold. (2) The major shift in the postwar years from village to town, from peasant to worker or white-collar-cum-administrator, was spearheaded by party members, who were the most mobile. What this meant, of course, is that the most active, articulate, and talented activists in the villages left. (3) The sharp drop, both absolute and relative, in peasant membership, a trend never to be reversed, occurred between 1952 and 1954. This reflects the end of the drive for collectivization and the consequent demobilization of the activists in the villages.

The continued decline of peasant membership coincides with the end of the party-league organized drives in the countryside aimed at fighting illiteracy, establishing cooperatives and collectives, and recruiting workers for the new industry. In effect, there was little for the league to do in the villages, and the peasant members became a passive section as the focus firmly shifted to the cities, to industry and the system of self-management. (4) The dramatic urbanization in the postwar years revolutionized the lives of many in the cities as the Yugoslav population shifted from a make-up that was 25 percent urban and 45 percent rural at the end of the war, to 63.4 percent urban and 36.6 percent rural by 1971. As noted before, the more ambitious and energetic respond to the urbanization and modernization drives and leave their villages. The process leaves many villages without young people and, above all, underlines the image of the village as primitive, backward, and stagnant. In short, the revolutionary shift in social relations and the dramatic modernization of life style are urban phenomena: no real revolution took place in the countryside. By stressing the role of self-management—which applies to the socialist sector—and by basing the representation of interests as well as the structure of local and higher governmental bodies on this sector, the system cuts the peasants off from the political stage. The league increasingly reflects the more dynamic strata central to the functioning of the system.

The proportions of employed persons in various categories who were members of the League of Communists of Yugoslavia in 1966 are given in table 12.[9] As Branko Horvat points out, the most

Table 12

League of Communists Membership Rate among Employed Persons

Employees with two-year college education	58.0%
Employees with university education	43.0
Employees with secondary education	39.0
Employees with primary education	37.0
Highly skilled workers	34.8
Skilled workers	20.6
Semiskilled workers	12.0
Unskilled workers	5.0

9. Branko Horvat, *An Essay on Yugoslav Society* (New York: International Arts & Sciences Press, 1970).

striking thing about these figures is the fact that the percentages for *all* categories of white-collar employees are higher than the average percentage for all categories of workers.[10] The second interesting phenomenon is the higher membership rate among those with a two-year college education than among those with a university education in the membership. The two-year college was designed as an instrument for mobility for late starters and for those who did not have the background necessary for the regular university. This figure therefore reflects the fact that the league has attracted and held the interest of a disproportionate number of extremely mobile persons. The more alarming figures are those for skilled and highly skilled workers—also for the most part persons who have improved their skills and status in postrevolutionary Yugoslavia. Given the ideology of the league, the higher membership rate among employees with secondary and even primary education than among skilled workers is a danger sign. This acts as a pressure against genuine attempts to solve one of the problems of the Yugoslav society and economy at this stage of development—the overexpansion of white-collar and administrative personnel, and their greater rewards compared with those of the skilled industrial working class.

RECENT TRENDS IN THE LEAGUE OF COMMUNISTS

Developments in the League of Communists of Yugoslavia are an extremely sensitive barometer for general developments in Yugoslav society as a whole, given the key role of the league in the institutionalization of the system. Recently the league has been described as an organization in search of a role. The problem is reasonably clear. A party of the classic Stalinist type when it took power, it has evolved voluntarily and consciously into the first among equals in a society with increased institutional pluralism and with participation of both institutions and the general public on various levels of power aggregation. Perhaps most critical has been the gradual withdrawal or atrophying of the functioning party units in the working institutions of the society and economy.

The point has already been made that the drastic decline of party membership in the rural sector seems to be associated with the end of the mobilization period in the countryside. It began to taper off

10. Ibid.

when there ceased to be a specific task for the party in that arena. With that as a precedent, the tendency until 1971 to limit the scope of league activity in social and economic organizations posed a major problem. It was not at all clear what the league *as an institution* was to do as distinct from the activities of the league members in these other institutions. Since 1958 the league has explicitly given up the right to issue directives or to work out a specific and detailed line in mass organizations. This policy has been followed to the extent that the league organization's inside industry and institutions may not discuss or act on matters that are supposed to come up on the agenda of the workers' council or the managing board. That is, the league local units in these organizations are not supposed to work out an agreement beforehand. The bulk of the preelectoral activities in the elections since 1958 have been handled by the Socialist Alliance, and again the league is explicitly barred from taking an active organizational role.

The tendency thus has been for the league to develop into something resembling an honor society, membership amounting to recognition of one's services in the society and political system as a whole. It is an organization of political and social activists distributed through the other institutional sectors of society. In this context we can understand two efforts launched since 1971: the campaign by the league's center to give local organizations greater cohesion and to link them more closely to the center, and the insistence on repoliticization of the league membership. The formal steps taken involve the reconstitution of the basic league organizations in the enterprises and neighborhoods, and a campaign to both rejuvenate and shift the social structure of the league. The campaign to shift the social structure of the league's elected bodies appears to be a lost cause, since, with the activization of the trade unions, the tendency will probably be for workers to center their activities around those organizations.

On the other hand, the campaigns to recruit the young appear to be reasonably successful. Recent trends in league membership are illustrated in table 13, which gives a breakdown by occupation of new members admitted since 1968. The table reflects a major effort of the league to recruit workers, since the category "workers, peasants, and craftsmen" is a misnomer (few craftsmen and peasants actually being recruited). Even more impressive is the league's success in maintaining a high rate of recruitment among the intelligentsia, university students, and high school students, all three of which normally present a problem for ruling communist parties. The figures should also be viewed in the light of the fact that there is considerable membership turnover, and that league membership has in fact dropped from the 1968 high of 1,146,082 to 1,025,476 in 1971. This is in good part a reflection of the pressure on inactive members to retire; in 1971, for example, 40,000 members were dropped— 20,000 for inactivity, 13,000 on their own initiative, and 7,000 excluded for specific reasons.[11]

Table 13

New LCY Members since 1968, by Occupation

Occupation	1969 (N = 49,537)	1970 (N = 31,885)	1971 (N = 47,000)
Workers, peasants, and craftsmen	41.0%	42.9%	43.5%
Intelligentsia and university students	19.0	17.5	20.0
High school students	13.0	22.0	18.0
White collar, management, and security	12.0	12.7	13.5
Other	5.0	4.6	5.0
	100.0%	100.0%	100.0%

SOURCES: *Radio Free Europe Research*, no. 1647 (December 22, 1972); "Report to Central Committee LCY," *NIN*, no. 1135 (October 1972).

Given the content of league activities, which tend to focus on discussion and propaganda rather than on specific tasks, even the present league membership is probably too large, and there is little for a relatively inarticulate person to do within the present league organization. This is all the more the case because, with the large number of alternative focuses for activity and for personal careers,

11. *NIN*, October 15, 1972. This includes those censored in the crackdown on league members involved in the purges against the nationalists, liberals, and technocrats. As the figure indicates, the number is hardly large.

league membership is no longer a precondition for employment and advancement. Yugoslav society, if anything, appears to suffer from an excess of participatory possibilities; a common complaint is that there are too many meetings to go to. League membership adds yet another realm of activity.

In the context of the general trends in the league's recent organizational history, that is, from 1958 until 1970, the campaign launched by the center in 1971 appears to have been a departure. The 1960s were characterized by a gradual depoliticization of the league and by increasing decentralization within it, so that by 1969 it seemed to be a federation of communist parties, each of which ruled its own republic. A number of observers of varying political colorations (including the Rand Corporation in its 1973 and 1974 reports) had expressed alarm at the pace of decentralization in Yugoslavia. It was decentralizing on all fronts. The federation was delegating increasing authority to the republics and their governments, the social and economic institutions were increasingly rooted in the republics, and even the league itself became part of this process.

The question of Yugoslavia's future was thus posed. The solution apparently adopted by the league center was to continue the present level of decentralization in the formal governmental sphere, especially in the relationship between the republics and the federation, while pressing for political centralization of the league. In terms of social content, such a policy can be described as a turn toward egalitarianism and against the social differences that developed in the last decade, reflecting the general feeling among league leadership that no *institutional* restructuring of the league makes sense without stronger *political* emphasis on a special role for the communist organization. The special role is that of a watchdog, guarding the social goals and norms of the system in a context where the economy is to be granted even greater autonomy in the future.

No proposals have been made to reverse the trend toward divorcing league officers from formal institutionalized power in the government and the economy: the hierarchies are to be kept separate. Paralleling the new political stress on egalitarianism, a rotation system is being used both to rejuvenate the top league bodies and to separate them from the hierarchies in the government and industry. This is the specific content of the campaign against bureaucracy and technocracy. The league makes a sharp distinction between technical intelligentsia, which it regards as desirable, progressive, and necessary, and technocracy, which it defines in almost Weberian terms as "the combination of bureaucracy with technical knowledge which is to be found in the House of Power." [12]

There is a perhaps naïve feeling that the Yugoslavs may find acceptable formulas for combining technical efficiency and progress with debureaucratization of the polity and economy, and that the league as an institution can play a major role in this development. This implies considerable tensions and struggle within the league itself, since the present bureaucratic and technocratic forces are also based in the league.

PARTY AND LEAGUE MEMBERSHIP POLICIES

Membership in the Communist Party of Yugoslavia, later the League of Communists, has meant different things at different times. Some of the changes were formally institutionalized at various party congresses, others gradually evolved with the development of the party and the league, and changes in the size and composition of its membership.

The prewar Yugoslav party, small and illegal, was perforce a cadre party, intensely active and tightly knit. Membership in the party organization was recruited through two different channels. Recruitment from the SKOJ, or Communist Youth League, was the preferred mechanism, since a young activist would be able to develop politically under the direction of communist youth bodies over a period of time before taking the next step. This step, for all but the SKOJ leaders, was becoming a candidate party member; after a minimum of eighteen months a candidate could be voted into membership by his local unit.

The second method, used more rarely, was direct recruitment of

12. Yugoslav theorists like Ljubo Tadic, Rudi Supek, and Svetozar Stojanovic stress that bureaucracy was produced by the advance of formal democratic principles against arbitrary rule and special privileges during the dismantling of the centralized administrative system. However, that bureaucracy later came into conflict with further development of democratization of social relations. Technocracy is the political consequence of functional rationality and is therefore linked to the social division of labor; thus it must continually fight any genuine attempts at workers' self-management (see chapter 7). It also must seek to extend the process of rationalization and routinization to the league itself.

adult workers, usually through the communist-dominated illegal trade unions or the communist factions inside the legal trade unions. There, too, candidate membership was used as a transitional stage. Members of both party and youth organizations operated within a framework where there were more sympathizers than members, and where membership in the party signified entrance into a revolutionary elite modeled after the Stalinized version of Lenin's Bolshevik Party.

During the war, a number of changes occurred under the pressures of Partisan warfare. To begin with, many of the party's better-known cadres were arrested in the big cities; the largest and best-organized section in Zagreb suffered major losses, in good part because of an attempt to carry on party activity in the cities where the police, both German and collaborationist, were active and effective.

The desperate need to fill out the cadres was then met by moving a number of youth organization members directly into the party, rapidly expanding the number of candidate members within the combat units, and systematically attempting to recruit the more active Partisan fighters directly into the party. The standards of political and theoretical competence naturally were compromised, although throughout the war the party organization held courses in party history and political theory for candidate members and newly recruited members. The courses were generally the responsibility of the political commissar of the given unit, although there were cadre courses on a higher level, particularly for the commanders and commissars of Partisan units. The formal criteria for party membership did not change, but the shift in membership was drastic: by autumn 1944 there were some 100,000 party members, including candidate members; after the consolidation of power in 1946, membership rose to 253,000. Of course party seniority relates very much to both the age of the person joining and to the circumstances under which he joined. Thus a loose stratification exists: prewar members who joined before the fall of Italy in September 1943, members who joined between 1943 and the fall of Belgrade in September 1944, members who joined before the end of the war, and, finally, postwar members who joined in the period between 1945 and the break with the Cominform. This stratification is more or less informal, unlike the formal distinction made in the case of Partisan War veterans between combatants who joined the original uprising in the summer of 1941, those who joined before the fall of Italy, and the rest.

Party membership in the postwar years expanded quite rapidly, although the formal structure from the prewar years was retained. Thus, by the time of the Cominform split, there were almost half a million members, and the subsequent development of the party can be seen in table 11 (see above in this chapter). The major institutional change, however, took place at the Sixth Party Congress in 1952, when the name of the party was changed to the League of Communists and a major attempt was made to open up the party. The new party statutes introduced four basic changes in party (league) practice. First, league meetings were henceforth to be public, and nonmembers, particularly those who were active in the Socialist Alliance or the trade unions, were encouraged to attend. Second, the league units in government branches and nongovernmental organizations were abolished, and league members were to function in those frameworks only as individuals. The organization from this point on was based on production and territorial divisions. Third, the party organs were decentralized so that the higher party organs no longer had the authority to assign operational tasks to lower units but could only lay out broad policy guidelines. Fourth, local autonomy of party units and the division of authority between the party and governmental bodies was formalized by barring heads of party organizations from simultaneously being heads of local bodies; and the Central Committee was no longer empowered to appoint party organizers to take over functions in local activities. The requirement of an eighteen-month period of candidacy was also abolished, and applicants were voted directly into membership.

Practice lagged somewhat behind the institutional changes, although a spurt in membership growth did occur and formal entrance into the party merely required two sponsors who were members of the local branch. Subsequently party membership was diluted still further, and by 1968 the formal practice changed even in this respect: membership in the League of Communists is now open to all citizens of Yugoslavia over the age of eighteen who choose to apply. Their membership is still passed on by the local organization, and in practice previous activity in student or youth organizations, trade unions, or the Socialist Alliance is the norm rather than the exception. This is modified in part by the recurrent membership drives, which are designed primarily to alter the composition of the party membership either by lowering the average age of the party units or by getting more workers and women to join.

Special legal privileges of party members were abolished as far back as 1950, although informal ties, particularly in the case of the older veterans, are still of considerable importance, particularly in government jobs and to a lesser extent in managerial appointments. The general rule seems to be that expertise is adequate to assure an appropriate career without party membership, but political activity still requires active membership in the League of Communists.

6

The Institutionalization of Multinationalism

A major challenge for the builders of the new socialist Yugoslavia lay in the multinational character of the country itself, a problem central to the failure of the prewar elites to establish a stable polity. The nationality problem was particularly salient at the end of World War II because it had been skillfully used by the occupying power as well as the various collaborationist groups to fan national hatreds during the civil war. The tradition of the Yugoslav Communist Party in this respect was helpful, since it had consistently fought against the control of the prewar Yugoslav state by the Serbian military and political establishment. It had in point of fact entered and fought the war with the slogan of a federal Yugoslav state in which the various units would be treated as sovereign entities voluntarily merging into a new Federal Republic of Yugoslavia.

Prewar Yugoslavia

Some very simple statistics, which can be contrasted with the postwar figures, illustrate the overwhelming Serbian domination of the pre-World War II Yugoslav state and its institutions. The military establishment was large and powerful, and it was jealously controlled by the Serbian officer corps. Out of 165 generals in active service in 1941, 161 were Serbs, 2 were Croats, and 2 Slovenes. Even if we allow for the fact that in prewar Yugoslavian statistics Montenegrins were considered as Serbs, this Serbian predominance is out of all proportion to the population figures. It shows that, among other things, no serious attempt had been made by the interwar Yugoslav military establishment to integrate the large number of Croatian and Slovenian officers who had served in Austro-Hungarian forces. That there was a pool of skilled officers from the other nationalities is clear from the fact that, at the outbreak of World War I, out of 375 generals and admirals in the Austro-Hungarian armed forces, 57 (over 15 percent) were Croat;

the Croatian population in the dual empire was thus over-represented. To be sure, the attitude of the military establishment reflected to some extent the ambivalence of the interwar Yugoslav governing elite toward all officials and officers inherited from Austro-Hungary. The official state-building myth regarded the Austro-Hungarian Empire as a foreign oppressor and the Serbs as the liberators of its South Slav peoples. Therefore, the officials and officers of Austro-Hungary of South Slav nationality were implicitly considered to have been disloyal. What this meant in practice was that a military career in prewar Yugoslavia was reserved to the Serbs and Montenegrins, with only slight representation by other national-ities. This was so firmly institutionalized by 1941 that out of 1,500 military cadets—the only possible candidates for the permanent officer corps in the last year of prewar Yugoslavia—there were 1,300 Serbs, 150 Croats, and 50 Slovenes.[1]

The situation in the governmental apparatus was no better. In 1939 the permanent high civil service officials of the various ministries were predominantly Serbian, as is shown in table 14. The rest were drawn from the two national groups with which the Serbian politicians tended to collaborate during the prewar period, Slovenes and Bosnian Moslems.

The picture is even clearer if we examine the occupants of the cabinet posts for the entire period of presocialist Yugoslavia. The interwar period can be broken down into two rough sections: from

Table 14

Serbs in Higher Administration, 1939

Ministry	No. of Posts Available	No. of Serbs	Percent Serbs
Office of the Premier	13	13	100%
Interior	127	113	89
Foreign Affairs	219	180	82
Education	156	150	96
Justice	137	116	85
Transport	26	15	58

SOURCE: Adapted from Rothschild, pp. 278–79.

1. Joseph Rothschild, *East Central Europe between the Two World Wars* (Seattle: University of Washington Press, 1974).

Table 15

Rate of Serbian Occupation of Major Ministries, 1918–41

Post	Constitutional period (121 months)	Authoritarian period (147 months)
Premiership	97%	100%
Defense	100	100
Interior	92	88
Foreign Affairs	83	100
Finance	98	67
Education	83	86
Justice	87	90

SOURCE: Rothschild, pp. 278–79.

December 1918 to December 1928, the period of constitutional government; and from January 1929 to March 1941, a period of authoritarian government under the royal dictatorship and the regency. Table 15 lists the major ministries. The figures give the percentage of time during which the given post was occupied by a Serb. A glance shows that the Ministry of Defense was never held by any other nationality and that the lion's share of all posts was held by Serbs.

NATIONAL AND REPUBLIC REPRESENTATION IN THE FEDERAL GOVERNMENT

The tradition of Serbian domination placed a major burden of proof on the postwar Yugoslav central government to show that it would attempt to divide federal posts fairly among the major nationalities of Yugoslavia. The problem is somewhat complicated by the location of the federal capital in Belgrade, which means that because of housing problems, if for no other reason, Serbs have tended to occupy at least the lower echelon posts in disproportionate numbers. However, the most recent figures illustrate major successes on the part of the Yugoslav postrevolutionary leadership in integrating the various nationalities on the federal level. To begin with, nominally the most important state institution on the federal level is the Federal Presidency, which is the collective body specifically designed to handle the problem of succession after Tito's death and which has considerable executive prerogatives (latent to be sure, but giving it legislative powers in emergencies). Its composition is by republics, as shown in table 16; for comparison, the nationality breakdown of the republics is given in table 17. The present make-up is a clear reflection of the federal structure of Yugoslavia on the highest level, the smaller republics having the same representation as the major one. The autonomous provinces have a smaller representation than the republics.[2] Bosnia, being multinational itself, gives all three of its major groups equal representation; Vojvodina overrepresents its Hungarian minority vis-à-vis the Serb majority; while Croatia overrepresents its Serbian minority by giving it one out of three posts. At the same time, Kosovo does not represent its Serbian minority at all. These figures show that, at the very least, a serious attempt is being made to work out some kind of reasonable balance.

Going further into republic representation in top institutions, we turn to the federal cabinet (Savezno Izvrsno Vece or SIV, translated as the Federal Executive Council) and the highest federal civil servants. The figures in table 18 show an attempt to maintain a rigid republic "key," or quota system, in appointments to the top federal

Table 16

Composition of Federal Presidency by Republic and Nationality

Republic	No. of members	Nationality of members
Bosnia-Herzegovina	3	1 Serb, 1 Croat, 1 Moslem
Croatia	3	2 Croats, 1 Serb
Macedonia	3	3 Macedonians
Montenegro	3	3 Montenegrins
Slovenia	3	3 Slovenes
Serbia	3	3 Serbs
Vojvodina	2	1 Hungarian, 1 Serb
Kosovo	2	2 Albanians

SOURCE: *Radio Free Europe Research*, no. 26 (June 1972).

2. Two "keys" are used in Yugoslav federal institutions; for major posts the unit considered is the republic or autonomous province, the units themselves working out the nationality breakdown internally. For other posts, the unit used was ethnic nationality. With increasing republic autonomy, the system has evolved into one of republic nomination and delegation for higher posts.

Table 17

Nationality Breakdown by Republic, 1971

Republic	% of Yugoslav Population in Republic*	Nationality breakdown (by percent)
Bosnia-Herzegovina	18.3%	Moslem 39.6; Serb 37.2; Croat 20.6; other 2.6
Croatia	21.6	Croat 79.4; Serb 14.2; other 6.4
Macedonia	8.0	Macedonian 69.3; Albanian 17.0; Turk 6.6; other 7.1
Montenegro	2.6	Montenegrin 67.2; Moslem 13.3; Serb 7.5; Albanian 6.7; other 6.3
Slovenia	8.4	Slovene 94.0; Croat 2.5; other 3.5
Serbia	25.6	Serb 89.5; Moslem 2.5; Albanian 1.2; other 6.8
Vojvodina	9.5	Serb 55.8; Hungarian 21.7; Croat 7.1; other 14.6
Kosovo	6.1	Albanian 73.7; Serb 18.4; Montenegrin 2.5; other 5.0

SOURCE: Adapted from *Popis stanovnistva Jugoslavije* (Belgrade: Savezni Zavod za Statistiku, 1971).

* Total Yugoslav population in 1971 was 20,522,972.

administrative bodies and suggest that this key is most effective on the highest level of all, that is, in the Federal Executive Council, though even when one totals up the next three levels a remarkably balanced composition results. Some leeway appears to exist but no republic is grossly overrepresented, and the republics of Bosnia and Croatia are only slightly overrepresented.[3] One can question whether or not the representatives of the republics at the federal level do in fact represent their republics, but that is a different type of argument from the one that bedeviled interwar Yugoslavia. Balancing the posts not only is clearly the goal but also works out in actual appointments.

The general use of a nationality and republic key in appointments

3. The "representation" sought is based not on the familiar one-man one-vote concept but rather on the principle of equal representation for each nationality as embodied in its home republic.

Table 18

Breakdown of Top Administrative Bodies by Republic

| | I | II | III | IV | | Relation |
	Members of SIV	Deputy State Secys.	Under- Secys.	Aides and Dept. Chiefs	Total II–IV	to Ideal Representation* (23)
Bosnia and Herzegovina	4	3	9	13	25	+2
Montenegro	4	2	4	15	21	−2
Croatia	4	5	4	16	25	+2
Macedonia	4	4	6	12	22	−1
Slovenia	4	5	5	13	23	—
Serbia	4	4	7	12	23	—
Kosovo	2	2	3	5	10 ⎱	−1
Vojvodina	2	3	2	7	12 ⎰	

SOURCE: *Radio Free Europe Research*, no. 19 (July 1972).

* The ideal figure is obtained by dividing the total number of posts by the number of republics and provinces (each of the latter counting as half a republic). This is the formal way in which the quota system is supposed to work.

extends beyond the top posts. As table 19 shows, the nationality key remains effective even in the administrative apparatus of the federation, although it begins to disintegrate at the level of "all employees." As previously stated, one of the problems for federal employees—especially lower-ranking ones—from outside Belgrade is the difficulty of finding housing in the capital; this is compounded by the reluctance of representatives from other republics who have school-age children to move there. For senior officials this is a minor problem, and by now the phenomenon of commuting higher officials has become quite common.

To round out this picture of the upper-level federal officialdom and civil service, table 20 gives a breakdown by republic of functionaries appointed by the Federal Assembly. The key working in the Federal Assembly is of course based on the republics and autonomous provinces and not on nationality as such. However, the existence of these two different criteria—republic and nationality—which are applied variously at different levels, poses a troublesome question. The general norm seems to be that a rigid key based on the

Table 19

National Composition of Federal Organs of Administration
in 1969

	Leaders	All employees	1971 Population
Serbs	39.4%	66.6%	39.7%
Croats	19.1	8.9	22.0
Slovenes	10.0	4.0	8.3
Macedonians	7.8	3.3	5.8
Montenegrins	15.1	7.2	2.5
Hungarians	0.2	0.4	2.5
Albanians	0.8	0.9	6.4
Moslems	5.1	2.9	8.4
Other (or unknown)*	2.5	4.8	4.3
	100.0%	100.0%	100.0%

SOURCE: *Izborni sistem u uslovima samoupravljanja* (Belgrade: Institut Drustvenih Nauka, 1969), p. 104.

* By 1969 definite pressure existed to declare oneself as a member of a specific nationality. Nevertheless, a substantial number of older officials persisted in using the definition "Yugoslav," which was placed under the rubric "other."

republics is used for the top policy-making functions; in point of fact these appointments are usually made in consultation with the republics, while the other higher officials are appointed by a nationality key. The Federal Assembly functionaries hew fairly closely to a republic key; however, it does slightly underrepresent

Table 20

Republic Origin of Functionaries Appointed
by the Federal Assembly in 1968

Bosnia-Herzegovina	13.6%
Montenegro	17.6
Croatia	19.3
Macedonia	11.4
Slovenia	10.8
Serbia, including Kosovo and Vojvodina	27.8%

SOURCE: *Izborni sistem u uslovima samoupravljanja*, p. 84.

Serbia, because Serbian representation under this type of a key would be double that of any other republic, as it includes the two antonomous provinces of Kosovo and Vojvodina.

The whole issue of the application of the "key" has troublesome implications in some ways resembling the debate on affirmative action in the United States. Obviously a trade-off has been made, the determined priority of assuaging the fears of the smaller republics and nationalities being considered more important for the institutionalization of the state administration than any abstract criterion of competence. Any serious attempt to provide a federal center whose legitimacy is accepted by the population at large in a multinational polity like Yugoslavia will have to maintain such a key for the foreseeable future since its emotional and symbolic importance is great, and since it represents a major argument against the development of local nationalism. To be sure, even the most representative federal structure will not be able to defuse all possible nationalist demands, but a reasonably representative structure can, at the very least, isolate the more extremist and antisocialist nationalists by making it clear that a genuine attempt is being made to represent the various components of the federal state in its administrative apparatus.

Competence is, after all, quite often a very tricky and subjective concept. Guerrilla communist regimes, such as that out of which the current Yugoslav system has evolved, have a tendency to promote more rapidly persons without formalized backgrounds to posts of major organizational power. Since the early postwar experience and the period of rapid development in the first decade of self-management were both directed by persons with little if any formal training, the argument of specialized competence is probably less acceptable in Yugoslav political debates than it is in more stable social and political systems. This is not to say that a specialized, competent, and routinized bureaucracy is not developing. What we have here, in a different form, is the familiar distinction made in the United States between appointed and civil service officials. The appointed officials in Yugoslavia or their specific equivalents are chosen by republic or nationality keys, a system hardly less efficient than appointments based on political affiliation in systems designed as pluralist. The real contrast between Yugoslav administration and others is more likely to be found in a comparison between Yugoslav officialdom and that of states like Italy, France or Japan, where the career officials move up much higher in the hierarchy than they do either in Yugoslavia or, for that matter, in countries with Anglo-Saxon traditions.

The growing pool of university-educated experts in all republics provides a base from which the civil service can be renewed, and the general tendency in any case, key or no key, is toward a gradual but steady upgrading of the formal training of officials on all levels.

THE NATIONAL COMPOSITION OF
THE YUGOSLAV PEOPLES' ARMY

A generalization can be made here that applies not only to the national make-up of the army but also to that of the League of Communists, discussed later: the higher the post, the easier it appears to maintain a national or republic balance; or, to put it somewhat differently, the less the posts in question are subject to inclination, tradition, voluntary decision of the candidates, or simple factors like geographic proximity, the more likely it is that the body in question will maintain a balance. Thus, it is no problem to maintain an ethnic or republic balance in the top levels of the League of Communists and other sociopolitical bodies on the federal and republic level. However, it is difficult, as will be shown, to maintain that balance in the lower ranks since the number of persons entering either the League of Communists or the officer corps depends on the number of candidates available, which in turn is affected by a whole series of factors over which conscious policy has limited influence. This is most marked in the officer corps itself, as shown in table 21. These figures should cast some light on the recent nationalist polemics inside and outside Yugoslavia about the degree of representativeness of this important institution. Even a cursory glance makes several things quite clear. The least representative level is that of the officer corps itself; career officers are not representative of the national make-up of the Yugoslav federation, despite attempts to create some kind of balance. Thus, on that level, the Serbs and Montenegrins are heavily overrepresented, reflecting in both cases, I believe, the military tradition of those two nationalities, but even more the ethnic make-up of the areas that were most intensively involved in Partisan warfare. A disproportionate part of the Partisan fighting occurred in mountainous areas where these two nationalities are concentrated, and the service

Table 21

Officer Corps of the Yugoslav Peoples'
Army by Nationality,* 1971

	Total Population	Officers	Generals	High Command
Serbs	39.7%	60.5%	46.0%	33.0%
Croats	22.0	14.0	19.0	38.0
Moslems	8.4	3.5	4.0	4.1
Slovenes	8.3	5.0	6.0	8.3
Albanians	6.4	2.0	0.5	—
Macedonians	5.6	6.0	5.0	8.3
Montenegrins	2.5	8.0	19.0	8.3
Hungarians	2.5	1.0	0.5	—
Other	4.3	—	—	—
	100.0%	100.0%	100.0%	100.0%

SOURCE: *Radio Free Europe Research*, no. 12 (April 1972).

* Nationality here means *declared* nationality, irrespective of republic origin.

military corps reflects this. Also noteworthy is that the Macedonians appear to have maintained an almost exactly proportionate share on all levels. There are probably two additional reasons for the underrepresentation of other nationalities, the two reasons operating differently for different groups. Because of their higher economic and cultural level and therefore the more varied opportunity structure for these three national groups, the Croats, Slovenes, and Hungarians probably view a military career as being less desirable. My guess, and it would be difficult to do more than guess, given the absence of more detailed figures, is that, if one were to add the number of Serbs from Croatia to the number of Croats in the officer corps, the resulting percentage would be fairly close to the percentage of the population of that republic in the military corps.[4] But that would, in turn, reflect again the fact that the Serb-inhabited areas of Croatia tended to be more active in the civil war. In any case, these are the least developed areas of that republic.

In the case of the Moslems and Albanians, other factors seem to be

4. No breakdown by republic was available. My guess that the disproportionate percentage of Serbs is based on Serbs outside of Serbia is an extrapolation from the areas most active during the Partisan War.

at work. For example, these two groups have the highest natality rate, and therefore, at least in the case of the Bosnian Moslems, the percentage within the officer corps is probably closer to the percentage of Moslems in the Yugoslav population who were the appropriate age for entry into the officer corps. This same factor holds for Albanians; in addition, from the end of the war to the political purge of the secret police apparatus and its leader, Alexander Rankovic, in 1966, there was admittedly discrimination against Albanians. One can assume that for both of these groups the figures will rise in the future.

The national composition of generals is much more representative, with the exception of the Montenegrins, who are here greatly overrepresented because of the large number of Montenegrin wartime officers who have stayed in the armed forces, having fewer alternative careers within that underdeveloped republic. Since this level of army leadership is exclusively populated by wartime Partisan cadres, it will probably shift in the direction of greater representativeness as the younger men move in. This is bound to create tensions within the military establishment since an attempt to balance out the nationalities at the level of generals will mean, for a large number of career officers, that promotions will be affected by political considerations and will be disproportionately more difficult for those whose national groups are now overrepresented among lower-ranking officers. More simply stated, it will be a good deal more difficult for a Montenegrin or Serbian colonel to be promoted to general than for their Slovenian, Croatian, or Moslem colleagues.

One factor that militates against excessive tensions arising against a quota system thus applied is the great sense of solidarity deliberately inculcated in the officer corps as a whole, and the jealously preserved autonomy of the officer cadres from their republic political structures. One of the reasons for the crackdown on the nationalist leadership of Croatia in 1971 was that it attempted to influence Croatian officers within the Yugoslav military establishment.[5] The army will almost certainly attempt to preserve its all-Yugoslav character for the time being.

The third level, the high command, is balanced with scrupulous

5. The best background discussion of the rise and fall of Croat nationalist leaders within the League of Communists is in Dennison Russinow's *The Crisis in Croatia*, in four parts (New York: American Universities Field Staff, 1972).

attention to ethnic make-up. Since the percentages are based on a relatively small number of persons, a word about the detailed composition of the high command is appropriate. The data given are for 1973. At the very top is the military section of the Presidency of the federation, including the supreme commander, the chief of staff, the secretary of the Council for National Defense, the secretary of the Council for State Security, and the secretary of the League of Communists organization in the Yugoslav Peoples' Army (YPA). These five posts were occupied by 3 Croats, 1 Slovene, and 1 Moslem. The next level is the State Secretariat for National Defense, composed of 9 persons: 4 Serbs, 4 Croats, and 1 Macedonian. Finally, there is the ten-member higher operative command of the YPA, composed of the chief of staff, the deputy chief of staff, and the commanders of the army districts. The breakdown there in 1973 was 4 Serbs, 2 Croats, 2 Montenegrins, 1 Macedonian, and 1 Slovene. The picture of the top military elite can be rounded out by the fact that there were 4 four-star generals in the Yugoslav army, of whom 1 (already mentioned as the secretary of the State Secretariat for National Defense) was a Serb and 3 were Croats. By virtue of their rank, they sit in the Council for National Defense.

The high command is, therefore, scrupulously balanced to prevent any possible suggestion of Serbian domination. In fact it is, if anything, disproportionately balanced against the Serbs.[6] In my opinion, given the fact that we are talking here about a Partisan cadre politically socialized in the party in the period of the greatest emphasis on Yugoslavism, given the emphasis in the internal political education of the army on its nonparticularist character, and, finally, given the fact that this cadre is explicitly a communist cadre, the national make-up is of secondary importance for the functioning of the institution. It is, however, of great symbolic importance for the future of the Yugoslav federation that one of the pillars of institutional stability of socialist Yugoslavia is at its top levels a reflection of the multinational character of the state.

A clearer picture of the make-up of the high command can be seen from a brief examination of the personnel of the State Secretariat for National Defense, the equivalent of a defense ministry in Yugoslavia today. The secretariat itself is headed by Marshal Tito himself, but

6. This is my opinion; no official statement to such effect exists.

the ten persons occupying the other posts reflect the general make-up of the high command. A breakdown for 1968, with thumbnail biographies, follows:[7]

> *State Secretary for National Defense:* a Serbian from Serbia, born in 1916. Finished military academy before the war in Belgrade; participant in NOB since 1941; helped organize revolt in his region. Moved up from a commander of detachment to a brigadier and a chief of staff of the Second Proletarian Division. After liberation, was commandant of division, corps, and, finally, all border units of Yugoslavia. Member of party bodies in his unit since 1941; also member of the Central Committee of the League of Communists (CCLCY) and the CCLCY's Commission for the Army. Deputy in the Federal Assembly from 1963 to 1969. Three-star general.

> *Chief of Staff, YPA:* Serb from Croatia, born in 1918. Schoolteacher before the war. Active in party front organizations. War of liberation. NOB participant since 1941, party member since 1942. Commandant of Partisan units in his region. Political commissar of a brigade, chief of staff of a division by 1943. Political commissar of a division same year. November 1944 became commandant of army corps. After war, commandant of army. Finished military academy in the USSR in 1947. Three-star general.

> *Assistant Secretary for National Defense:* Croat, born in 1915. Finished law school in Zagreb before the war. Member of Communist Youth Organization since 1937; illegal underground worker till May 1942. Party member since 1942. Entered active Partisan combat units in fall of 1942. Moved through army ranks. By 1944 commandant of Army Corps and deputy commandant of the Third Army. Finished war as the commandant of the Tenth Army Corps, which liberated Zagreb. Completed war as two-star general; now admiral. Completed military academy in Moscow 1946 to 1948. Commandant of the navy since 1962. Member of the CCLCY Commission for the Army since 1950.

> *Assistant Secretary for National Defense.*[8] Croat, born in 1918. Completed technical school in 1937. Reserve officer in prewar army; member of the party since 1939. Active in the underground and NOB from 1941. Moved up through various ranks. Completed war as the commander of

7. Detailed data were available for that year in "Jubilarno izdanje drustveno politicke zajednice," *Federacija* (Belgrade: Interpress, 1968), 1:321–24.

8. Later became chief of staff, YPA. Replaced in 1971 by a Serb.

a division. Three-star general, commandant of the Army Air Force. Member of the CCLCY Commission for the Army.

Assistant Secretary for National Defense: Croat, born in 1916. NOB participant since 1941, joined the party in 1942. Moved up through Partisan ranks as combatant and army commander. Completed the war as chief of staff of an army corps. Completed military academy in Yugoslavia. Elected to various party bodies. Three-star general.

Assistant Secretary for National Defense: Croat, born in 1918. Machinist in Split before the war. Member party organization 1933, party 1935, NOB from 1941. Held both political and military positions throughout the war. Commissar of a division by 1943. Political commissar of a corps till 1944. Moved out of the army at the end of the war to hold various party positions. Returned to the army in 1950. Held various posts in both republic and federal League of Communists and in the army party organization. Three-star general.

Assistant Secretary for National Defense: Montenegrin, born in 1920. Student of mathematics before war. Member of party student organization since 1939; joined party at the end of 1939. Head of his party cell. Organized NOB uprising in his area. Held various military and political functions throughout the war. Party leader of the Third Proletarian Brigade 1942–44. Moved up to secretary of the party's Committee of the First Proletarian Division. Moved to USSR in 1944 as political commissar of the First Yugoslav Brigade, organized in the Soviet Union. Upon return moved into the political section of the Ministry of Defense. Held additional posts as commissar of the Yugoslav navy and army. Member of the Central Committee of the party and league; member of the CCLCY Commission for the Army.[9]

Assistant Secretary for National Defense: Slovenian, born in 1921. Worker before the war. Joined the party in 1941, participated in illegal activities. Active Partisan since 1942; moved through various functions to the political commissar of a division by the end of the war. After the war completed party higher school and Military (Air Force) Academy. Held various functions, particularly commissar of division and head of the Military Academy. Member of the Central Committee of the league; member of the CCLCY Commission for the Army.[10]

Assistant Secretary for National Defense: Croat from Dalmatia, born in 1916.

---

9. Moved to commander of Eastern Frontier. Replaced by a Serb.
10. Promoted to Military Committee of the Presidency. Replaced by a Macedonian.

Construction painter, before war. Party member since 1939; organized uprising in his region; throughout the war held major political and army posts. Moved from political commissar to commandant of battalion, brigade, and finally division. In 1944 sent to USSR, where he finished military academy. Subsequently completed military academy in Yugoslavia. Member of the CCLCY Commission for the Army.

Assistant Secretary for National Defense: Serb from Croatia, born in 1919. Law student and member of party youth organization before war. Helped organize uprising in his region; member of the party since 1941; member of the regional party committee and political commissar of brigade. Held various political posts in Croatia throughout the war. Completed war as staff officer. After war, completed Military Academy. Basically involved work as publicist.[11]

These sketches make it clear that the use of a nationality key has not even been attempted. There was, for example, only one Serb from Serbia. The group is so homogeneous in background that the biographies become almost monotonous. All participated in the war of liberation from the beginning. All basically tested their mettle in the bitter years of the Partisan warfare, and all ended up as high officials of the Partisan army by the end of the war. Whether one should speak of this body as a party body in the army or as an army body in the party is an open question. Clearly they have maintained linkages with both organizational structures, and even during the war they shuttled between commandant and commissar appointments. A number completed military academy in the Soviet Union, but what was crucial was that they passed that second test with as high marks as the first, the first being of course the Partisan War. There was considerable pressure on Yugoslav communists studying in the military academy in the Soviet Union to break with Yugoslavia and back the Cominform. These men did not do so. They subsequently held high military and political posts, and from the point of view of institutional stability the only major problem that can arise in examining this group is their relative age homogeneity, which means that they will face retirement at approximately the same time.

While data on the army in Yugoslavia are less accessible than data on the party and civil service, I would be surprised if the next layer below these men was markedly different in terms of the balance

---

11. Moved to staff work, not replaced.

of political and army experience. A different situation exists with the lower-ranking officers who are basically postwar products. However, I believe political factors are probably crucial in the make-up and attitudes of this older group, modified by only one major consideration, and that is that their institution (the army) is based on the federal state itself and not on any republic; in all probability they are hostile to any particularist demands, either nationalist or economic, which would threaten the unity of the state they are to defend.

THE NATIONAL COMPOSITION OF
THE LEAGUE OF COMMUNISTS

The Composition of the League of Communists is often the subject of serious discussion within the Yugoslav establishment. As I will show further on, much of the discussion focuses on its social make-up, where it is clear that the league is increasingly representative of the existing modern sector of Yugoslav society and of precisely those strata that have the greatest stake in the system and its preservation. However, the national make-up is somewhat skewed by factors not dissimilar to those affecting the make-up of the officer corps. However, since the league is a mass organization with over a million members, the imbalances are less flagrant (see table 22).

The league figures tell a story similar to the army's but one that deserves some discussion nonetheless. In the first place, our breakdown is by nationality, not by nationality and republic, since the latter figures are not yet available. The tendency in previous censuses was for the Serbs, who are overrepresented in the Serbian league, to be somewhat likely to be similarly overrepresented outside of the republic of Serbia proper. That is, the Serbian minorities in Bosnia and Croatia have a higher tendency to be members of the league than the Bosnians and Croats around them.[12] These are the areas with the deepest Partisan tradition. This also explains the fact that the Montenegrins are most overrepresented; but in addition almost a quarter of the Montenegrin population of Yugoslavia now lives in Serbia, and among them are found a disproportionately high number of persons who occupy high posts on the ladder of postwar

12. In 1968, 26 percent of the members of the league in Croatia were Serbs although Serbs comprised only 15 percent of the population. In Bosnia the respective figures for that year were 55 and 42 percent.

Table 22

National Composition of LCY Membership, 1968 and 1971

	1971 Population	1971 LCY Members	1968 LCY Members*	% Change
Serbs	39.7%	49.4%	50.7%	−1.3
Croats	22.0	17.4	17.2	+0.2
Moslems	8.4	4.6	3.9	+0.7
Slovenes	8.3	6.3	6.1	+0.2
Albanians	6.4	3.4	3.2	+0.2
Macedonians	5.8	6.2	6.4	−0.2
Montenègrins	2.5	6.3	6.3	—
Hungarians	2.5	1.17	1.1	—
Other	4.3	5.3	5.1	+0.2
	100.0%	100.0%	100.0%	

SOURCE: Composite table using figures from the 1968 and 1971 censuses, *Radio Free Europe Research* (February 1970), and *NIN* (October 1972).

* Notably small changes have occurred despite the fact that between the two party censuses both the nationalist wave in Croatia and the crackdown by the federal center occurred.

social mobility. Croats and Slovenes are underrepresented, as are the two major minorities, Albanians and Hungarians, and the Moslems.

In the case of the Moslems and Albanians, the age make-up of the league probably tells part of the story, since two factors are at work here. The two basic age groups where the bulk of the league's membership was to be found in 1971 are 28–40 years and 41–55 years, which account for 39.8 and 32.9 percent of the membership respectively. In terms of experience, these groups include, first, those who matured during the postrevolutionary period and are already securely employed and, second, the revolutionists. Younger league members are less numerous: only 16.8 percent were 21–27 years old and only 3.9 percent 20 or under in 1971. Thus, the fact that the Moslem and Albanian subpopulations are disproportionately young may be one reason for the underrepresentation of these nationalities. Two other factors are relevant: these two national groups are concentrated in the traditional rural sector and are therefore least subject to the impact of modernizing values, the carrier of which is the league. In the case of the Albanians and the Hungarians, because they are minorities living in compact areas adjacent to Albania and Hungary, they were viewed with suspicion until 1966.

One other element that bears on the national make-up of the league is the growing percentage of pensioners within it: they now amount to 8.9 percent of its total membership. This is higher than the percentage of retirement-age (55 and older) party members, who account for only 6.6 percent of party membership; but this is explained by the fact that a substantial number of pensioners were permitted to retire early because of their years of wartime service, which counted double. In turn, such early retirers tend to be from mountainous areas and are often those members of the league who did not develop skills suitable to rapid social mobility in the postwar revolutionary society.

As a general rule, all Yugoslav institutions tend to become more representative in terms of republic, nationality, and even sex as we move up in the hierarchy. That is, the closer we move to the levels where conscious manipulation of the make-up of the institution is possible, the more likely we are to find that the normative description agrees with the actual distribution of posts. As Yugoslav society emerged from the period of harsh centralism, the processes of normalization and routinization began to affect the league as well as the various governmental bodies. The league, and particularly its lower echelons, has become more a reflection of its base and less of a transmission of directives from the center. This positive feature of the development and evolution of the League of Communists has certain negative consequences. On one hand, it means that in the least developed areas the league is likely to reflect the patriarchal and traditional attitudes of the members who have not been socialized through the cadre-party period and revolution into socialist values. It also makes possible the penetration of the league by the sentiments and values of forces hostile to the league's program. Such forces, representing either a nostalgia for the "more orderly and stable" period when the party acted as the cutting edge of a hard-boiled communist dictatorship,[13] or latent nationalist sentiment, or even managerial and technocratic values, can develop and will undoubt-

13. Arrests in the spring of 1974 of members of a pro-Soviet conspiratorial group that had held an organizing conference and begun to build a national organization show that this current still exists. Most of the arrested were pensioners from the security service.

edly continue to grow within a decentralizing organization. This is why the league itself is bound to be subject to spasmodic organizational drives to alter its balance and to make the league's base organizations conform to the norms of its program.

This lies at the root of much of the current debate. The problem is that consensus reached at the top levels is often evaded or blocked at the grass roots. A good example is the failure of the league to alter its composition successfully along the lines that were universally agreed to at the top levels. Campaigns to increase the percentages of industrial workers, young people, students, and women meet continual resistance by present members of the league's base organizations who do not relish the notion of sharing the great latent power still found in the league. In particular, the latter can hardly be expected to recruit from age groups likely to challenge the present leaders. On the other hand, the party leadership on higher levels, working with different criteria, engages in continuing campaigns to break down such resistance and to develop a league that represents the dynamic strata—which need to be recruited in order to maintain effectiveness—within what is, after all, the crucial system of organization in contemporary Yugoslavia.

THE FORMAL POLITICAL SYSTEM

The political and representative institutions of postwar Yugoslavia have evolved through a number of successive stages, some of which represented a drastic discontinuity with previous ones. While this is not the place for a descriptive history of postwar constitutional developments, a number of themes require a fuller exposition.[14]

The consolidation of power by the Yugoslav communists at the end of World War II on the state level was preceded by the development of a wide network of local National Committees of Liberation (NOO) which represented the new state authority locally and which had, by and large, consolidated their power before the formal communist takeover. The history of these institutions varied from region to region so that in some areas local quasi-governmental

14. The Yugoslav authority on the institutionalization and development of the constitutional system in postwar Yugoslavia is Jovan Djordjevic; see especially his *Ustavno pravo* (available in many editions) and *Politicki sistem* (Belgrade: Savezna Admistracija, 1970). See also *Izborni sistem u uslovima samoupravlijanja* (Belgrade: Institut Drustvenih Nauka, 1969).

units were set up and functioning by 1942, but the major period of development was from the fall of Italy in September 1943 to the fall of Belgrade in October 1944. In that one-year span, disregarding the constitutional niceties that preoccupied Yugoslavia's allies, the Yugoslav Communist Party convincingly replaced the old organs on the communal level with new Liberation Committees, and as the territories were liberated from the occupiers and their quislings new Liberation Committees were established to create the first network of governing institutions. These National Liberation Committees were set up to support the Partisan resistance and were supposed to provide a broad political base of support for the combat units. However, no other organized movement, party, or group was permitted to operate within the National Liberation Committees, and as it became evident that the Partisans were winning the civil war the organs of repression of the nascent state—the army and the police—made it clear that no political challenge to the authority of the party would be tolerated. It is important to stress that the NOOs were broad at least in that they involved previously passive sectors of the population in local administration—women, the young, and the poor.[15]

Throughout the war there was a gradual development of first quasi-governmental and then formalized legal structures in the areas under Partisan control, resting on the base of the National Liberation Committees in the liberated territory and on the armed units. The first of the "republic" structures was set up in Slovenia by September 1941, followed very rapidly by republicwide institutions in Serbia, Bosnia, and Croatia. (These "republicwide" institutions anticipated the future republics of the new federal constitution, adopted much later.) In November 1942, in the town of Bihac, in the center of the liberated territory in Bosnia, the first attempt to set up a statewide political structure was made at the First Congress of AVNOJ—the Anti-Fascist Council of National Liberation of Yugo-slavia. AVNOJ claimed to be the holder of supreme political authority in the resistance, though without the attributes of a legal government, and at least in theory its directives were only advisory

---

15. Jack Fisher's *Yugoslavia: A Multi-National State* (New York: Chandler, 1966), is the handiest English-language source on the Yugoslav communes. Yugoslav sources are too numerous to cite.

to the National Liberation Committees in what were to become the republics.

The Second Congress of AVNOJ was far more significant. It was held in the town of Jajce in Bosnia, in November 1943, which is generally considered to be the date of the foundation of socialist Yugoslavia. The Second Congress followed the fall of Italy and a major expansion of the Partisan-held liberated territory. It made a number of decisions that anticipated the future constitution. The most significant were its denial of authority to the government in exile in London, and its claim to be the representative institution of Yugoslavia and the one with which the Allies would have to deal. It also formally pledged to establish a federal structure after liberation. The basic resolutions on this question in theory guaranteed full equality to the peoples of Serbia, Croatia, Slovenia, Bosnia-Herzogovina, Macedonia, and Montenegro and stated that the federal Yugoslav state could be developed only after liberation, by the voluntary adhesion to the federation of those units. The new name adopted was Democratic Federal Yugoslavia (changed in 1946 to the Democratic Federal Republic of Yugoslavia). The structure set up by AVNOJ at its second Congress became the de facto if not the de jure political authority on which the party rested, and the future negotiations between Tito and Prime Minister Churchill in 1944 involved merely the addition of a few presumably uncompromised ministers from the prewar government to a committee elected by AVNOJ to set up the Provisional Government of Yugoslavia which was recognized by the Allies.

The constitutional development of postwar Yugoslavia was enormously complex, involving drastic redefinitions of the formal organization of the system. The first constitution, promulgated in 1946, was clearly modeled on the Russian model and created a bicameral legislature representing the republics in the upper chamber and smaller geographic constituencies—roughly equal in population—in the lower chamber. The Stalinist period of mobilization that coincided with that particular parliamentary structure determined that the Yugoslav parliament was a typical showpiece, taking little or no initiative in policy definition.

As a consequence of the break with the Cominform, three major institutional developments occurred. First, primitive legislation established a system of workers' councils, albeit with poorly defined prerogatives and still operating within a basically centralized economy. Second, the Economic Reform of 1951 stressed decentralization and delegated considerable authority to republic, regional, and communal governmental and party cadres. Third, coinciding with this decentralization was the first, most successful, and most realistic of the Yugoslav postwar plans—the long-range ten-year plan of 1951–61.

The consequences of these changes took the form of the Organic Law of 1953[16] which began an experiment that proved abortive. While there was again a two-chamber legislature, the first chamber combined representation of both republics and geographic constituencies, while the second, a Chamber of Producers,[17] was supposed to reflect the changes in the economy. Within the first chamber, the delegates of the republics were supposed to meet separately as a Council of Nationalities in cases involving the autonomy of the republics. However, they never did meet as a separate chamber, and the Organic Law of 1953 can be described as a centralist document which was accompanied by a stress on "Yugoslavism" and on the development of centralized institutions in the federal administration. Many if not most of the subsequent reforms were directed at reversing the consequences of this recentralization of Yugoslavia.

The period 1953–63 is referred to by current would-be centralizers with considerable nostalgia, since it combined an economic growth rate second only to that of Japan with a cohesive governmental apparatus and a League of Communists that operated primarily as a statewide institution. This was also the period of the greatest development of the southern and underdeveloped regions, resulting in a drastic shift in the proportion of the industrial working force in these two regions. Thus, while approximately 23 percent of all workers were in the southern regions[18] at the end of World War II,

16. Djordjevic, *Ustavno pravo*. A solid discussion can be found in Woodford McClelland, "Post-war Political Evolution," in Wayne S. Vucinich, ed., *Contemporary Yugoslavia* (Berkeley: University of California Press, 1969).

17. Elected by all employed in the socialist sector of the economy, including administrators and government services within the same *geographic* units as the regular legislators.

18. I use here R. V. Burks's division, roughly the Sava-Danube line, with the Belgrade area included in the North. See Burks, "The National Problem and the Future of Yugoslavia" (mimeo., Santa Monica, Cal.: Rand Corporation, 1971).

by 1964 that percentage had risen to 43.2 percent, which represents an even greater expansion than the figures suggest, given the much higher birthrates in the southern region and therefore the higher percentage of economically inactive persons. The period from 1953 to 1963, as a whole, was characterized by a gradual development of the institutions of self-government and communal autonomy, with little emphasis on the republics as aggregating centers, and with relatively structured planning emphasizing modernization of the underdeveloped regions. There was also a massive expansion of the institutions of higher learning, and a general though slow liberalization and institutionalization of the political system.[19]

The next stage was marked by the constitution of 1963 and a series of measures following soon after, known as the Economic and Social Reform. The constitution of 1963 and the changes made in the League of Communists at its Eighth Congress in 1964 drastically altered the balance between the federation and the republics. The legislature was transformed into a five-chamber body with a Chamber of Nationalities and a Federal Representative Chamber,[20] to which were added three chambers with indirectly elected delegates representing what the Yugoslavs define as the social communities: the Economic Chamber, the Chamber of Health and Welfare, and the Cultural-Educational Chamber.[21] Legislation in any given area was supposed to be initiated in the relevant chamber and became law when both it and the Federal Representative Chamber passed it. This constitutional reform was followed by party reforms, the most important of which was a proposal that the republic parties meet in congress before each statewide party congress, and the introduction to the League of Communists itself of a system of delegations from the republics. Indeed, the Ninth Congress, in 1969, was so conducted, and it institutionalized a new Executive Bureau, consisting of Marshal Tito, two representatives from each of the republic parties, and one from each of the autonomous provinces. Thus the leadership of the party itself was federalized and the now familiar six-plus-two formula (i.e., six

19. Ibid.
20. Elected from geographic units roughly equal in population.
21. These chambers were elected from the persons employed in those respective sectors in the same geographic units used for the Federal Representative Chamber.

republics plus two autonomous provinces as a basis for representation) was applied to the league organs, giving birth to the quip that Yugoslavia was indeed moving toward a multiparty system. Paralleling these changes was a deemphasis on the concept of Yugoslavism with a stress on the unifying concept of a Yugoslav "commonwealth of nations," membership in which was through membership in a republic, each republic being the national home of one of the major Yugoslav nationalities—a distinct and implicit allusion to the Swiss system. The Economic and Social Reform had even more drastic consequences by delegating further authority to the enterprises and the workers' councils, and by limiting the role of central planning to stating general goals without giving directives.[22]

Considerable resistance toward both sets of changes developed inside the league. One center of resistance was the police apparatus in alliance with the large number of persons who had served in the police agencies and regarded themselves as the party Old Guard, with a special role in defending Yugoslav socialism. Opposition was particularly directed toward economic decentralization but it also focused on the growing liberalization of the system and the increasingly free-wheeling discussions in the press and public. The covert resistance of this group led by the designated successor to Tito—Alexander Rankovic—and his allies came to a head at a league plenum of July 1966, when he and his major supporters were removed from party posts and expelled. In the months that followed the police institutions were subjected to a wide purge and were much reduced in size and influence.[23]

One of the forces instrumental in bringing the police to heel was the army. It was army intelligence that produced evidence that Rankovic and his allies had been regularly tapping the phones of the members of the Central Committee, the Presidium and the government, including even the phone of Marshal Tito himself. Years later, as the process of democratization created considerable tensions and exposed a number of underlying conflicts and cleavages in Yugoslav society, a popular joke went like this: Tito to Rankovic: "Look, after

22. The most influential work on the dismantling of the central planning system in Yugoslavia is Miladin Korac et al., *Politika dohotka* (Belgrade: RAD, 1972). See also Branko Horvat, *An Essay on Yugoslav Society* (New York: International Arts & Sciences Press, 1969).

23. Burks, "National Problem."

all, we have been friends for these many years. I understand that we could have had a few differences, but why on earth were you tapping even my phone?" Rankovic to Tito: "Tito, when I and my lads were listening to you, all Yugoslavia heard and obeyed you."

The removal of Rankovic remains historically important both to those sectors of the league leadership that sought to continue the process of decentralization and democratization, stressing this action as a break with the administrative intervention of the political police, and to the remnants of the Old Guard, who traced most of the troubles in later days to the removal of the "watchdog of the revolution" from its post. The atmosphere was also envenomed by the fact that the fall of Rankovic was viewed in part as a defeat for those forces in the league and government who sought to maintain the pace of rapid development of the underdeveloped areas and was viewed as a victory for those who would make major concessions to the egoism of the more developed regions which had been chafing at what they considered uneconomic and wasteful investments in the underdeveloped regions. It did not help matters that Rankovic was the only Serb in the top leadership circle and that his fall was viewed by Serbian nationalists as a strike against their republic and people.

The elimination of the political police as a force in the political system and economy has been followed by attempts to reach a new equilibrium between the republics and the federal center. The best-known and sharpest dispute arose in 1970 and 1971 between the new leadership in Croatia and the federal center. This dispute starkly outlined the dilemma of a federal polity that seeks to maintain both consensus and development. Perhaps there is a point in Seymour Martin Lipset's argument that pluralism, and therefore Western-style political democracy, requires a "low temperature" of political discourse.[24] A better way of putting it, perhaps, is that the "normal," that is, parliamentary, decision-making processes work when there is no major decision on the agenda threatening the interests of any substantial class or group in the society. A revolutionary regime, by definition, is committed to changing social and class relations and is obviously driven to seek other, nonparliamentary means.

What is in dispute here is the nature of the democratic decision-

24. Seymour M. Lipset, *Political Man* (New York: Doubleday, 1969).

making process itself. Most Western political scientists deal with modernizing and communist regimes from a background that identifies democracy and democratic political theory with the development of liberal parliamentary institutions informed by the Anglo-Saxon tradition. The whole purpose of the institutional development of parliamentary democracy in postrevolutionary America was to minimize the possibilities of rapid social and economic change. And the main theoretical reason for the separation of powers was to prevent the "mob" from having access to the tools of political change. In the Yugoslav case, the institutionalization that occurred was more analogous to the experience of the Jacobins in France, and the balance-of-power mechanisms modify the untrammeled rule of the political party only insofar as they take into account the special multinational character of Yugoslavia.

In an established bourgeois society, at least theoretically, the degree of initiative required by the political institutions in order to maintain the status quo is quite limited. Parliamentarianism itself implies the acceptance of a given political order and of orderly and therefore quite often very gradual change. In contrast, mobilizing regimes, irrespective of their degree of representativeness or popularity, are more analogous to emergency legislatures and tend to maximize the output or the results of the political process rather than focusing on the process itself. Simply stated, the question is: Is democracy judged by adherence to a set of rules, or by the results of the working of a political system?

The development of an alliance between the nationalists and the local leadership in Croatia signaled a new approach to negotiating between the republics and the center. Because of the de facto veto power that any republic has, the Croatian leadership during the two years of "national euphoria" was able to block the resolution of an increasingly urgent set of federationwide questions and hold up decision making on that level until its specific demands were met. The problem was twofold: each success of the leadership in Croatia tended to make it more intransigent and unwilling to negotiate with the other republics on questions like the Five-Year Plan, the development of transportation infrastructure, and the foreign currency regime. This in turn isolated the Croatian leadership from the other republic centers which were potential allies on some issues and forced it into an increasingly open alliance with nationalist forces operating outside the formal political system. Thus it appeared to threaten the one unnegotiable pillar of authority in postrevolutionary Yugoslavia—the League of Communists itself.[25] After several attempts to resolve the dispute at the federal level, each of which was blocked by the refusal of the Croatian leadership to accept any compromise, a split developed in that leadership itself which was deftly utilized by President Tito at a meeting of the party Presidium in December of 1971. The result was a major shake-up which forced several hundred local Croatian officials, including some of the leading figures, to resign. It appears now that this leadership had already lost its working majority on the Executive Committee of the Croatian League before the meeting in December.[26]

The political crisis posed by the Croatian developments has led to two new institutional departures in Yugoslavia. First, there has been revitalization of the league bodies, particularly of its Executive Committee on the federal level, accompanied by a systematic revival of the basic league organizations in plants and communities. Second, an even more explicitly federal structure has been developed in governmental institutions. Most of the 1970–71 demands of the Croatian leadership for greater autonomy of the republics and for the introduction of the system of republic delegations into the federal structure have been met. For that matter, many of the economic demands have been satisfied in that a greater proportion of the hard currency earned by a given industry is now retained by it rather than going into the central bank, and the central banks have been "republicanized." The party elite seems to be saying that it is willing to negotiate greater decentralization, always provided that the leadership of a given republic is firmly in the hands of the local League of Communists, which is in turn committed to Yugoslavia. This remains unnegotiable.

In the restructuring of internal league relations that followed the crackdown on the Croat leadership, a new theme emerged which has apparently become more important in the thinking of the league center. What is basically involved is a redefinition of the respective weight and importance to be given to the two modern strata on which the party rests its power: the workers and the technical

25. Russinow, Crisis in Croatia.
26. Ibid.

intelligentsia. While the technical intelligentsia does not appear to have been actively engaged in the nationalist movement in Croatia —most of the participants were students, members of the traditional intelligentsia, and lower-level party officials—neither did substantial numbers of the technical intelligentsia actively oppose this development. Such opposition as was generated to the alliance with nationalism in Croatia came from trade unions, enterprises with large numbers of industrial workers, Partisan veterans, and part of the Marxist intelligentsia.

This lesson has not been lost on Tito and his immediate entourage, and present policy therefore stresses social egalitarianism, greater influence of trade unions and workers, and an attempt to create political allies in the universities.

Evolution of the Political and Social System

The development of stable political institutions in postrevolutionary Yugoslavia can be measured by a number of indicators, formal and informal. After the break with the Soviet Union, the Federal Assembly gradually developed from a typical sounding board to a body that assumed ever greater initiative in proposing legislation in Yugoslavia. This is clear from table 23, which shows that in the period from 1953 until 1967 there was a substantial shift in the balance of initiative between the Federal Executive Council and the legislature. By the period of the reform, 1963–67, more measures were initiated in the legislature than in the cabinet. This development of the legislature was accompanied by a number of parallel developments, not all of which are considered positive by the theoreticians of the system. As table 23 shows, there has been a measurable increase of activity by individual deputies as well as by the legislature as a whole, and the number of interpolations to the cabinet members proposing measures increased drastically in the period 1963–67.[27] However, as the legislature has grown more important as an arena for decision making and bargaining within the system, it has become less representative of the population as a whole. The reason is obvious: as a real center of power it attracts

27. This fact was rather painfully brought home when one such interpolation was raised in 1969 about the opinion-makers project in Yugoslavia, which I was directing at the time (see the Appendix).

Table 23

Federal Legislative and Executive Activity in Yugoslavia, 1953–68

	Parliamentary Session		
	1953–57	*1958–62*	*1963–68*
Laws and decisions of the Federal Assembly	254	475	782
Decisions and Regulations of the Federal Executive Council	1373	1085	686
Interpolations by deputies in the Federal Assembly to the Federal Executive Council	58	243	475

SOURCE: *Dokumentacija Savezne Skupstine*, 2 vols. (Belgrade: Savezna Admistracija, 1969).

increasingly the real holders of power in the system. This is most clearly shown by table 24, which examines the occupational background of the deputies of the Federal Assembly from 1953 through 1969. Two trends are evident: a sharp reduction of the number of deputies whose professional base is the league and/or some other mass organization, and an increase of managerial personnel reflecting the greater autonomy of the economy. There has been a corresponding drop in the percentages of workers and peasants, to a point where in 1969 there were fewer workers and peasants in the Federal Assembly than in prewar Yugoslavia.

This trend became the focus of much debate after the political offensive of the League of Communists against nationalism, technocracy and "liberalism" was launched in 1971. The trade unions as an increasingly autonomous organization are pressing for more direct representation of the producers on the federal level, and new constitutional changes provide for direct representation of the trade unions and working collectives on all levels. As I will show, the representation of workers in the workers' councils and the trade union structure remains high,[28] which is the reason the councils are now used as a base for representation in the legislature. Nevertheless, these figures mean that the legislature developed increasing auton-

28. See the data in chapter 7.

Table 24

Occupational Background of Parliamentary
Deputies in Socialist Yugoslavia

Occupational Background	Election Year					
	1953	1958	1963	1965	1967	1969
Party and mass organization functionaries	73.0%	68.5%	30.8%	41.0%	34.1%	29.4%
Managerial personnel	16.6	18.1	41.5	32.8	41.8	44.9
Specialized or professional personnel	0	0	20.5	19.9	19.0	21.1
Workers and peasants	3.4	6.8	5.5	3.9	1.9	0.6
Others	7.0	6.6	1.6	2.2	3.1	3.9
	100.0%	100.0%	100.0%	100.0%	100.0%	100.0%
N:	(552)	(587)	(670)	(670)	(670)	(620)

SOURCES: D. Tozi and D. Petrovic, "Politicki odnosi i sastav skupstina drustveno-politickih zajednica," *Socijalizam* 11 (1969), p. 1594; *Statisticki bilten: Predstavnicka tela drustveno-politickih zajednica; izbori e sastav* (Belgrade: Savezni Zavod za Statistiku, 1964, 1965, 1967, 1969).

omy and that this was paralleled by the understandable desire of the electorate to have the most powerful possible legislators acting for them at the center. This explains why the campaigns to increase the percentages of the young, women, workers, and the like have failed.

As the development of the Federal Assembly brought into the legislative arena more of the strata that manage Yugoslav society, and as those groups in turn began to differentiate functionally, making the legislature the focal point of outside interest-aggregating centers, two other developments occurred. The first, a function of the general emphasis on higher education as the major legitimate path for social advancement in the system, can be seen in the dramatic changes in the educational background of the deputies from 1953 to 1969. Table 25 shows that the percentage of deputies with elementary school educations or less shrank from 46.1 percent in 1953 to 2.6 percent in 1969, while the number of persons holding university degrees or their equivalents rose from 23.6 percent to 82.3 percent.

It is important to note here that both the change in educational background and the change in occupational background reflect more than a change in personnel. The politically active Partisan veterans who held positions of importance in 1953 were under

Table 25

Educational Background of Parliamentary Deputies

	1953	1958	1963	1965	1967	1969
Elementary school or less	46.1%	38.0%	9.1%	7.3%	4.3%	2.6%
Secondary and vocational schools	30.3	31.8	24.6	22.1	20.6	15.1
Higher schools and university faculties	23.6	30.2	66.3	70.6	75.0	82.3

SOURCE: Adapted and prepared by Lenard Cohen from *Dokumentacija Savezne Skupstine*.

increasing pressure to upgrade their educational backgrounds as a condition for maintaining their status. We have, therefore, in the Yugoslav broader leadership a substantial number of persons who obtained their higher education after they began to play a political role. (This is the case even with the higher leadership group studied in the International Study of Opinion Makers in 1968–69; see the Appendix.)

A further indicator of the normalization and routinization of the system is the slow but continual change in the age structure of the federal legislators. This change, which parallels similar ones throughout the system, has gone through two phases: first, the gradual aging of the unusually young revolutionary elite that came to power in 1944, and, second, the spasmodic attempts by the party leadership to rejuvenate the now aging cadres. This second phase has had limited success at the very top, where the average age of the collective Federal Presidency is now 49.[29] However, returning to the deputies, table 26 shows that the percentage of deputies 50 and over

Table 26

Yugoslav Parliamentary Deputies by Age, 1953–69

	Parliamentary Session					
	1953	1958	1963	1965	1967	1969
Under 40	56.4%	45.7%	45.8%	40.4%	26.9%	24.1%
40–49	32.8	44.4	44.1	41.5	52.1	55.0
50 and over	10.8	9.9	10.2	18.5	20.0	20.9

SOURCE: *Dokumentacija Savezne Skupstine*.

29. *Radio Free Europe Research*, June 26, 1972.

almost doubled between 1953 and 1969. This trend is, I believe, linked to the changes in social composition, in that managerial leaders tend to be older than the political cadres.

In examining the shifts that have occurred in the Federal Assembly, there are at least two other points that need to be stressed. The first is that the changes affecting the legislators were much more rapid than those affecting the top federal civil service. Given the application of the system of rotation[30] to legislators, this means that the overwhelming majority of legislators were elected to their present posts *after* the Economic and Social Reform of 1964, while a slight majority of the higher federal administrators were recruited during the period of administrative socialism, that is, from 1945 to 1951. Changes in the federal administration are slower but they are speeding up in pace as a greater proportion of the top federal posts become subject to nomination from the republics. This represents a source of tension between the civil servants and the legislators since the period of recruitment and adult socialization of the federal civil servants coincided with the period when the federal center had more initiative and when the state itself was more centralized. This makes the information in table 19 even more interesting, and I interpret it as evidence of a continual expansion of the prerogatives of the federal legislature vis-à-vis the higher civil service.

The second point of considerable long-range importance is the trend away from one-candidate elections on both the republic and federal levels. In federal-level elections since 1969, although there has been considerable variation between the republics, as a whole there have been almost 50 percent more candidates than posts.

The Federal Assembly appears to have passed through its golden period, which can be loosely defined as 1963–70. Developments since 1971 have introduced new factors: on the one hand, because of a greater delegation of authority to republics, there is more emphasis on the republic legislatures as policy-making bodies; on the other hand, the development since 1970 of informal conflict-resolving bodies within the Federal Assembly reduces it to a creature of the republics. Legislation of a fundamentally noncontroversial character

30. A deputy may not be elected more than twice to the same body. He may, however, move back and forth between the federal and republic legislatures, or, though this is rare, between various chambers of the Federal Assembly.

still goes through the old institutionalized channels, being generated either in the committees of the legislature or in the commttees of the federal executive council (SIV), and then referred to the appropriate chamber which enacts it into law. However, as the federation's prerogatives diminished, so also did the number of noncontroversial issues dealt with by federal legislation. With typical Yugoslav disrespect for formal structures, a whole new set of bodies has been set up which to the amazement of both Yugoslav and foreign observers appear to function reasonably well.[31] These are the five federal committees dealing with the five major areas of federal competence other than the army. The committees are composed of one representative from each republic or province, chaired by the appropriate member of the SIV. The committees hammer out compromises among the republics themselves by referring the controversial legislation back and forth to the republic centers, and when they finally report out a piece of legislation it represents the consensus of the eight centers and the federal government. If no compromise is reached within the committee, the matter is kicked upstairs to another informal body, called the Coordinating Committee, which consists of the Yugoslav premier and the presidents of the eight republics and provinces, occasionally coopting other personnel, such as the head of the trade unions or a member of the party Executive Committee. In theory, if no resolution were found on this level, the matter would be referred to the federal Presidency which has the right to enact legislation. This has not happened to date, and the Coordinating Committee has apparently been able to function to the satisfaction of all concerned. According to one well-informed observer, in a period of less than one year, between September 1971 and March 1972, 124 controversial issues were settled; 92 of these issues, which included highly sensitive economic questions, were basically settled in the committees, only 32 being referred to the Coordinating Committee. This stands in stark contrast to the near paralysis of the federal center in the preceding two years. The effect, however, is that when a piece of legislation is proposed to the Federal Assembly after this long, delicate process of negotiations, there is

31. Dennison Russinow, *Yugoslavia 1969* (American Universities Field Staff Report, Southeast Europe Series, vol. 16, no. 8) has a lengthy and informed discussion of this development.

enormous pressure on the individual deputies not to rock the boat, since so much haggling has already taken place.

An additional effect of this is that the Federal Assembly acts more and more as a rubber stamp, legalizing agreements already reached among the republics. It would be naïve to attribute the break in the logjam of decisions solely to this organizational innovation. It is obviously true, however, that the constitutional and political crises created by the Croat leadership in 1970 and 1971 served as a serious object lesson to all republic leaderships about the necessity of working out more effective mechanisms for reaching consensus, and therefore the development of these bodies merely represents the institutionalization of the new reality of legislative power in Yugoslavia. It also puts pressure on local republic leadership not to move out of this framework, since they are consulted at every step of the way and share political responsibility for legislation with the SIV.

The most recent constitutional changes have somewhat altered the election process by developing an intermediary body between the voters and the elected bodies higher up. This institution, called the County Conference, is elected by the voters directly and by the working collectives, trade unions, and other mass organizations. The conference delegates in turn elect the higher bodies. In theory the conference facilitates the recall of deputies to the republican and federal levels and places considerable pressure on the deputy to keep contact with his base. The long-range consequences of the system are as yet unknown, since these changes were only introduced in 1973–74.

ECONOMIC AND SOCIAL DEVELOPMENT

The evolution of the political system of Yugoslavia, while representing a major effort to deal with the problem of legitimizing a revolutionary regime in a multinational state, tells only part of the story. For understandable reasons, political sociologists, particularly in Anglo-Saxon countries, tend to place more emphasis on the processes than on the outcomes of a political system. Thus, the general working definitions of democratization usually stress plurality of parties as aggregators of interest and well-regulated procedures for defending the rights of dissidents. A number of studies of other systems indicate that this definition is parochial. Thus, Samuel Barnes, in his *Party Democracy*,[32] points out that Socialist Party activists in Italy define democracy in terms of substantive outcomes rather than process features. This issue is further complicated by the fact that revolutionary regimes and new governments in developing countries often come to power in situations where resources are scarce and tasks enormous. Therefore, the legitimation of a revolutionary government seems to require substantive progress in accomplishing the tasks of industrialization, development, and political modernization. Whether or not these tasks are met does not by itself tell us whether a regime will become legitimate, but it seems reasonably clear that if the tasks are not accomplished the tendency for a regime to turn to coercive means for obtaining compliance will increase.

The Yugoslav revolutionary leadership, upon coming to power, not only faced the task of rebuilding and developing the country—and for the communist elites economic development is a sine qua non of success—but this task was further complicated by the fragmentation of the polity they had taken over and the powerful particularist and nationalist traditions present. Thus development could not be pursued simply by considering Yugoslavia as a whole and maximizing investment where the return would be the highest. Of necessity, development involved the double task of developing the country while attempting to close the gaps between the richer and poorer regions. Following the split with the Soviet bloc, an additional consideration affected developmental policy. Remembering their experience with the German invasion, the Yugoslav leadership stressed development in regions far from the frontiers, in the mountainous and inaccessible regions, that is, in those areas likely to form the backbone of resistance in the case of another invasion. This coincided with and reinforced the need to develop the backward areas. In addition to these major considerations, a simple appreciation of services rendered during the war required that the least developed areas should receive special consideration, all other things being equal.

The impetus toward legitimation of the regime provided by the revolutionary élan of the postwar years, and the patriotic support

32. Samuel Barnes, *Party Democracy* (New Haven: Yale University Press, 1967).

during the early period of the split with the Eastern bloc, could not be maintained after the new generations began to enter the political scene. In point of fact, considerable resentment exists on the part of the new, younger technical cadres against the Partisan generation. The legitimation of the Yugoslav revolutionary regime, therefore, rests squarely on its ability to solve societal tasks in a manner convincing to sufficiently broad sectors of the population so that support for the regime does not merely coincide with the politically active population organized in the League of Communists. The claims of the Yugoslav regime are that it has healed the basic national cleavages that bedeviled prewar Yugoslavia and has provided a pace of economic and social development that is exceptional for polities of its type. It also claims to have developed social and political institutions that are more participatory than those of either Western or Eastern European states—self-managing bodies in the economy and the communes—and contends that this solution represents a novel way of handling the general problem of the development of technocracy and the bureaucratization of modern industrial states.

The actual figures on development are critical to the arguments of both supporters and critics of the Yugoslav system. Table 27 shows

Table 27

Annual Growth Rate of Social Product per Capita
for Various Countries, 1952–66

	1952–66	1952–60	1961–66
Japan	7.91%	7.77%	8.16%
Yugoslavia	7.75	8.78	6.19
Bulgaria	7.66	8.14	6.96
Rumania	7.33	7.55	7.71
Greece	6.36	5.97	6.96
E. Germany	5.64	7.32	3.01
Poland	5.35	5.80	4.56
Hungary	5.06	5.63	4.23
W. Germany	5.06	6.05	3.54
Austria	5.02	5.97	3.54

SOURCE: Z. Popov, "Zemlje najbrzim privrednim razvojom," *Ekonomska Analiza* 1–2 (1967): 120.

Table 28

Growth of Social Product in Yugoslavia,
by Republic, 1952–68

	1968 level (1952 = 100)	Annual growth rate, 1952–68
Yugoslavia	328	7.70%
Bosnia-Herzegovina	273	6.48
Montenegro	340	7.95
Croatia	334	7.83
Macedonia	356	8.26
Slovenia	335	7.83
Serbia	331	7.77
Vojvodina	363	8.39
Kosovo	296	7.02

SOURCE: Stipe Suvar, "Da li je hrvatska eksploatirana," *Naše Teme* 12 (December 1969): 2055.

the social product per capita[33] from 1952 until 1966 for a number of rapidly developing states. These figures show that Yugoslavia, for the period 1952–66, was second only to Japan in its rate of growth, and that, while the growth rate did slow somewhat in the period 1961–66, it remained convincingly higher than that of most East European countries and, for that matter, higher than that of West Germany and Austria. This in itself represents a success for the Yugoslav development policy, particularly when one considers the fact that Yugoslavia began with a countryside and industrial capacity deeply damaged by the civil war. However, an important consideration in a multinational polity like Yugoslavia is not merely the rate of development but its breakdown by republics. Table 28 shows the growth of the social product by republic for the period 1952–68, with 1952 taken as 100. Clearly there has been an attempt to spread growth across the republics and to maintain a pace of growth in the less-developed republics similar to that of the already industrialized Slovenia and Croatia. Unfortunately, while the Yugoslav growth rate is adequate, and even superior to that of most other developing countries, the tasks of development are made more difficult by the inexorable demographic pressure which has acted as an anchor

33. Yugoslavs give their figures in "social product per capita," which differs from GNP in that it represents the GNP *less* the value of amortization.

dragging on the underdeveloped. Some relevant figures regarding the population problem, which I have referred to previously, are given in table 29. Two things can be seen: (1) there is a major difference between the developed and the underdeveloped regions in rates of population growth; the Vojvodina rate is more than five times that of Kosovo; and (2) the rate of growth has declined, for all regions, from the postwar highs of 1950–54. Nevertheless, the overall pattern is that the least developed regions have the highest percentage of economically inactive persons, and the development policy is skewed by this factor. The best way to show this is to look at the effect of this growth on per capita income by republic, which is shown in table 30. This table shows that, despite the rapid development in all regions and the fact that Kosovo, which is at the bottom of all of these scales, increased its social product enormously (from 100 in 1952 to 296 in 1968), Kosovo's relative share of national income per capita has in fact fallen. That is, income has increased even in Kosovo, but the gap between the most developed and the least developed republics is widening. Incidentally, table 28 also shows that the more developed republics of Slovenia and Croatia have not been adversely affected by the policy of stressing the development of underdeveloped areas; the income gap between both republics and their less fortunate partners has increased.

There are many other indicators that can be used. A special

Table 29

Population Growth in Yugoslavia, by Republic

	New births per 1,000		Pop. increase per 1,000
	1950–54	1968	1968
Yugoslavia	28.8	18.9	10.3
Bosnia-Herzegovina	38.2	23.1	16.5
Montenegro	32.7	20.7	14.3
Croatia	23.2	15.2	5.1
Macedonia	38.4	25.6	17.6
Slovenia	22.4	17.4	6.7
Serbia	26.1	14.9	6.6
Vojvodina	23.3	13.8	4.6
Kosovo	43.5	37.4	28.5

SOURCE: *Statisticki godisnjak Jugoslavije, 1970* (Savezni Zavod za Statistiku, 1970), pp. 48–50.

Table 30

Relative Per Capita Income, by Republic, 1952–68
(index: Yugoslav-wide per capita income = 100)

	1952	1964	1968
Bosnia-Herzegovina	87	65	62
Montenegro	71	65	64
Croatia	114	118	125
Macedonia	66	77	69
Slovenia	164	176	183
Serbia	96	98	100
Vojvodina	100	122	120
Kosovo	47	36	33

SOURCE: Special edition of *Ekonomist* (Zagreb, 1969), English version, p. 54.

problem in Yugoslavia is posed by the openness of the Yugoslav frontier. The Yugoslav population appears to compare the performance of Yugoslavia not with underdeveloped countries but with the neighboring West European countries. This creates a set of expectations probably impossible for any regime to meet. To be sure, the rate of development of Yugoslavia—7.9 average annual rate of growth for 1952–66—compared with its two Western neighbors, Italy and Austria—5.36 and 5.11 respectively—is quite impressive. However, since the base from which the latter two countries began was so different, the gross figures obviously still favor Italy and Austria. Thus, Yugoslav professionals and workers comparing their standard of living with that of Italy or Austria continue to express resentment. While the rate of development of Yugoslavia remains high, this is generally not being felt in the form of immediate rises in the individual standard of living. Therefore, the Yugoslav regime is working against time, hoping the rate of development will begin to assert itself and satisfy demands, which are now expanding more rapidly than the economy. The irony, of course, is that comparisons with East European neighbors, which are favorable to Yugoslavia, tend to be rejected as irrelevant. The Yugoslavs appear to accept their differences from the East European states as normal; the East European societies are not a general reference point.

Other indicators of social advancement in Yugoslavia are similar to the economic ones and reflect the effects of a rapid rate of

Table 31

Illiteracy Rates in Yugoslavia, by Republic, 1970

	Illiterates over 10 years of age, as % of population		
	Male	Female	All
Yugoslavia	7.7%	22.5%	15.2%
Bosnia-Herzegovina	10.1	34.6	22.7
Montenegro	7.4	26.3	17.2
Croatia	4.5	13.0	8.9
Macedonia	11.0	25.1	18.0
Slovenia	2.5	2.5	2.5
Serbia	7.5	27.6	17.7
Vojvodina	5.3	13.2	9.4
Kosovo	21.3	43.5	32.2

SOURCE: Adapted from *Statisticki godisnjak Jugoslavije, 1972*, pp. 84–88.

development on a series of regions that started at very different levels. A graphic illustration of the gap between the republics is found in the literacy figures for 1970. The figures in table 31 for illiterates over the age of ten show a wide gap between the most developed and least developed republics, a gap not duplicated in any other European country. The illiteracy rate of 2.5 for Slovenia makes it similar to advanced Western countries, while Kosovo, with a rate of 32.2, is more similar to Asia Minor. The figures also show an interesting feature of Yugoslav development: the campaign against illiteracy must now be directed at what remains of the traditional sector of society in the countryside and, above all, at the women traditionally subjugated in Balkan peasant societies. Between the illiteracy rates for males and females there is an enormous gap: in Yugoslavia as a whole, illiterates outnumber males 3:1, and even this understates the problem since illiteracy is concentrated in precisely those areas where women are least likely to be participating in the economy and least likely therefore to be under economic and social pressure to change existing conditions. There the Yugoslav government faces a continual dilemma, for modernizing policies are perceived by national and religious groups as an attack on traditional ways. Attempts to introduce compulsory education for women in the predominantly Moslem regions of Kosovo and Bosnia are resisted widely, and enforcement would require far greater coercion by the central authorities than is customary in Yugoslav social relations today. This is one of the areas where the liberalization of the system has created a long-range problem since it means that the pace of modernization of social relations may be increasingly affected by the local political cultures.

The last point to be made quantitatively about the rate of development in Yugoslavia and its effects on interrepublic relations concerns the wide disparities now existing in the employment situation. Table 32, which shows the employment structure by republic, vividly illustrates the now familiar Yugoslav development dilemma. There are many more people employed in industry in Slovenia than in Kosovo and many more wage earners in Slovenia. These figures rather than major differentials in pay lie at the root of the wide disparities in per capita incomes. When one considers the demographic variations, it appears that the salary structure is a good bit more egalitarian than one would expect, even taking the regional factor into account.

Underlying the whole problem of development are a series of policy considerations for the Yugoslav Communists. The country is too poor to be able to provide sufficiently massive injections of funds and resources to industrialize the underdeveloped regions at a more rapid rate. It has to consider the problems of overall development,

Table 32

Employment Structure by Republic,* 1968

	Wage Earners as % of Republic Population	% of Wage Earners Employed in Industry
Slovenia	30%	48%
Croatia	22	36
Vojvodina	21	32
Serbia	19	37
Macedonia	15.8	32
Montenegro	15	33
Bosnia	14	46
Kosovo	8	38

SOURCE: *Statisticki godisnjak, Yugoslavije, 1972*, pp. 106–11.

* This covers only the employed population, that is, those earning wages. Self-employed peasants are excluded from these calculations.

and a clear difference of opinions is possible. The technocratic groups in the more advanced republics by and large believe that the development of the most developed regions, which is of course economically most efficient since regions begin with an existing infrastructure and a more skilled work force, presents the optimal policy of development and that interrepublic migrations will gradually shift the population centers to the developed regions. Here it is useful to remember that while unemployment in Yugoslavia is generally high, it ranges from only 2 percent in Slovenia to over 20 percent in Macedonia and Kosovo.[34] Unfortunately this view ignores the reality of multinationality, and the very real and understandable desire for modernization in each of the republics that is a home for a nationality.

There is an even more pressing ideological consideration. The Yugoslav Communists, after all, regard themselves as a party based on the modernized sectors of the economy and society, that is, on the industrial working class, the general and technical intelligentsia, and the modern administrative services. Therefore, they find it essential to develop a working class in each of the national republics and provinces. The alternative would be to assume that certain regions would increasingly withdraw from the Yugoslav political system and would never be able to play an appropriate political role in the federal system as a whole. This situation is somewhat eased by the fact that two of the major underdeveloped regions—Bosnia and Kosovo—are rich in minerals and have a high potential for development.

The self-interest of the more advanced republics is mobilizable for the development policy of the central government on two levels: ideological, where the criteria mentioned above play a role in the League of Communists in all of the republics, and economic, since the existence of a unified Yugoslav market benefits the more developed regions—it not only provides them with a protected market for their goods but until recently it has also aided them by maintaining federal price controls for raw materials and agricultural products which discriminated in favor of the more developed regions.

The recent turns in policy since 1971, stressing the role of the trade unions and the workers' councils, will in all probability increase the

34. Stipe Suvar, *Nacije i medjunacijonalni odnosi* (Zagreb: Nase Teme, 1970).

tendency to invest in the underdeveloped regions, for two reasons. The proportion of workers living in or coming from the underdeveloped regions has increased rapidly so that it is now over 40 percent of the entire work force.[35] Any restructuring of institutions that gives the blue-collar workers more power within the system will probably lead to a balance favoring the underdeveloped, who have tended to develop labor-intensive industries.

The Yugoslav socialist regime has tackled the problem of multinationality with considerable success on the level of formal institutions and has probably given more representation and more leeway for cultural autonomy to its component parts than any other system in Europe except that of Switzerland. It has resolutely moved away from any "melting pot" conception of Yugoslavia and has legitimized national and republic centers for power-aggregating purposes to a point beyond which it probably cannot go. This has defused what had been the major source of tension in Yugoslavia, the national question, although nationalist sentiments will probably exist on the periphery of political life for some time to come.

The nationalist sentiments that still exist cannot focus on making reformist demands on the system, demands likely to be perceived as reasonable by the representatives of the other nationalities. After all, representation in the federal institutions is already reasonably fair, all languages are treated as legally equal, and no evident discrimination exists in the development policy against any particular national republic. To argue against the present policy is not to argue against discrimination but rather to insist on the right of the more developed republics not to aid the less fortunate ones, that is, to argue for a dissolution of the Yugoslav federation itself. This means that such nationalism as will be found will tend either to act as a surrogate for anticommunism, which was, in my opinion, what occurred in 1969–71 in Croatia, or to become the property of traditionalist intelligentsia who would use it as a vehicle to protest their loss of relative power and importance.

The institutionalization of the parliamentary system has reached a point where new changes can be anticipated. The federal and particularly the republican legislatures have developed far beyond

35. Burks, "National Problem."

serving as a sounding board for the party, speaking as an undifferentiated whole. The intrarepublic committees play a major role in debating and formulating federal policy within relatively flexible guidelines. One problem here, however, is that the social composition of the legislatures is increasingly ideologically distasteful to the party leadership. This in my opinion will lead to further legal and institutional changes designed to increase drastically the proportion of workers in the legislature. However, these workers would not be elected as atomized representatives of the growing Yugoslav industrial working class. Rather I believe they will represent existing organs that wield considerable economic, social, and political power—the workers' councils.[36] The consequences of such a development, while congruent with the official ideology of the system and legitimate in terms of the values expressed by broad strata of the population, will take Yugoslavia into an uncharted area, since the polity will then rest on institutional structures whose base is unlike those of any other industrial society. The future development of Yugoslav institutions lies in this delicate balance between the representation of legitimate national and local interests, and the representation of the industrial working class and the technicians in the modern sector of the economy.

36. One must keep in mind the fact that at least two-thirds of the members of workers' councils must, by law, be workers. The remaining third can be white-collar and managerial personnel.

7

The New Political Culture

Yugoslav self-management has been studied by both Yugoslav and foreign scholars for over two decades. The study of Yugoslav self-management, initially begun because of the uniqueness of this institution which the Yugoslavs themselves realized was moving them into a hitherto uncharted area, was of particular interest to three groups of Western social scientists. First were those very few Western social scientists who come from a socialist tradition. They sought in the system of self-management a solution for the problems of alienation from the work process and disenchantment with the authority structure in nationalized industry in the West under social democratic governments, problems they were all too aware were also present in Eastern Europe and particularly in the Soviet Union. Simply stated, they looked for *social relations* in the economy appropriate to a nonreformist working model of socialism.[1]

The second group studied self-management from a narrower perspective, that of industrial relations and managerial techniques. This group approached the problem of self-management by attempting to isolate it from its general political and ideological framework, hoping to discover in self-management insights applicable to other industrial systems. They were particularly attracted to the notion of self-management as a form of codetermination, or workers' participation which would be transferable to industries remaining under private ownership or ownership that was diffused or mixed. Of special interest to this group is the question of participation as a method of avoiding conflicts and providing "job enrichment." They are also interested in productivity and the ticklish and complex

1. A good example of this approach can be found in the journal *Autogestion* and in two books by Albert Meiser: *Socialisme et autogestion: L'experience yougoslave* (Paris: Seuil, 1964), and *Ou va l'autogestion yougoslave?* (Paris: Anthropos, 1970).

problem of the role of technical cadres and of management itself within the framework of self-managed industry.[2]

The third group studied self-management in a more general framework, particularly the economists from the United States and Great Britain who studied self-management as one aspect of a socialist market economy. For them self-management is primarily *plant or enterprise autonomy* from the centralized plan, and Yugoslavia is most interesting as a unique experiment within a socialist market economy. The political mobilizing aspect of self-management in industry or democratization of industrial authority patterns is secondary to this group. Self-management is viewed as a necessary instrument for breaking down the previous centralized planning system, which had proven all too inefficient, and for establishing an economy based on the market and therefore free from the vagaries of political pressure or individual whims.[3]

The same three emphases can be found in the work of Yugoslav social scientists who have devoted themselves to the study of self-management. The bulk of the relevant literature on self-management is in the Yugoslav languages, primarily Serbo-Croatian or Slovenian, and very little is therefore accessible to the scholars who do not command these languages. The few works that are available in English and French tend to be dated or based on partial studies, with the possible exceptions of Branko Horvat's *An Essay on Yugoslav Society*,[4] Svetozar Stojanovic's *Between Ideals and Reality*, and the collective papers of the conference on self-management in Amsterdam organized by M. J. Broekmeyer.[5] Political scientists such as Robert Dahl have also addressed themselves to some of the social and political implications of self-management,[6] but it is clear from

2. This is, I believe, characteristic of the work of Jiri Kolaja, of Adolf Strumthal's *Workers' Councils* (Cambridge: Harvard University Press, 1964), and of Ichak Adizes, *Industrial Democracy Yugoslav Style* (New York: Free Press, 1971).

3. The best example of this approach is Benjamin Ward's essay "Political Power and Economic Change in Yugoslavia," *American Economic Review* 58, no. 2 (May 1968). See also Oscar Lange, *Papers in Economy and Sociology* (London: Pergamon, 1970), esp. pp. 95–99.

4. This is a translation of a book originally published in Serbo-Croatian.

5. *Yugoslav Workers' Self-Management*, ed. M. J. Broekmeyer (Dordrecht, Netherlands: D. Reidel, 1970).

6. See Robert Dahl, *After the Revolution* (New Haven: Yale University Press, 1972).

Dahl's writing that his acquaintance with the system is very limited and comes primarily from secondary sources.

I begin with the assumption that self-management in Yugoslavia cannot be isolated from those other aspects of the Yugoslav socialist system which make it unique. Five main characteristics of Yugoslav socialism can be roughly summarized as follows:

1. In international affairs, independence and nonalignment
2. In economics, a socialist market economy with indicative planning
3. Politically, a multinational state with no dominant nationality; decentralization and a unique party system
4. Historically, a case of a successful war of national liberation, that is, of guerrilla communism legitimized over three decades of power
5. Socially, a new political culture based on self-management in the form of workers' councils, self-managing bodies in institutions and in the communes

These characteristics exist within a society—and this factor has been of growing importance—marked by a high rate of social and political modernization which has been slowing down as Yugoslavia emerges from the mobilization phase dictated by the backwardness of the destroyed traditional society.

It is clear when one considers Yugoslavia that self-management can be taken as only one part of what is an integrated whole, or rather an integrating whole, since the system is still in the process of evolution. Self-management itself can be broken down into three components: workers' councils or self-management in industry proper; self-managing bodies in social institutions such as schools, quasi-governmental bodies, and the like; and finally self-management on the level of the commune. All three elements should be considered jointly as it is all but impossible to treat workers' councils as an isolated phenomenon in Yugoslavia. The workers' councils are perhaps the most interesting aspect of the Yugoslav experiment and the one that may appear easiest to transfer to other situations; but, as the experience of Algeria, India, and other countries has shown,[7] attempts to establish workers' councils in isolation without an

7. See articles on Algeria in *Autogestion*, and Zivan Tanic's *Workers' Councils in India* (Belgrade: Institut Drustvenih Nauka, 1965).

accompanying change in the fabric of society itself are likely to lead to failure and a cumulative inefficiency in the economy and society.

A HISTORICAL NOTE

One of the more puzzling facts about the establishment of self-management in Yugoslavia is that it appears to have had no preexisting roots in the historical experience of Yugoslavia or of the Communist Party that led the revolution and directed postwar developments. The Communist Party of Yugoslavia became, in the process of the war and revolution, a mass party. However, the predominantly peasant masses who entered the party from 1941 to 1945 joined a party that remained one of the most orthodox communist parties even after the dissolution of the Communist International—a party that consciously, perhaps all too consciously, held the Russian model as the only desirable one; and, although the party had come to power independently, it sought to copy political, economic, and military structures from the existing Russian model wholesale. The political literature most of the party cadre were brought up on would have to be examined in great detail to discover any references to self-management or workers' councils. One need only remember that perhaps the most important text in party courses even in the war years was Stalin's *History of the Communist Party (Bolshevik) U.S.S.R.* It was the first book to be typeset in the printing shops of the first Partisan Republic in Uzice in the fall of 1941, and the unused plates were painstakingly transported in the retreat that winter.

In the socialist tradition itself the theme of participation and workers' control weaves through much of the classic literature—from Fourier through Marx, Lenin, the guild socialists and the various leftist opposition groups in the social democratic and communist parties. Lenin himself in *The State and the Revolution* presented a model based on directly elected councils, and the very slogan "All Power to the Soviets" represented, before their atrophy, an attempt to institute forms of direct democracy as a substitute for traditional state power. The most fully developed theories of workers' control are found in the writings of the Workers' Opposition in the early 1920s in Russia,[8]

8. See Robert Daniel, *The Conscience of the Revolution* (New York: Simon & Schuster, 1960), particularly chs. 4, 5, and 6, for a summary of the views of the Workers' Opposition.

but it would be difficult to trace the influence of the destroyed and vilified Workers' Opposition or its program on the leaders of the Communist Party of Yugoslavia in the early 1950s.[9] Furthermore, the grim tasks of the period following World War II, particularly in an underdeveloped society confronted by the hostility of the Soviet bloc, hardly made it the best time to introduce social experiments that had no previous record of success. Therefore, the evolution of self-management should be considered as the specific form that Yugoslav socialism took in counterposition to the familiar Stalinist model of development.

This lack of historical roots did not apply to one form of self-management, communal self-management. It had been developed during the revolution itself, at least in a nascent form in the National Committees of Liberation (NOO) which held wide-ranging authority in the Partisan-held areas and even in the enemy-occupied areas. These communal councils drew on a very active tradition of communal self-government, especially highly developed in those parts of Yugoslavia that had been exposed to Turkish influence. Therefore the communal councils were not only a convenient micro-organization for the Partisan army to use and develop in extending its authority but were also rooted in genuine local loyalties, since the highly fragmented traditionalist societies of the mountain areas had a centuries-old tradition of communal assemblies which had been harnessed by both the Turks and the Venetians in their respective areas of dominance. For that matter, even the highly centralized and bureaucratic Austrian regime utilized local communal bodies at least in the area of the military frontier. The NOO's were a way of bridging the gap between the younger, more politicized combatants and the broader population base which increasingly supported the resistance movement. It thus created links through participation with what would otherwise have been passive segments of the population. Not incidentally, it also involved those segments in the development of the new authority by in effect forcing them to take sides even if they did not participate in combat.

9. The theme of participation was also pursued by Antonio Gramsci, most specifically in his *Soviets in Italy* (London: Institute for Workers' Control, 1973), but his views were all but unknown to the Yugoslav theorists up to the late 1950s.

In view of the discontinuity with earlier practices and with immediately preceding organizational tradition that the introduction of self-management represented, it is no wonder that it took over a decade to develop, and that it created a series of stresses and contradictions still present in the society. For the classic advocates of workers' control, workers' councils were not a parallel form but the only form of organizational power that should exist in a socialist society. In Yugoslavia the workers' councils were initially introduced into an economy still highly centralized, with fully developed state administrative organs and a monolithic party structure, all of which had a great deal more real power than the councils themselves. This was the case even in those matters that would have been assumed to be under the jurisdiction of the councils.

It was not until the introduction of a market economy that the councils began to assert at least minimal *enterprise autonomy*, and it was not until the councils began to dispose autonomously of the major part of their income that real economic power began to shift. This shift has been a major source of tension, since it naturally implies decentralization in economic decision making, which is hardly consistent with a powerful centralized state apparatus. Consequently, there have been continuing pressures to alter the political and party structures in such a way that they would reflect the new social relations and modes of political behavior developing through self-management.[10] These pressures of course do not always produce the desired results, if for no other reason than that they are not consciously directed.

Historically, the introduction of workers' self-management within a market economy must therefore be viewed as a means of dismantling the old state apparatus and of shifting the bulk of economic decision making into nonstate bodies. This is why much of the debate about the socialist market economy is actually a debate about workers' self-management in Yugoslavia today. The criticism directed at the enterprise egoism[11] that has developed in certain

10. That is, the norms of self-management are participatory and the decision making stresses consultation and consensus, while the state and league are organized hierarchically with directives flowing from the top down. The models of behavior in the two domains—self-management, and the state and league structures—are in direct contradiction.

11. Enterprise egoism refers to the tendency of persons in self-managed industry to

branches misses the point. In a self-managed society, the workers inside their self-managing institutions would have to be *convinced* through discussion to make the sacrifices required for the community as a whole. Here of course the role of the League of Communists in developing the needed socialist consciousness would be central. Well-meaning critics often find themselves taking a posture that implicitly assumes that societal priorities are better determined by experts, governmental bodies, or for that matter "disinterested" intellectuals than by voluntary participation of the workers themselves. To put it more simply, they do not trust the workers to work for the interests of the wider community. Implicit in this mistrust is the acceptance of the continual existence of dual power and therefore of a limitation on self-management.

The major economic theorists in Yugoslavia have been preoccupied with the problem of guiding the self-managed economy in a direction that would require little or no outside intervention for regulatory purposes. That is, they have sought to develop via the market and the alliances of branches of industries mechanisms that would be self-regulating. At the same time, they have been concerned with providing a material basis for participation in the self-managing bodies, conceiving as they do of the worker and man in general as primarily, if not exclusively, an economically rational being. Therefore, the tendency has been to stress the direct effects of the decisions made by workers' councils on the incomes of the members of the working collectives. This tendency has sharply increased since 1971 in an attempt to increase the degree of control exercised by workers in the elected bodies over the managers. The councils are told, in effect, that wrong decisions by the managers in the field of investment and market choice will directly affect the incomes of all workers in the collective. This is not an abstract consideration: in the fall of 1972 over half a million workers were receiving minimal incomes, that is, 80 percent of their nominal incomes, because their enterprises were losing money. As a result, pressure to remove inefficient managers has obviously increased and a growing demand for an almost day-to-day accountability by the

---

subordinate social and societal goals to the needs of their specific enterprise. Generally it takes the form of socially irresponsible decisions which would maximize the enterprise income.

managers is becoming institutionalized as a norm in the more successful collectives.

The tendency to increase the prerogatives of the elected self-managing bodies has taken surprising forms in recent years. For example, there has been considerable pressure on the large collectives which have an expanding need for technically trained experts to provide scholarships for university students in the relevant disciplines. The trend since 1968, however, has been for the collectives to prefer to give fellowships to workers of their own who choose to become engineers rather than subsidizing middle-class students in the major cities. This has gone to such an extent that the large and successful mining collective of Bor has not only insisted on financing its own workers in the attempt to develop trained cadres but has successfully fought for and obtained the development of a Metallurgical and Mining Faculty right in the mining area. Such developments do tend to increase the tensions between the university-based intelligentsia and the working collectives, which regard university training instrumentally and are unwilling to let the university faculties decide who should receive their fellowship funds.

The Dimensions of Self-Management Today

Before discussing the general relevance of Yugoslav self-management, it is useful to examine the current extent of popular participation. There are three areas of self-management: enterprises (including cooperatives), communal councils and bodies, and social services and institutions. In the economic sphere, where self-management is most widely developed, great numbers of persons are involved on various levels. Four specific groups of participants in self-managing bodies can be distinguished in the economy. (1) The first group consists of workers' councils elected in enterprises large enough to have councils and managing boards; there were 145,488 members of councils in this category in 1972. (2) The second group includes managing boards of enterprises too small to have a council and a board; there were 10,016 members of such boards in 1972. (3) The third and largest group consists of members of self-managing bodies in *parts* of enterprises. This group can be expected to grow for a number of reasons, one of which is the growth of large complex enterprises in Yugoslavia. In 1972 there were a total of 308,328 persons participating in self-managing bodies on this level. (4) The fourth group, numbering 35,469 persons, consists of self-managing bodies in agricultural coops. The grand total for the economy in 1972 was therefore close to half a million persons participating in various self-managing bodies.

In the field of communal self-government, the communal assemblies (there are 500 communes in Yugoslavia) included 40,791 persons in 1972, roughly half of whom were elected at large, the other half being elected by the working communities. In addition, there were local community bodies on a lower level with a membership of 92,275 persons. The total was thus 133,516 persons.

The third area, defined for the purposes of statistics as "social self-government in institutions of social services," includes primary and secondary schools; higher schools and universities; scientific institutions; cultural, educational, art, and entertainment institutions; health institutions, and social welfare institutions. The self-managing councils here included 210,384 persons in 1972, of whom roughly half came from the primary and secondary schools.[12]

The point of all these figures is to show the enormous numbers of people involved in one way or another in the institutions of self-management and thus participating with various degrees of intensity and effectiveness in managing some aspect of their social existence.[13] It is important to note that, while the largest number are in the enterprises, vast numbers are found in the other two fields. This wide involvement of nonprofessionals in managing major institutions in their society, albeit pro forma in some cases, obviously affects the entire political culture over time. Self-management thus becomes not an instrument of the society but its very fabric. This is not to say that abuses do not exist, that participation is not sometimes merely nominal, or that the general political climate of the society at a given moment does not also affect the workings of these bodies. All I am asserting is that the norm of participation is now firmly rooted, and the system of rotation used in electing representatives to self-managing bodies means that a major part of the working population participates at one point or another in running its own institutions.

12. *Statisticki godisnjak Jugoslavije, 1970* (Belgrade: Savezni Zavod za Statistiku, 1970), pp. 66–69. The figures are somewhat dated (1969–70) but adequate.

13. In all, 838,201 persons participate in some type of self-management, out of an employed population of approximately 4 million!

This confirms my earlier point that self-management is not a partially transferable system.

Accompanying self-management itself has been a process of decentralization from the federal to the republic and provincial governments down to the communes. This process began relatively early in Yugoslavia and can be seen in the decrease in personnel in the federal administration from 47,300 persons in 1948 to 10,326 persons by 1956; the trend continues to this day.[14] There are two underlying theoretical approaches to this process of decentralization. The first emphasizes the sovereignty of the republics and regards decentralization as primarily a reflection of the multinational character of Yugoslavia. The second stresses structural decentralization and thus favors decentralization to the level of the self-managing bodies in the communes and the enterprises. While the two processes are simultaneous, they are in my opinion ultimately contradictory, and it is the second process that seems to flow most naturally from the basic needs of a self-managed society. It can, however, be argued that the second stage of decentralization necessarily required an emphasis on the republics in order to dismantle the central federal structure. I think the future will show a greater emphasis on the second process, accompanied in all likelihood by attempts to solidify statewide institutions such as the League of Communists, the unions, and the unified market.

The contradiction between the two processes is clear from the republics' autarchic tendencies and their attempts to centralize. However, I believe that on balance the league's needs for integrating institutions that cut horizontally across the republic levels are better served by developing a common political culture based on workers' councils cutting across the republic and regional levels, and that the increasingly modern nature of the Yugoslav working class will tip the probabilities in the direction of the workers' councils.

The decentralizing processes in Yugoslavia have basically gone through four stages. The first stage, coinciding with the immediately postwar constitution, nominally placed major emphasis on the republics in what was de facto a highly centralized system. From 1952 to 1963 decentralization occurred primarily through the

14. Dusan Bilandjic, *Borba za samoupravni socijalizam u Jugoslaviji, 1945–1969* (Zagreb: RAD, 1969), p. 73.

delegation of increasing responsibility and authority to the enterprises and the communes. From 1963 to 1971, the tendency was to increase the prerogatives of the republics as centers of power aggregation and sovereignty; this was formalized by the constitutional amendments of 1971. In part it was a reflection of the growing conception of Yugoslavia as a commonwealth of nations and in part a concession to the development of national self-assertion in the component republics.[15] Two negative consequences of this process, however, probably mark its end. The first was the well-known escalation of nationalist demands from 1969 to 1971, but the second and less noted one was the tendency of the leaders of certain republics to treat their economies as autarchic economic components of what should have been a unified Yugoslav market. Therefore, the central leadership today is stressing structural decentralization and economic reintegration, giving more power to the communes and the local enterprises, while at the same time using the instrument of the "social agreement," [16] where branches of industry, for example the entire metal working industry in a given republic (Serbia in 1972), set up common indicative directives regarding the permissible income gap and the acceptable range of salaries. This process is of a piece with the general policy of avoiding direct state intervention in matters perceived as the business of the working collectives.

A major debate has developed over the alleged trend toward greater income disparities since the economic reform of 1966. However, the more recent studies by Berislav Sefer and Miladin Korac[17] indicate that on the contrary the trend since 1966 has clearly been toward a lowering of the differences in salaries between various levels of skills and training, and, further, that the main reason for the differences in wages between the various republics is the different sizes of families supported by the wage earners. Sefer's figures, for example, show that the general income range in given branches of industry is on the order of 1:2.6, the first figure

15. The emphasis on republics is rooted in the specific historical needs of a multinational Yugoslavia, not in self-management as a system.

16. A "social agreement" is a voluntary agreement between a group of enterprises or a whole branch of industry. It is reported to the legislature, not enacted by it.

17. Berislav Sefer, *Dohotak i primanja u Jugoslaviji* (Belgrade: Zavod za Iztrazivanja Trzista, 1972), and Miladin Korac et al., eds., *Politika dohotka* (Belgrade: RAD, 1972).

representing unskilled workers, the second the wages of the university educated.

A similar trend can be observed even in the universities, where the existence of self-managing bodies has had the long-range effect of narrowing the gap between the lowest- and the highest-paid academic employees. Thus at present the largest salary differential between instructors and full professors is 1:2. This is partly because even in academic hierarchies there are more lower-level employees voting on such matters than higher-level ones.

RECENT YUGOSLAV SURVEY DATA ON SELF-MANAGEMENT

The findings of Yugoslav studies on self-management are numerous and difficult to summarize. For a brief time it appeared that the most rapidly growing cottage industry in Yugoslavia was studying of workers' participation and self-management, which were almost innumerable. The 1968 bibliography on self-management published by the Institute of Social Science has over four hundred pages.[18] Certain facts, however, do stand out. It is clear that in terms of actual participation skilled workers are overrepresented. They show a higher participation rate than both unskilled workers and nontechnical white-collar staff, as can be seen in table 33. This finding holds for all republics. The table also shows that, while the white-collar employee groups are slightly overrepresented in the councils, the group most overrepresented, at a ratio of almost 2:1, is highly skilled workers.

A second general point that can be made is that different strata relate to different participatory forms. Thus, peasants and independent craftsmen tend to rank the Socialist Alliance and the communal self-management organs first as places where they can sound off and push their demands. Skilled workers give primacy to workers' councils and trade unions; unskilled workers to the trade unions and the league but less as participatory bodies than as agencies for voicing complaints. Intellectuals naturally enough relate to the professional associations and their work collectives, and finally directors and managers find the collegium, that is, the body of the

18. J. Acimovic, *Bibliografija o radnickom samouprojljanju* (Belgrade: Institut Drustvenih Nauka, 1968).

Table 33

Social Composition of Workers' Councils, 1970

	Composition of Workers' Councils	Employed Population as a Whole, 1970	Representation Rate (ideal = 100%)
Blue-Collar Workers[a]			
Highly skilled	17.2%	6.6%	260%
Skilled	33.7	25.2	134
Semiskilled	9.0	12.7	71
Unskilled	7.4	24.5	30
Apprentices	0.3	—	
Total	67.6	68.9	
White-Collar Employees[b]			
Jr. college and college educated	10.1	9.6	105
Secondary schooling	15.9	14.3	111
Elementary schooling	6.4	7.9	81
Total	32.4	31.1	

SOURCE: *Statisticki godisnjak Jugoslavije, 1970*, p. 134.

[a] Highly skilled workers are the equivalent of craftsmen in the United States, that is, they usually have completed secondary school plus a 4-year apprenticeship. Skilled and semiskilled workers usually are trained on the job. These categories are probably expressions of seniority more than anything else.

[b] White-collar employees are stratified by educational level. The junior college and college category can be broken down into 3.8 and 5.8 percent respectively of the employed population.

technical experts in the enterprises, and the league committee in their enterprise, most relevant.[19]

The Institute of Social Research of the University of Zagreb put an identical question to a general sample of the Croatian population for three years in a row. The question is: "Some people believe that self-management is the most important basis for the development of socialism while others believe that socialism can be developed in other ways. What do you think?" Some of the results can be seen in

19. This is an impressionistic summary based on discussions with Yugoslav sociologists and political activists and recollections of scattered survey data from 1968 and 1969.

table 34. More interesting than the gross figures for responses is the breakdown of responses by league membership, shown in table 35; and even more significant are the responses by age, shown in table 36, where the trend is clear.

Confirming other findings, these responses show that positive attitudes toward self-management correlate with league membership (which could have been anticipated), and that the views of the younger groups are closer to the norms of the system than those of the older groups. Incidentally, in the republic of Croatia there is also a marked difference between males and females on this and other political questions, a total of 65.7 percent of the males holding that self-management is indispensable, in contrast to only 45.9 percent of the females. This reflects a number of factors, including the greater influence of traditional institutions like the church over women, and the more private nature of the lives most women still lead, which does not favor their chances of being employed in the socialist sector.

More specific data are available from a series of studies of worker participation organized by Professor Rudi Supek in Zagreb.[20] Two findings stand out. First, there was a major difference in the actual power wielded in the collectives, which relates to the level of automation or modernization of the given plant. Simply stated, in those industries where the bulk of the labor was still manual, the director was perceived as the most powerful figure in decision making, with the technical staff second, the League of Communists third, the management board fourth, and the workers' council fifth. In the mechanized plants, on the other hand, the perceived power distribution was radically different. There the League of Communists was seen as first, the workers' council as second, the director third, the management board fourth, and the technical staff fifth. In the automated plants, the technical staff was seen as occupying the first rank, the director second, the management board third, the workers' council fourth, and the league fifth. This confirmed one of the hypotheses of the researchers, namely, that in the automated industry the management of "men" is being increasingly replaced by technical expertise, which is of course widely distributed in such plants.

20. Published in Josip Obradovic, *Participacija i motivacija u radnickom samoupravljanju* (Zagreb: Institut za Drustvena Iztrazivanja, 1968).

Table 34

Self-Management and Socialism

	1967	1968	1969
Self-management is most important	46%	50%	55%
Socialism is possible without self-management	5	8	5
No opinion	49	42	40

SOURCE: *Javno mnenje stanovnistva S.R. hrvatske, 1969* (Zagreb: Institut za Drustvena Iztrazivanja, 1970).

Table 35

Self-Management and Socialism, by League Membership

	League Members	Nonmembers
Self-management is most important	85.9%	51.0%
Socialism is possible without self-management	3.6	4.7
No opinion	9.4	44.3

SOURCE: *Javno.*

Table 36

Self-Management and Socialism, by Age

Age	Self-managment is most important	Socialism is possible without self-management	No opinion
Under 26	65.4%	4.1%	30.5%
26–30	64.8	6.7	28.5
31–35	62.8	3.7	33.5
36–40	60.3	5.1	34.6
41–45	61.7	2.3	36.0
46–50	50.0	6.1	43.9
51 and over	44.9	4.4	50.6

SOURCE: *Javno.*

A second interesting finding was the contrast between the desired power structure and the power structure as perceived in the twenty plants studied. As table 37 shows, respondents were unanimously agreed that the workers' council should rank first, and, while the importance of the technical staff is not at all underestimated in the respondents' desired rank order, this group is clearly subordinate to the authority of the workers' council. Interestingly enough, both the League of Communists and the trade unions rank higher in the desired rank order than in the actual rank order as perceived by the workers. These attitudes, observed in 1967 and 1968, would probably be more pronounced today, particularly since the league has been energetically pursuing a more egalitarian policy and has weakened its linkages with the managerial personnel. As argued previously, the trade unions are on their way up in the political hierarchy of groups for similar reasons.

Underlying these findings are two demographic factors, which give them a growing importance: the increasingly skilled composition of the growing working class of Yugoslavia, and the general rise in the educational level of the blue-collar workers. I have argued elsewhere that this rise in the educational level of workers is a disrupting factor in industry where it is not accompanied by growing authority and participation.[21] Conversely, the availability of struc-

Table 37

The Power Structure within Enterprises

Desired Rank Order		Perceived Order	
Workers' council	1.0	Director	2.1
Technical staff	2.8	Managing board	3.1
League of Communists	3.0	Technical staff	3.3
Workers	3.5	Workers' council	3.5
Trade unions	5.3	League of Communists	3.7
Director	5.8	Workers	6.5
Managing board	7.1	Supervisors	6.9
Supervisors	7.3	Trade Unions	7.9
Administration	9.0	Administration	8.1

SOURCE: *Participation and Self-Management* (Zagreb: Institut za Drustvena Iztrazivanja, 1972), 1:172.

21. See my essay "Is There a New Working Class?" in *Workers' Control*, ed. Gerry Hunnius (New York: Random House, 1973).

tures for participation in the Yugoslav social and economic system will probably mean an increasing activation of the workers' councils as workers who view themselves as educated and competent become more numerous. It is this factor that gives a special impetus to the continued drive toward the activation of the workers' councils, and makes self-management increasingly important in all spheres of Yugoslav social and economic life.

Attitudes toward self-management among Yugoslav workers, judging from survey results, appear to be correlated with the level of mechanization in the plant. In the technologically more advanced plants, the salaries and the working conditions are superior, and one can assume that the directorial prerogative is more important, given the complexity of the decisions made. Table 38 shows that the degree of support for self-management increases markedly with the level of mechanization and automation of the industry, and that participation in workers' councils, not surprisingly, strengthens support for workers' self-management. The table is based on the responses of workers from twenty plants in Croatia in 1967 to the question: "Would the elimination of workers' councils and the return to previous ways of managing create dissatisfaction among workers and employees?"

Table 38

Degree of Dissatisfaction Elimination of Workers'
Council Would Cause

Type of Enterprise	Workers' Dissatisfaction				Workers' Council Members' Dissatisfaction			
	Great	Some	None	DK	Great	Some	None	DK
Handicraft	27.7%	21.8%	6.9%	39.6%	53.8%	19.8%	5.4%	19.4%
Mechanized	43.0	18.0	5.0	30.0	78.2	8.0	3.5	9.2
Automated	51.5	18.8	8.9	19.8	80.5	2.4	2.4	12.2

SOURCE: Rudi Supek, "Two Types of Self-Managing Organizations and Technological Progress," *Participation and Self-Management*, 1:171.

The assumptions behind the increasing emphasis on self-management in Yugoslavia are similar to those expressed by Nancy C. Morse and Robert S. Weiss in "The Function and Meaning of Work":

4. The average human beings learn, under proper conditions, not only to accept but to seek responsibilities. Avoidance of responsibility, lack of ambition, and emphasis on security are generally consequences of experience, not inherent to human characteristics.

5. The capacity to exercise a relatively high degree of imagination, ingenuity, and creativity in the solution of organizational problems is widely, not narrowly, distributed in the population.

6. Under the conditions of modern industrial life, the intellectual potentialities of the average human being are only partially utilized.[22]

More recent research on the population as a whole shows that attitudes toward self-management stress primarily the role of the workers in controlling industry rather than the notion of the autonomy of the enterprise. The fall 1972 survey of public opinion in Croatia posed two questions.[23] The first was "What, in your opinion, is self-management?" and the responses, chosen from a closed list of alternatives, are instructive (see table 39). Several remarks are appropriate here. To begin with, considering the fact that this is a general population sample, including housewives and peasants, there is a remarkably low rate of "no answer, do not know, no response," which usually range from 18 to 20 percent. The two answers most often picked were the two normative descriptions of self-management, and these answers also represent two of the Yugoslav regime's major claims to legitimacy. Answer 6 stresses communal self-management while 5 emphasizes the rule of the working class of the system as a whole through the mechanism of self-management. If replies 4, 5, and 6 are added together, 76.2 percent of the respondents describe self-management in terms close to those used by the official ideologists *but* stress the aspect least stressed in the recent press and media description of the Yugoslav system, that is, the rule of the working class.

22. Nancy C. Morse and Robert S. Weiss, "The Function and Meaning of Work," *American Sociological Review* 20 (1955): 191–98.

23. Reports on the study are found in *Svaraoci Javnog mnenja u Jugoslaviji* (Belgrade: Institut Drustvenih Nauka, 1969) and a version in English of the major papers in *Opinion-Making Elites in Yugoslavia*, ed. Allen H. Barton, Bogdan Denitch, and Charles Kadushin (New York: Praeger Special Series, 1973).

Table 39

The Meaning of Self-Management:
Responses to a 1972 Survey in Croatia

1. State management of the means of production   4.8%
2. Management of the means of production and the
   results of work by individuals   2.3
3. Management of the means of production and the
   results of work by elected groups   5.9
4. Management of the means of production by workers'
   councils and managing boards   10.4
5. Management of the means of production by the
   working class   43.8
6. Participation of citizens in decision making in
   all aspects of life and work of the community   22.0
7. No answer, don't know, no response   10.9

SOURCE: *Javno.*

The second question was: "Are there any groups that have significantly improved their living conditions through self-management?" The responses are shown in table 40. While these answers were also chosen from a closed list of alternatives, the workers easily took first place as beneficiaries of self-management. Second were the directors of enterprises, who are beneficiaries at least in that they have gained greater autonomy from the state organs. And the response for "political leaders" should probably not be overempha-

Table 40

Beneficiaries of Self-Management:
Responses to a 1972 Survey in Croatia

1. Production workers   35.3%
2. Independent peasants   1.6
3. White-collar workers   8.5
4. Intellectuals   2.4
5. Engineers and technical intelligentsia   5.0
6. Directors of enterprises   20.4
7. Political leaders   11.7
8. Pensioners   1.8
9. Housewives   0.8
10. No answer   12.5

SOURCE: *Javno.*

sized, since a section of the public is of the opinion that *every* change benefits political leaders in Yugoslav society. Respondents realistically perceived that those groups that do not benefit from the introduction of self-management include not only the obvious ones—pensioners, housewives, and private peasants—but also the intellectuals and, more significantly, the technical intelligentsia.

These findings confirm the general picture that self-management is viewed by the population as a whole as benefiting primarily the industrial working class, and the working class reflects that feeling, particularly when faced with the question of what would happen if self-management were to be abolished. A number of old-time communists have remained ambivalent about self-management, thinking it chaotic and semianarchistic, and the intelligentsia has, at the very least, been neutral to those aspects of self-management which stress workers' control. However, the attitudes of the Yugoslav population toward self-management indicate that the norm of participation in industry is widespread, especially among its participants. Given the central position assigned by Yugoslav political leaders and institutions to self-management as the cementing and legitimizing value system, these findings go a long way toward making a case that the indigenous Yugoslav variant of socialism has been successfully grafted to what must have seemed unpromising roots.

An extensive study of attitudes toward self-management was undertaken in Zagreb in the spring of 1969, utilizing a sample with six subgroups: students, secondary school youth, trade school youth, young workers (under 30), older workers, and a control sample of adults. Table 41, where some of the results are given, is interesting in that the alternative of multiparty democracy is among the possible replies, as is rejection of self-management insofar as it is linked with a market economy. The younger groups and both groups of workers were consistently lower than the control sample, by at least a 1:3 ratio, in picking a multiparty system as being more democratic than self-management. Similarly, a higher number picked self-management as the desirable direction for further development of Yugoslav society. If the two replies that are pro–self-management but criticize it either from the point of view that it is acceptable without the leading role of the League of Communists or that the problem is that the Yugoslav society is insufficiently mature for self-management are

Table 41

Attitudes toward Self-Management among Six Subgroups of Yugoslav Society, 1969

	University Students	Secondary School Students	Students at Industrial Workers' Schools	Young Workers	Older Workers	General Control Sample of Adults
1. Self-management is the proper direction for the development of our society.	58.2%	67.0%	60.8%	53.6%	51.1%	38.3%
2. Our society is not sufficiently mature for self-management.	21.4	17.0	16.7	25.0	20.7	20.1
3. Self-management, when combined with a *market economy* is unacceptable for our society.	7.5	7.0	8.3	10.7	14.1	12.8
4. A multiparty system is more democratic than self-management.	3.0	3.0	4.2	1.2	3.3	13.4
5. Self-management is acceptable but without the leading role of the League of Communists.	10.0	6.0	10.0	9.5	10.9	15.4

SOURCE: Ivan Siber, "Idejna orientacija mladih," *Politicka Misao* 6, no. 4 (1969):44.

combined with the unequivocally pro–self-management replies, an overwhelming majority of the students and workers accept self-management as a norm. The significance of the high level of acceptance of self-management among workers and the two groups who are the future technicians and employees of the society—high school and college students—is obvious.

Yugoslav economists today by and large argue that self-management is not only socially desirable but, and this is significant for a developing country, inherently efficient. That is, they do not believe that a dichotomy exists between participation and humaneness on one side, and technical efficiency on the other. Branko Horvat, one of the leading Yugoslav economists, presents his argument graphically in table 42. This is a thorny and complex question, and chapter 5 presented some other indicators of development that could strengthen Horvat's case.

While one may have reservations about the indicators used, since economists themselves are not in agreement on this, Horvat's figures are significant even if wrong since they represent the assumptions of economic policy makers in Yugoslavia. This is their perception of the relative performance of the systems.

Two things in the table stand out. The self-managerial form appears superior or equal in performance in all categories except the growth of fixed capital, and even there it is respectable by comparative indicators. The minor drop in the increase rate of employment under self-management can be explained by the

Table 42

Comparative Analysis of the Efficiency of Economic Systems in Yugoslavia, 1911–67

| | Growth Rate of: | | | |
System	Gross Domestic Product	Employ-ment	Fixed Capital	Technical Progress
Capitalism, 1911–32	3.28%	1.87%	3.52%	+0.71%
Capitalism, 1932–40	4.67	0.72	2.59	+3.16
State socialism, 1944–54	5.91	4.76	9.99	−1.04
Self-management, 1956–67	10.31	4.44	7.84	+4.44

SOURCE: Branko Horvat, *Privredni sistem i ekonomska politika Jugoslavije* (Belgrade: Savezna Admistracija, 1969), p. 173

Table 43

Ownership of Fixed Capital in Economic
Organizations, 1955–69

Year	Enterprises	Banks	Sociopolitical Communities*
1955	44.0%	0.8%	55.2%
1960	37.4	1.0	61.6
1965	36.8	31.7	31.5
1969	34.8	49.4	15.8

Source: Neca Jovanov, "The Relationship between Strikes and Self-Management," in *Participation and Self-Management*, 1:16.

* Federal, republic and communal governments and regional planning agencies.

growing development of Yugoslav industry and the consequent shift from extensive to intensive development, which would produce a slower rate of growth in employment. The significant columns are those for gross domestic product and for technical progress. So long as Yugoslav economic planners accept these figures, dramatic shifts away from self-management are highly unlikely. However, there is a problem in the growing concentration of fixed capital funds in banks, creating a force outside the self-managing structure of the enterprise which inevitably influences the policies of those enterprises.

The figures in table 43 reflect the dismemberment of the direct economic power of the state agencies in the economy. They also show that most Yugoslav enterprises are, like many enterprises elsewhere, unable to generate sufficient fluid capital for investment purposes, and that capital in Yugoslavia is becoming concentrated in the banks. While the banks also have self-managing bodies, they are in an anomalous position since they do not "produce" money. A major debate has been under way since 1971 about the role of the banks in the economy, sparked in part by the development of nationalism in Croatia. The banks have been accused of usurping the decision-making powers of enterprises and even local and republic governments, since they sometimes attach conditions to their loans which affect the prerogatives of the workers' councils. It is argued that, while the sociopolitical communities are subject to political pressures from the trade unions, the league, and other citizens' organizations, the banks use self-managing autonomy to protect themselves from such "outside" pressures. As a result there was a major crackdown on the holdings of the banks in 1973 and the spring of 1974, and the bulk of their funds were transferred to the enterprises.

The dilemma of the Yugoslav policy makers is that they wish to create controls over the banks without reverting to central state control of the banks or the economy. This is currently being resolved by two mechanisms: (1) the break-up of the federal banking centers and the transfer of their funds to republic and regional banks; and (2) the trend of groups of enterprises and entire branches of industry to pool funds so that they are freed from dependence on banks. One side effect of the debate has been to revive a call for the regulatory role of the League of Communists itself in setting norms for "socialist economic morality," and an increase of the power of the trade unions in the economy.

The sharpening debate about self-management in the period from 1969 to 1973 strengthened the tendency toward egalitarianism, particularly within the industrial working class. A fall 1971 survey of workers' attitudes in Slovenia provides some interesting documentation of this trend (see table 44). When examining these figures, one must keep in mind the fact that egalitarianism[24] has not been supported by either the media or the political leadership, especially

Table 44

Attitudes toward Existing Income Differences (Slovenia, 1971)

	1966	1968	1971
Differences are too great	54.1%	60.0%	64.9%
Differences are appropriate	29.0	23.0	22.4
Differences are too small	6.8	6.0	4.9
Don't know, no answer	10.8	11.0	7.8

SOURCE: Sasa Micki, "Socijalna diferencijacija: Diferencijacija stavova," *Sociologija* 3 (1972): 499–508.

24. Excessive egalitarianism (*uravnilovka*, or "leveling down") has been the target of repeated press and political campaigns. It is attacked as primitive communism or primitive egalitarianism. The official line is that everyone should be paid according to the results of their work, that is, that differentials based on skill and hard work are legitimate; only illegitimate differentials are unsocialist and wrong.

Table 45

Desired Income Differences, by Educational Level (Slovenia, 1971)

Schooling Completed	A*	B*
4 years of elementary school	15%	1:1.7
8 years of elementary school	14	1:1.6
School for skilled workers	26	1:1.5
Gymnasium and secondary school	27	1:1.8
Junior college, college	34	1:1.8
Averages for all	25	1:1.6

SOURCE: Micki, p. 503.

*See explanations in text.

in Slovenia, where the leadership has stressed the importance of technical experts and engineers, who have been demanding greater differentials. The trend shown in table 44 is all the more interesting, given that Slovenia is by any indicator the most advanced republic and is regarded by the leadership of the other republics as a model of their own futures.

Even more relevant are the opinions of the workers and other professional groups in Slovenia about desirable income differences. In table 45, column A shows the percentage by which the given group feels *its* income should be increased from its present level, while column B represents the ratio the group feels should exist between the salaries of unskilled workers and technical experts. The less skilled workers (that is, those with only elementary school educations) apparently have modest aspirations for increasing their own salaries, while the skilled workers are the most egalitarian. Column 1 shows that it is the better educated and more highly trained workers who feel that their wages should be substantially increased; this is most marked in the case of the employees who have junior college or college educations. There are two reasons for this: one is that the trend has been toward equalizing wages, despite the apparent increase in social stratification, inflation contributing to this trend by placing the burden of inflation mainly on higher income groups, and the second is that this group is most likely to compare its standard of living with that of neighboring Austria or Italy. The more important fact that stands out is that even those most discontented with their current wages favored a modest 1:1.8 ratio between the wages of an unskilled worker and an engineer.

The other somewhat surprising finding is that the difference between the desirable range of incomes cited by the most egalitarian and by the least egalitarian groups is amazingly small—only 0.3 percent. Thus, although egalitarian tendencies are stronger among the skilled workers, there is no great gap between them and the other strata, at least when responses to this question are expressed in specific ratios. This strengthens my conviction that the trend toward egalitarianism will grow in Yugoslavia despite the arguments of a number of experts on modernization and political development who insist that greater modernization involves greater functional differentiation and therefore greater income differences.

Data in the last table from the Slovenian survey seem to contradict table 44. Table 46 gives the breakdown by educational level of those who answered that income differentials are too great. Two things stand out in this scale of what I will call "verbal egalitarianism." The percentage for the most educated stratum, probably reflecting the official line against *uravnilovka* ("leveling down," or excessive egalitarianism) is consistently the lowest. The skilled workers are not only the highest on both the verbal egalitarianism scale and the "real" scale (in table 45) but are increasingly homogeneous on this question. This, when linked to the growing stress on skilled workers as the strategically most significant group in Yugoslav society—the group on which the party desires to base itself—supports my view that policies aimed at egalitarianism and increased egalitarian rhetoric can be anticipated.

Table 46

Verbal Egalitarianism by Educational Level (Slovenia, 1971)

Schooling Completed	1967	1968	1971
4 years of elementary school	45.6%	55.2%	48.5%
8 years of elementary school	53.5	63.0	70.5
School for skilled workers	62.9	69.8	70.6
Gymnasium and secondary school	39.3	42.3	55.3
Junior college, college	24.1	16.2	16.3
Averages for all	53.8	60.0	64.9

SOURCE: Micki, p. 505.

The findings, incidentally, also argue against a fairly common assumption about Yugoslav self-management: that it increases the egoism of the strategically more powerful groups since the wage gap between the skilled workers and the unskilled workers is of the same order as the one between the skilled workers and the engineers and technicians. It could have been expected, based on this, that the skilled workers would desire greater income differentiation, particularly in advanced, highly industrialized Slovenia. However, if Slovenia does represent the future of the other Yugoslav republics, one can expect a trend toward egalitarian policies throughout the federation, particularly if the political and social weight of the workers' councils increases in the coming years.

DIFFERENT APPROACHES TO SELF-MANAGEMENT

Self-management can mean very different things to different groups. Managers and technical experts stress plant and enterprise autonomy and their right to manage without interference of the government or central economic bodies. Politically conscious workers interpret self-management as their right to control the managerial staffs and to make the significant day-to-day decisions affecting their lives. Socialist intellectuals regard self-management as an alternative to a highly structured, party-dominated political system, and one that will create new norms and therefore hopefully a new socialist man. These themes of course represent ideal types, but it is clear that, although self-management was an unexplored possibility when introduced, it has become attractive to wider publics in both Western and Eastern Europe, at least as a slogan. What should be stressed is that this slogan is passed on with all of the ambiguities implicit in the different approaches named.

In Hungary and Poland in the mid-1950s and among the Czech reformers in 1968, very different approaches to self-management were present. In the first two cases, the demand for self-management came primarily from the workers themselves. This demand was made more urgent by the fact that they felt that they did not control and were not represented by their parties and trade unions. In Czechoslovakia, however, attitudes among the reformers were more ambiguous, since many were hesitant about self-management because they wanted to move toward greater income differentiation and a society in which managers and experts would be free from the political structure.[25] They rightly assumed that in any industrial situation where genuine power resides in the elected workers' councils, the pressure will be toward greater wage equality and against special privileges for the managerial and technical cadres.[26] This is why partial self-management in the form of codetermination or joint consultation is far more attractive to managers and industrial relations experts, whose views are usually similar to those of enlightened management among liberal or social-democratic reformers.

A further problem which the discussions about self-management tend to obscure lies in the relationship of the other representative workers' institutions to self-management. I refer primarily to the trade unions. Self-management can be related to the trade unions in three typical ways. First, in some forms of co-consultation, the union itself represents the interests of the workers on a joint body with managers and technicians. While this implies a conflict of interests between the management and workers, in practice it all too often turns out that the trade union representatives on such bodies become more "reasonable" than the rank and file they represent. They come sensitized to the problems of management and production, which often clash with their normative role as the advocates of the direct interests of the workers. A second type of relationship is one in which the trade union, or rather the shop stewards, *are* the workers' council. This is the syndicalist model and it has at least the virtue of simplicity. Managerial and technical staffs at that point work for the workers' council, and the problem of representation is solved because of a single line of representation. A third model is one where the trade union is, rightly or wrongly, perceived as unrepresentative and the workers' council as being more directly representative. This can occur either in situations where a fragmented trade union movement

25. See Ivan Svitak, *The Czechoslovak Experiment, 1968–1969* (New York: Columbia University Press, 1971), esp. pp. 52–59. An excellent discussion of the views of Czech reformers on the question of equality is in Ernest Gellner's "The Pluralist Anti-Levelers of Prague," *Dissent* (summer 1972), pp. 471–83.

26. See the interesting discussion by Kiro Gligorov at the Session of the Presidium of the League of Communists of Yugoslavia on October 30–November 1, 1972 on economic differences, as reported in *Politika*, November 2, 1972. The point I want to stress is that income differences within specific branches of the economy are becoming smaller. This is also seen in the work of Berislav Sefer.

exists, divided between politically competing unions, or in cases where the trade union leadership asserts no independence from the rest of the hierarchy of the society. In such cases the trade union is not regarded as the instrumentality through which grievances and personnel questions are settled, and it often appears on the management side of the table in the managing board. This describes the limited councils in Poland and Hungary, and the early stage of Yugoslav development.

When the trade unions begin to assert greater independence as representatives of generalized interests of the workers, their relationship to the self-governing structure is one where they defend the societal interests of the workers as a quasi-political lobby, while the councils themselves take on the functions that are in part carried out by the shop stewards' committees in some of the unions in Western Europe and the United States. While conflicts exist in these situations, they need not be endemic.

Industrial self-management in Yugoslavia must be distinguished from the classic workers' councils in that it includes the managerial and technical experts as well as workers, who constitute a majority. However, self-management or workers' control is an increasingly attractive slogan in many different countries and social situations. As noted before the content given to that slogan will vary widely. Some view the councils as a way of winning worker participation in mediating conflicts, improving productivity, and supporting an "incomes policy"; others view the workers' councils as proto-soviets, that is, instruments for the revolutionary transformation of a capitalist (or, for that matter, state socialist) society to a socialist society. It is therefore important to specify very carefully what one means by participation and self-management, since those slogans are by now used at least as widely as "democracy." The slogans become most popular in situations where the workers do not feel that their parties and trade unions are sufficiently militant in transforming the conditions and the social organization of work. In these cases economic demands are rare, and one can assume that, when wage settlements are determined on a higher level without a direct confrontation of the workers and the employers, the demand for some form of workers' participation or workers' councils will increase. This trend in advanced industrial countries will undoubtedly be strengthened by the rising educational level of the working class and the increasing complexity of work. The old division between the experts on the management side and the relatively uneducated workers on the other is breaking down, and an intermediate group, sometimes designated the "new" working class[27] has arisen. The existence of this stratum in the working class will make the demand for some form of self-management more and more general in advanced industrial societies.

In developing societies, on the other hand, the function of self-management or workers' control is different. To begin with, it represents a major attempt to mobilize the newly industrialized peasants and socialize them in the norms of factory life. It is also an instrument for recruiting new managerial strata in societies without adequate cadres. Finally, it is ideologically useful—even in situations where the power of managers is almost unaffected by the existence of councils—because it justifies, or seeks to justify, the transformation of revolutionary political activists into managers. That transformation is ideologically more acceptable if at least the form of participation is maintained. However, forms that do not reflect social reality can prove to be a dangerous luxury. When workers are told that they own the factories and that they are to manage them, they sometimes seek to act as if this were so. Under these circumstances, conflict can develop between workers operating within the official ideology of the system and the system itself.

Prospects for Self-Management

The development of self-management in Yugoslavia has had the effect of reviving discussion of the possibilities of workers' control in contemporary society. Previous programs, even when they appeared to be spelled out in considerable detail by the anarcho-syndicalists, guild socialists, and the Workers' Opposition in Russia, were after all abstract models. All assumed, at least implicitly, that the workers'

27. The best discussion of the implications of this development is in Serge Mallet's *La Nouvelle Classe ouvriere* (Paris: Seuil, 1963). See also Denitch, "Is There a New Working Class?" and Michael Harrington's essay on the same question in the special summer 1970 *Dissent* issue, later published in book form as *The World of the Blue Collar Worker* (Chicago: Quadrangle, 1972). In Yugoslavia this idea was popularized by M. Pecujlic in *Buducnost koja je pocela* (Belgrade: Institut za Politicke Studije, 1969).

councils themselves would be the focus of governmental power. One could, after observing the Yugoslav experience, outline three possible approaches which flow from the application of self-management to complex polities.

The first model would assume a revision of the traditional Marxist definition of the working class, and its replacement by the concept *working people.* In this case self-managing bodies in the economy and society would represent the entire working population—the managerial, white-collar, and technical strata as well as blue-collar workers. Implicit in this model is the assumption that organic changes are occurring in the composition of the working force which will substantially reduce the proportion of blue-collar workers in the economy. Therefore, a self-managing system and the corresponding political structure have to be based on other broad strata in addition to the working class. The notion that there are no major social conflicts within the category "working people" and that harmonious self-managing bodies can represent the group as a whole within a given sector is also implicit in this model.

The second model, which seems to be closer to the classic model and is now popular in sections of the French and Italian working class, conceives of workers' councils as organs of dual power in a class society where the working class parties do not necessarily rule. That is, workers' councils or shop committees are instruments of struggle for that power and are primarily conceived of as substitutes for the traditional trade union structure. They bargain and speak in the name of the blue-collar workers and their allies and do not necessarily have any connection with the state structure itself.

In the third model, workers' councils represent the blue-collar working class and its immediate allies and run the industry and the economy in a framework where the society itself is ruled by a party of the working class. In this situation the workers' council would hire the experts, managers, technicians, and the rest. It also "hires" the secondary services, that is, banking, finance, and so on. Here the assumption would be, presumably, that the party of the working class which rules the society bases itself on the blue-collar workers in self-managing institutions. The party is, simply stated, the society-wide expression of the conscious will of the more advanced sectors of the working class, with its allies.

The troubling question in all three cases is of course the relationship of the workers' councils and other self-managing bodies to the state. The first case presents a model that can be developed within either a single- or a multiparty structure. Its essential characteristic is the assumption that there are no specific working-class interests as distinct from those of the other working strata. Therefore, implicit in that model are consultation, coordination, and consensus. The second and third models imply class conflict but resolve it on different levels. In the second, where workers' councils exist as an organ of dual power, the councils themselves are one of the contenders for power, and such a situation, particularly if the ownership of the economy is mixed, can lead either to the atrophy of the workers' councils and their reduction to mere consulting bodies or to an attempt by the councils to acquire state power. In the third case, while the councils would clearly dominate and control the economy, and the ruling party would be the reflection of their interests, it is not inconceivable that other strata—managers, technicians, private farmers, and the like—might nonetheless be represented in the political structure through their own organizations or even parties.

The Yugoslav system falls somewhere between the first and the third types. It is therefore, I believe, a model in the process of transition: it can move in the direction of stressing greater enterprise autonomy and the unity of the managerial, technocratic strata with the working class, or it can move toward the third model, a possibility that did not exist at the time the workers' councils were created, for the simple reason that there were not enough workers to constitute the primary group or base for industrial and state power.

What is overlooked in the discussions about the future structure of the working force in modern industrial societies is that, although technical strata and white-collar workers have been expanding at a rapid pace, blue-collar workers have not in any advanced industrial society declined to any statistically significant extent over the past five decades.[28] The percentage of blue-collar workers, even after the

28. Taking only the United States, where the trend toward elimination of the traditional working class would presumably be most advanced, we find the following percentage breakdowns of the total work force (male and female) by job category:

massive introduction of labor-saving devices and automation, has remained constant at around 35–40 percent in most advanced industrial polities. It is the percentage of people involved in agriculture that has diminished, while increases have occurred in the growing secondary sector. Furthermore, an unanticipated change has taken place in the sector of technicians and white-collar workers, where massive groups have become proletarianized, at least in the organization of the work process and the development of a trade union consciousness.

The point of this seeming digression is that the Yugoslav model, if applied to advanced industrial polities, would probably be a reflection of a radical working-class program rather than of proposals supported by the economic techno-structure, that is, an instrument of class conflict rather than class conciliation. To put it differently, the aspect of self-management that interests the techno-

	1900	1920	1940	1950	1960	1970
Managers, officials, proprietors, farm owners, etc.	25.6	21.9	17.7	16.1	15.5	12.7
Professionals and technicians	4.3	5.4	7.5	8.6	11.1	14.4
Clerical and sales	7.5	12.9	16.3	19.3	21.2	23.6
Service workers	9.1	7.9	11.8	10.5	12.5	12.4
Manual workers (all)	35.8	40.2	39.8	41.1	36.1	34.9
Farm workers	17.7	11.6	7.0	4.3	3.1	1.8

Three points should be made here: (1) the increased proportion of women in the work force, primarily in the clerical and sales category, probably means that the proportion of families where the major breadwinner is a blue-collar worker has not diminished at all. Among males only, the percentage of manual workers was 37.8 in 1900, 44.5 in 1920, 45.5 in 1940, 48.3 in 1950, 46.3 in 1960, and 46.8 in 1970. (2) Because of increasingly factorylike conditions, unionization efforts are now being directed at clerical and sales workers, service personnel, and some professional technicians. (3) The category "professionals and technicians" is really two categories:

	1900	1920	1940	1950	1960	1970
Professionals and technicians: independent	1.1	1.0	1.1	1.1	1.3	1.5
Professionals and technicians: workers	3.1	4.4	6.4	7.5	9.9	12.9(!)

Thus, this category includes groups that are sometimes designated as the "new working class."

All figures are from *Historical Statistics of the United States* (Washington, D.C.: Bureau of Labor Statistics, 1970), p. 225.

Also see A. Szymanski, "Trends in the American Working Class," *Socialist Revolution*, no. 10 (1972).

structures is its application to the struggle between the classic owners and managers in private and sometimes state-owned industry, and the working class which they attempt to buy off by giving it the illusion of participation through consultation, while the power stays in the hands of the technically better-trained strata. The Yugoslav model, with all its imperfections and contradictions, is on a different plane. It represents a major historical attempt to create a *society* based on self-management. The success or failure of this effort may reshape the future strategy of working-class parties throughout the world.

Self-management in Yugoslavia represents an experiment of sufficient duration for it to begin to answer some of the basic questions raised primarily within the workers' movements about the possibilities of workers' control in modern society. These possibilities in Yugoslavia were limited by underdevelopment, the complex political problems of the postwar state, and the large sector of the population that remained in private agriculture. Thus the experiment was successful since, even under conditions that were far from optimal, a working system of self-management developed, producing a dynamic economy and a degree of participation hitherto unknown in industrial society.

Yugoslav self-management applies to the socialist sector, which means that it affects roughly half of the working population. Three major groups are outside the system: private farmers, numbering approximately four million; people in the private sector, numbering some 90,000; and the large number of workers temporarily working abroad (almost one million). Pensioners, housewives, and those not employed are of course also excluded. Even with these limits, as I have shown, close to a quarter of the relevant population participates at any given time in the institutions of self-management. Since a system of rotation is used, this means that a major portion of the population in the modern sector is involved at one time or another. The other strata participate through the political process.

There is considerable evidence that self-management has entered into the basic value nexus of Yugoslavia and is generally accepted as a desirable social goal, despite existing imperfections. The processes of self-management have created new pressures in the society which will in all probability continue to alter the political cultures of

Yugoslavia in basic ways. Hostility to Yugoslav socialism—expressed as hostility to self-management—can be expected from a number of sources. In addition to the traditional ones, there will be two major new ones. The first is the new middle class, which seeks to enjoy a living standard close to that of Western Europe and whose values are increasingly technocratic and managerial. For them what is wrong with self-management is precisely that it does involve workers—persons who are viewed as having insufficient culture and expertise to make major decisions. The second group includes those who identify socialism with centralized planning and a unitary state. They object to the workers making major decisions because they view them as lacking political expertise. Both groups of would-be tutors will frame their attacks within a nominal support for self-management, but of a reasonable and limited form.

As the society continues to develop, the values implicit in the new set of social relations in the economy will increasingly clash with traditionalist values. These traditionalist values are most often expressed in the form of either nationalism or centralism (or rather statist socialism). This is because the processes of self-management tend to minimize the role of charisma and the special prerogatives of the traditional gatekeepers of societal values. Thus self-management will be viewed with suspicion by both traditionalist political cadres and the humanistic or traditional intelligentsia. The crucial determinant in the future development of self-management, therefore, will be the role and power of the growing industrial working class of Yugoslavia. It represents the major social group in whose unambiguous interest is the extension of self-management.

The social differences that have arisen in Yugoslavia are not the product of the system of self-management and a socialist market economy; rather they are the result of violations of the legal and political norms of the society. A major campaign against these abuses is essential to prevent the corrosive effect illegitimate privilege and wealth have on the morale of the society and thus on self-management itself. These privileges represent a threat not because they are widespread but because they underline an absence of social control and the fact that new socialist norms appropriate to the present stage of Yugoslav development have not yet developed. They are also a threat because of the widespread cynicism that results and in turn creates a political vacuum—fertile ground for nationalism and other platforms inimical to the whole Yugoslav experiment.

Self-management has created processes in the base of the society that have not yet produced an appropriate political superstructure. This is, if for no other reason, because the political structure has a history and tradition while the social system is new. It has, however, begun to shape that superstructure. One of the results is the form of pluralism of institutions now found in Yugoslavia. The continued process of change in my opinion is irreversible without outside intervention and will basically alter the state and the political institutions. The result can be a model of a democratic socialist society—a model with no real precedent.

8

The Question of Legitimacy

"History does *nothing,* it 'possesses *no* immense wealth,' it 'wages *no* battles.' It is man, real living man, that does all that, that possesses and fights; 'history' is not a person apart, using man as a means for its *own* particular aims; history is *nothing but* the activity of man pursuing his aims." [1]

This study of the revolutionary transformation of Yugoslavia, which involved the destruction of the traditional social structure and the development of a new political culture, is basically a case study focusing detailed attention on the consolidation of revolutionary authority in a single country. Thus it belongs in the general framework of studies of political modernization, social change, and the development of stable one-party regimes. This is a field in which a great deal of attention has been focused by American political and social scientists, although no generally accepted principles have developed even after three decades of discussion. [2]

1. Karl Marx and Friedrich Engels, *The Holy Family* (Moscow: Foreign Languages Publishing House, 1954), p. 105.
2. The most optimistic recent discussion of the utility of some of the available conceptual tools for analyzing social change in communist systems is William A. Welsh, "The Usefulness of the Apter, Easton, and Spiro Models in the Study of Communist Systems in Eastern Europe," *Newsletter on Comparative Studies of Communism* 5, no. 4 (August 1972).
   More sobering notes will be found in Karl de Schweinitz, Jr., "Growth, Development, and Political Modernization," *World Politics* 22, no. 4 (July 1970); T. H. Rigby, " 'Totalitarianism' and Change in Communist Systems," *Comparative Politics* 4, no. 3 (April 1972); Charles A. Powell, "Structural-Functionalism in the Study of Comparative Communist Systems: Some Caveats," *Studies in Comparative Communism* 4, nos. 3–4 (July–October 1971); and Alexander Eckstein, "Economic Development and Political Change in Communist Systems," *World Politics* 22, no. 4 (July 1970). The state of the relation of existing theories and models to the actual living systems as described in these articles is not encouraging for any attempts to construct macro-theories.

The initial approach to the study of communist systems, centered on the development of the totalitarian model, has been progressively refined from Hannah Arendt's work to the works of Zbigniew Brzezinski, Alexander Dallin, Carl J. Friedrich, and others. Friedrich, attempting to inject some badly needed theoretical vigor into the concept of totalitarianism, unfortunately all but defined it out of existence; a totalitarian system included:

> 1) a totalist ideology; 2) a single party committed to this ideology and usually led by one man, the dictator; 3) a fully developed secret police; and three kinds of monopoly or more precisely monopolistic control, mainly that of a) mass communications, b) operational weapons, c) all organizations including economic ones, thus involving centrally planned economy.[3]

If Friedrich's definition is accepted, and it does represent a departure from the older models which stressed the use of terror, it is clearly not applicable to the case of Yugoslavia. A centrally planned economy is not a feature of the Yugoslav system, nor are all organizations directly controlled by the league center, nor are, for that matter, mass communications. And, finally, the regime's very definition of Yugoslav Marxism as an open system means that, whatever else may be, it is not a totalitarian ideology. The League of Communists' policy of defining its area of dominance and concern narrowly leaves considerable areas of public activity and intellectual life to the autonomous forces within the society.

For that matter, one could question whether even this restricted model of totalitarianism is applicable to a number of East European regimes. Hungary and Poland at the very least come to mind as probable exceptions. However, if the now dated category of totalitarianism is not particularly useful in the study of communist systems, its most recent rival—authoritarianism—suffers from dif-

---

Much of the explanatory power of Barrington Moore's *The Origins of Dictatorship and Democracy* (Boston: Beacon Press, 1970) unfortunately seems to lie in the cases and period he picked. The advent of modern communist movements puts the whole question of conscious, organized intervention in revolutionary transformations on the agenda. That element—the role of the revolutionary party—is in my opinion inadequately dealt with in the existing literature.

3. Carl Friedrich in *Totalitarianism in Perspective: Three Views*, ed. Carl Friedrich, Michael Curtis, and Benjamin Barber (New York: Praeger, 1969), pp. 125–26.

ferent but equally pressing problems when applied to existing modernizing one-party regimes. The most commonly cited and influential definition of authoritarianism is probably that of Juan Linz:

> Political systems with limited, not responsible, political pluralism: without elaborate and guiding ideology (but with distinctive mentalities); without intensive nor extensive political mobilization (except at some points in their development), and in which a leader (or occasionally a small group) exercises power within formally ill-defined limits but actually quite predictable ones.[4]

Linz's definition suffers from a problem opposite to Friedrich's. While the latter is narrow and probably historically limited, the former covers far too wide a variety of essentially diverse regimes and societies. It could be applied to a range of societies from the post-Stalin Soviet Union (with some difficulty) to nonparty systems like Ethiopia, multiparty systems like Colombia, and of course single-party systems ranging from modernizing egalitarian socialist states to traditional one-party dictatorships like Spain. A category so broad in effect creates a continuum rather than a dichotomy between the authoritarian systems covering most of the polities in the contemporary world today and the presumably pluralist polities limited essentially to Western European and Anglo-Saxon states, with the possible addition of Japan. Even India could be forced into Linz's pattern, which it certainly resembles more than that of a developed pluralist polity, since even with the existence of rival parties a single party has dominated Indian politics since independence.

The difficulty becomes even greater if the output of the systems is examined and if the pluralist polities are examined with emphasis not on competing political parties and institutions but on the actual range of issues that meaningfully occupy the political and social agenda of those societies. That is, the range of issues that may be legitimately raised within the boundaries of a multiparty polity may not be wider than that existing in one-party polities.

4. Juan J. Linz, "An Authoritarian Regime: Spain," in *Cleavages, Ideologies and Party Systems*, ed. Erik Allard and Yrjo Littunan (Helsinki; distributor: Academic Book Store, 1964).

In any case, the application of Linz's definition of authoritarianism to Yugoslavia presents the researcher with certain difficulties. To begin with, it is a very dubious proposition—and one specifically negated by more recent developments—that Yugoslavia is a polity in which neither intensive nor extensive political mobilization takes place.

More importantly, one can argue that the entire purpose of the introduction of self-management into the Yugoslav economy and political system has been to institutionalize a permanent mobilization of broad layers of the populace in accomplishing the tasks of economic development and legitimizing the system. If self-management is conceived of as a long-range experiment in political participation and political socialization, then Yugoslavia is probably the country in Eastern Europe that has made the most extensive attempts to transform the political culture inherited from the past and to develop new values and norms in broad sectors of the population. The whole point of a participatory economy and society is that the party does not seek to rule alone and passively but places major emphasis on mobilizing processes which are channeled through the system of self-management in such a way as to reinforce the legitimacy of the system.

The concept of authoritarianism, while representing a healthy antidote to the more sterile paradigm of totalitarianism, appears to apply to stable polities that are not involved in drastic long-range attempts to transform existing social and economic relations, and above all to polities that seek to normalize and routinize the forms of dominion on which this economic and state power rests. In this respect the continual emphasis in Yugoslavia on deprofessionalization, debureaucratization, and rotation of personnel even within the formal political system represents an antipode to the routinizing processes, endemic though they may seem.

One of the problems with the loosely defined authoritarian model is its relative abstractness and concentration on the political superstructure, which may well be similar in very diverse social orders so that appreciation of this diversity requires a closer examination of the socioeconomic base. A further problem—with any model, of course—is that features of different types of social orders coexist in most polities.

To take the example of Yugoslavia alone, we can discern three different forms of dominion existing simultaneously on different levels of policy formation. These processes vary in importance at different points in time and on different policy issues and outputs. First, the charismatic mobilizing level is presently identified with the institution of the president and specifically with the person of Marshal Tito who has been elected president for an indefinite term (i.e., life). This level is characterized "by a very wide and undefined series of prerogatives which through time have nevertheless become predictable." [5] The second level is characterized by routinized bureaucratic processes, where institutionalization and normalization are characteristic. This level is best identified in the legal system and the federal and governmental apparatus as distinct from the sociopolitical organizations. A focus on this level would show a continual development of institutions with defined prerogatives and limited powers and legal dominion. [6]

The third level, absent in the polities usually described as authoritarian, I would call participatory-particularist. [7] This level is the specific product of the Yugoslav social revolution and is what gives the Yugoslav system its unique features. It is based on the institutions of self-management in both the economy and society, most specifically the workers' councils and the communes.

The presence of this third level makes it difficult to classify Yugoslavia as an authoritarian regime, although the first and second levels have features found in such regimes. With this triad of institutional levels or spheres, what generally occurs is a shifting set of coalitions between levels in response to different social problems and the ordering of priorities. Thus the period characterized by Western scholars as a liberalization period was basically one in

5. Ibid.

6. The second or bureaucratic-legal level in Yugoslavia has certain specific characteristics, such as the legal *managerial* autonomy of enterprises operating within a market economy, which make this level far more complex (involving considerable institutional pluralism) than has been the case in other East European systems.

7. The term "particularist" is not used here as the Parsonian pattern variable opposed to "universalism," focusing on traditional relationships as opposed to "modern" depersonalized bureaucratic relationships. Rather, the term here refers to the Yugoslav legalization and legitimation of particularist collectivities—communes, enterprises, and nationalities—as building blocks of the whole social system, that is, to their rejection of the Jacobin unitary conception of the nation state.

which the second level played a major role in day-to-day policy making and opinion mobilization. Therefore, Yugoslavia developed features analogous to those of other parliamentary regimes with a division of authority and function institutionalized in the governmental bureaucracy, the courts, and the different levels of administration. This represented a shifting alliance—initially between the charismatic president and the increasingly routinized bureaucracy—with a gradual surrender of the prerogatives of the charismatic process to the routinized one, although the latent power of the charismatic leadership remains. A breakdown in the ability of the routinized processes to handle cleavages, particularly the cleavages that arose in the period 1969–71 along national and republic lines, led to a reassertion of the unifying role of the president and activated the party centers.[8] This led to the present situation: an alliance was formed between the charismatic president and the third level (participatory-particularist), as a way of generating pressure on the routinized processes, which were not perceived as moving quickly and decisively enough to meet social priorities. Thus, the most recent period has been characterized by continual calls on the working class from the collective Federal Presidency and from league leadership to assert its power through the participatory institutions of workers' self-management, and to exert pressure on precisely those strata of society most able to utilize the routinized processes to establish their own status demands.

This can be found in a number of the features of present policy: the call for a mobilization of the popular base against the growing social differentiation resulting from the increasing complexity of the Yugoslav society and economy; the call for an assertion of the power of the workers' councils over the technocratic and managerial strata; the attempt to remobilize political sentiment in the base against the various currents that had developed within the routinized structures —particularly against those currents which sought to base themselves on either traditionalist nationalist sentiment or technocratic managerial demands for greater efficiency.

The campaign process that has been opened up, described as an

8. A very detailed discussion of this process can be found in Dennison Russinow's well-informed four-part study *The Crisis in Croatia* (New York: American Universities Field Staff, 1972).

offensive by the League of Communists, seeks to reverse a number of trends that developed through the routinization and legalization of social relations in the last decade. Thus, a campaign has been launched against social privileges, excessive differentials in income, and luxuries such as summer homes and extra apartments, which were found mostly among the educated class of experts and the small private sector, and which are therefore likely to be coveted by the broad mass of industrial workers and lower administrative employees. The privileges of the very top stratum, the political elite, are less vulnerable to this campaign for a number of reasons, not the least of which is the fact that those privileges do not express themselves primarily in the form of private property but take the form of access to and use of less visible privileges. In effect, what is sacrificed to the popular demands for greater egalitarianism are the privileges of that stratum which enjoys economic benefits without political power, and whose benefits were therefore regarded as illegitimate by both the mass base and the political elite.

The return of Yugoslavia to the campaign process as a way of handling the logjam of economic, social, and political issues must not, however, blind us to the fact that the other two levels continue to exist parallel to the charismatic presidency, and that it is increasingly unlikely that the concentration of charismatic power held by the present occupant of the presidency, Tito, is transferable. Another way of stating this is that the campaign process requires that the titular presidency of the state and the party be occupied by a person who still holds sufficient moral and political authority over the other institutions of society and who bases this authority on irreplaceable criteria. No new occupant or, rather, occupants of Tito's position in contemporary Yugoslavia are likely to have the same unquestioning authority in the party, the army, and among the people. It is far more likely that the charismatic presidency itself will be subject to the process of routinization and institutionalization, and in point of fact the present constitutional provisions explicitly so state, since what is envisaged as a successor to Tito is government by the collective Federal Presidency, with the individual post of president rotating among members of this body.[9]

9. Radio Free Europe Reports in Yugoslavia, June 27, 1972, pt. 2, *What Will Happen after Tito?* An individual president is to be chosen each year, from among the

The routinized processes, providing an atmosphere in which the rules of the game are predictable for the various actors, require a greater congruence between the participatory and particularist base of society and its formal superstructure. That requires above all two things: the growing articulation on a societywide basis of participatory self-managing institutions, and an increasing social weight for the strata resting on and using those institutions. In my opinion, the growing industrialization and modernization of Yugoslavia makes both possible. The institutions of workers' self-management are affected both by the size of the Yugoslav industrial working class and by its growing literacy. One could characterize the development of Yugoslavia as involving the establishment of participatory institutions from the top down at a time when the social class that was to rule through those institutions was neither massive enough nor sufficiently developed to make use of the possibilities existing within the system itself. Therefore, the system of self-management became institutionalized before it could assume the role assigned to it in the system itself, and as a consequence criteria of geographic representation and institutions with vertical hierarchies, such as the League of Communists, continued to have the greatest weight in the generation of policies, although implicit in the system itself were functional rather than geographic representation and participatory rather than hierarchical organization.

However, the institutionalization of self-management in Yugoslavia had as a direct consequence the development of self-management as the unifying social myth of the society, analogous to such broad terms in Western polities as "democracy." I stress the analogy because of course in the advanced Western polities, although a great emphasis is placed on the ideal of democracy, there is continual criticism of the gap between the real and the ideal. Similarly, in Yugoslavia much of the criticism of the system is expressed in terms of the norms of the system itself. This is one of the marks of the legitimation of a new norm, for it is evidence that even most of the

---

seven republic and province representatives who constitute the Federal Presidency, to serve a one-year term. The pattern of rotation by republic is pre-determined in such a way that a given republic will control the post of president only one year out of every seven. Also, since members of the collective Presidency are elected for five-year terms, it is very unlikely that an individual will ever hold the post twice, and most members of the Presidency know that they will never hold the highest office.

critics of the system take for granted the value of the norms, that is, of the rules of the game, and thus concentrate their criticism on what they perceive as the inadequacies of implementation.

POTENTIAL CHALLENGES TO SYSTEM LEGITIMACY

Challenges latent within Yugoslav society to the legitimacy of the present social order vary in intensity and importance. The most commonly identified ones fall into three categories: (1) those associated with the traditional prerevolutionary social order, particularly nationalism, separatism, and privatization of socially owned property; (2) those reflecting the pressures of the centralized state-socialist system, found particularly in sections of the party and in veterans' organizations, who are basically worried by what they perceive of as chaotic semianarchism, that is, an absence of order and direction; and (3) those arising within segments of the self-managing system itself, particularly currents identified as technocratic. There is a fourth category which, for reasons I will develop, is residual yet has no particular potential for threatening Yugoslav social order. That category covers the very visible and articulate student and intellectual groups identifying themselves as leftist critics of the existing society. This current in Yugoslavia will continue to exist as a gadfly but has neither the independent social weight nor the potential social allies necessary to have a direct political impact on the system. The students are subject to continual cooptation by the league and other institutions of society, and their radical critical stance is therefore mostly transitory. The intellectuals, mostly philosophers associated with the journal *Praxis*, have a policy impact only when certain of their themes and demands are adopted by sections of the establishment itself, and therefore should be regarded as a quasi-official loyal opposition.

Individual members of this group, or even subgroups such as the eight Belgrade philosophers associated with *Praxis*, may occasionally exceed the ill-defined boundaries of what is defined as legitimate criticism at a given point in time. They may thus find themselves in an uneven conflict with the league leadership either locally or on the federal level and may in the end be removed from the universities or find their journal placed in a situation that makes continued publication impossible, but they remain critics within the system. What is most characteristic of this group is its firm adherence to the

formal norms of Yugoslav socialism: nonalignment, self-management, dominance of the working class, and Marxism as the unifying
ideology. Therefore, they often play the role of explaining the
workings of the system itself to the Yugoslav establishment proper,
that is, of explaining some of the implications of the radical social
experiment implicit in the establishment of participatory democratic
institutions within a one-party system.

All of the more significant challenges to the legitimacy of the
present order in Yugoslavia potentially coexist and they often
combine. Thus the nationalist "mass movement" leaders in Croatia
in 1970 and 1971 sought a conscious alliance with the technocratic
currents in the modern self-managing economy.[10] In the same
period, centralist elements sought a similar alliance with technocracy. The technocrats were perceived as potential allies against the
status quo which by virtue of its emphasis on self-managing
institutions within the economy was perceived as inherently inefficient and as having usurped management prerogatives.

The alliance between centralists and technocrats has a fairly clear
logic. Their major social goal is rapid development—development
that requires technical expertise and stable central authority—and
therefore both the participatory forms in the economy and the
localist centers of authority are obstacles to rapid development. This
line of criticism, for that matter, has often been expressed by Western
scholars and observers of Yugoslav society, more recently by an
American economist, Deborah Milenkovich;[11] R. V. Burks, a political scientist, lectures the Yugoslavs about the general dangers of
excessive decentralization.[12] This is also the major line of criticism
from East European and Soviet sources, and it has a certain
resonance among older party cadres whose entire development was
shaped by the Stalinist phase of Yugoslav Communist Party history,
and who regard the mobilizing hard-boiled dictatorship of 1944 to
1950 as the golden era of Yugoslav socialism. Such elements hope

10. See particularly the speech of Mika Tripalo in the *Borba* supplement for
January 24, 1970, with its heavy stress on the role of managerial and technical cadres.
11. Deborah Milenkovich, *Plan and Market in Yugoslav Economic Thought* (New
Haven: Yale University Press, 1971).
12. R. V. Burks, "The National Problem and the Future of Yugoslavia" (mimeo.,
Santa Monica, Cal.: Rand Corporation, October 1971).

that in the post-Tito period the army league organization will join them in supporting a policy designed to bring order, stability, and development.

The nationalist current, which was most evident in Croatia but had its weaker analogs in Serbia and Slovenia, represents a peculiar amalgam of traditionalist-romanticist-nationalist intellectuals and sectors of the republic-based league who, through such an alliance, sought to provide themselves with a popular base against the federal center. The rationale of the local league leaders, who were allied to the nationalists, was crudely analogous to the official doctrine of self-management. One major justification for the establishment and development of self-management is that, by giving the producers a major right in disposing of their income, it prevents the alienation of the worker otherwise inherent in a state-socialist system. The nationalists took this point one step further and argued that, just as it was improper to take surpluses from self-managing enterprises without the consent of the workers of that enterprise, it was also improper to take the income of a republic without the consent of the republic's leadership. That is, they used the analogy of the enterprise and applied it to their republic.[13] Implicit in this analogy is a theory of social contract which considers the republics basic sovereign entities related to a federal government through a set of loose, voluntary ties; this would entail the evolution of the Yugoslav federation into a confederation. The basic problem faced by nationalist currents in Yugoslavia is not merely or even primarily caused by the repressive measures against nationalism taken by the league leadership and the presidency. Rather, the basic difficulty lies in the interdependence of the Yugoslav economy and the increasing development of peculiarly Yugoslav social and political institutions and norms. Also a problem is the almost impossible task of specifying what precisely is the outcome of a given republic since most of the major industries use raw materials and supplies from other republics.

The real income of the individual republics cannot be measured

13. The most explicit statement of the nationalist position, naturally dressed in Marxist terminology, is found in H. Sisic, *Za ciste racune* (Zagreb: RAD, 1970). Also see Sime Djodan, "Gdje dr. Stipe Suvar 'pronalzai' nationalizam a gdje ga ne vide," *Kolo*, no. 7 (1969).

simply on the basis of where the end-process of production occurs. A
good example in recent Yugoslav debates is the tourist industry, a
major hard-currency earner. Most of Yugoslav tourist income is
generated along the Dalmatian seacoast, in the republic of Croatia.
However, the hotels and the tourist centers have been built with
funds generated as often as not in other republics, and the food
supplies indispensable to the maintenance of a tourist industry come
primarily from other regions, most often from Vojvodina and Serbia.
The question posed therefore was why should the agricultural
producing areas—subject to controlled prices of agricultural production[14]—subsidize another republic and another region unless the
funds so generated were to be considered federally rather than
regionally.

A further problem in the attempt to utilize nationalism to
generate support for reforms within the system is the historically
combustible nature of nationalism in the Balkans. Given the tortured
history of this area, it is difficult even for its leaders to keep
nationalist sentiment, once aroused, within acceptable boundaries.
Thus nationalist demands escalate and very rapidly become a
surrogate for a general critique of the social system itself. In short, in
a situation of intensifying nationalism, the local communist leaders
will always be outbid by traditionalist, religious, and anticommunist
elements. They can never be sufficiently nationalist to satisfy the
aspirations of legitimist nationalism based on the diverse historical
traditions of the Yugoslav republics.

However, nationalism in Yugoslavia threatens the system only
when nationalist themes combine with economic and social demands
of strata broader than the intelligentsia. This is the inherent
weakness of nationalism and separatism in contemporary Yugoslavia. Slovenian nationalism, for example, ceased to be a problem once
it became known that Slovenia desperately needs the raw materials
and supplies it gets from the less developed republics at lower-than-
world-market prices. It also needs the protected Yugoslav market for
its finished goods. Similarly, Croatian nationalism is doomed, as is
Serbian nationalism, to become a residual problem because it does
not tend to mobilize the growing modern strata but rests instead on

14. Also limited is the right of agricultural regions to export food to hard-currency
markets unless local needs (i.e., those of the tourist industry) have been met.

an inherently weak alliance of traditionalist intellectuals, ambitious students, and disgruntled segments of the old middle classes.

The fact that nationalism was and is weakest within the industrial working class points to the very uncertain future of nationalism in Yugoslavia as the system keeps modernizing. This trend is accelerated by the increasing mobility of labor within Yugoslavia. Last and not least is the fact that, although segments of the league may be willing to make occasional tactical alliances with national sentiment, once the genie is out of the bottle the normal instinct of self-preservation of the league as an institutional instrument of rule reasserts itself, and it inevitably cracks down. In such a crackdown, it can apparently count on being viewed increasingly as an instrument of legitimate authority.

BASES OF AUTHORITY AND LEGITIMACY

The case of Yugoslavia is relevant to two major questions of social theory. One is the question of how successful revolutions develop and occur in countries in the middle range of development, such as Yugoslavia was in 1941–43. The second is of course the complex problem of the development by a revolutionary regime of legitimate authority and of an appropriate political culture embedded in sufficiently broad strata of the population to provide a basis for stable development.

Useful insights are provided by Richard Rose in his insufficiently cited "Dynamic Tendencies in Authority of Regimes." [15] For our purposes his middle-range approach is more useful than the macro-theories of Cyril Black[16] and Samuel Huntington.[17] Rose locates the tendency toward increasing legitimacy in regimes in the interaction between the regime and its subjects, whom he defines as that sector of the population actually demonstrating some compliance with and support of the regime. His typology is dynamic, not static, and is based on the levels of support and the levels of compliance to regime authority at a given point in time (see table 47). Rose defines authority as

15. *World Politics* 21, no. 4 (July 1969).
16. Cyril E. Black, *The Dynamics of Modernization: A Study in Comparative History* (New York: Harper & Row, 1966).
17. Samuel Huntington, *Political Order in Changing Societies* (New Haven: Yale University Press, 1968).

a universal term to label collectively the different patterns of relationship between regimes and the populations from which they seek obedience and allegiance. To say that a regime has authority tells nothing of itself. It may be discredited or fully legitimate authority. . . . *The type of authority that the regime exercises can be distinguished by the degree to which its population acts in accord with regulations concerning the maintenance of the regime and has diffuse cultural orientations approving the regime. The typology has two principal components—compliance and support—compliance emphasizes the power of the regime to get its nominal subjects to act as de facto subjects—support is the enduring and diffuse basis of voluntary obedience to a regime's regulations: a high level distinguishes some regimes from others, primarily based on coercion, calculation, or absolute ideological goals.*[18]

Postwar Yugoslavia can thus be seen as having developed from a revolutionary regime with divided legitimacy to a partially legitimate regime with mixed support and high compliance. The break with the Russian bloc led to a number of challenges that were in essence managed by measures designed to maximize support. There were some heuristic possibilities that were perhaps historically unique: a realistic external threat, which normally increases the support of a population for a regime but was in this case not sufficiently explicit to divide the population. The increasing support was reinforced by conscious measures designed to maximize it. The popular slogan of self-management in 1949, followed by the removal of pressures on the peasantry in 1953 and measures decentralizing

Table 47

Typology of Regime Authority

Fully Legitimate	*Intermittently Legitimate*	*Isolated*
high *s*; high *c*	high *s*; mixed *c*	high *s*; low *c*
Partially Legitimate	*Divided*	*Disrupted*
mixed *s*; high *c*	mixed *s*; mixed *c*	mixed *s*; low *c*
Coercive	*Semicoercive*	*Repudiated*
low *s*; high *c*	low *s*; mixed *c*	low *s*; low *c*

SOURCE: Rose, "Dynamic Tendencies," p. 83.

NOTE: *s* = support; *c* = compliance.

18. Rose, "Dynamic Tendencies"; italics added.

the state apparatus and democratizing public life in the mid-1950s, moved in the direction of increasing regime support. The evident successes of the development policy during the next decade (1954–66) provided an increasingly solid basis for the full legitimation of the regime and, above all, provided time for the new social relations and institutions based on self-management to enter into the normative nexus of the new political culture of the country.

The Yugoslavs clearly did not enjoy the optimal conditions for achieving full legitimacy presumably found in the cases of Britain, Sweden, and Switzerland, where it has been achieved by gradual evolution. However, again following Rose, regimes founded by a struggle for independence against a foreign invader or colonial overlord are likely to enjoy high support in the initial phase, although no long-range predictions are implicit. This is often contrasted with regimes founded by civil war, which are able to develop compliance proportionate to the thoroughness of their social and military victory but achieve only partial legitimacy. Yugoslavia is a case of a regime founded by a combination of two types of revolutionary struggle and thus blessed with conditions optimal for maximizing both support and compliance when the regime consolidates—the high support that comes with the waging of a war of independence, and the ability to win compliance which comes from a convincing victory in a civil war.

I have argued that it was the level of violence and the thoroughness of the defeat of the enemies, both present and potential, that gave the Yugoslav political elite a head start in establishing its regime and meeting the prerequisites for legitimacy. This point is also made by Rose, in a more general form: "Once badly beaten the losers in a civil war will be easily coerced even if their support cannot be gained. This hypothesis is supported by the maintenance of regimes for long periods after especially bloody civil wars in 19th century America and in 20th century Ireland, Spain and Yugoslavia."

Here Rose's assertion that "the longer a regime can remain in power, the more the turnover of generation works to its advantage for its present becomes normal in a cognitive sense and one may hypothesize in a normative sense as well" is particularly salient in the study of revolutionary regimes. With the traditional norms broken, the establishment of new norms and a new political culture, to provide both support for and compliance with a regime's aims, requires time. Here the Yugoslav data can be interpreted as being generally optimistic for the regime, if we define the regime in the narrow sense of the word as "that set of institutions coordinating and controlling the civil administration, the police, and the military within a state." [19]

The theory of social change and revolutionary transformation suffers from the lack of treatment of revolutionary processes by serious social scientists who would treat that process as a whole. The point is made very well by Stanley A. Kochanek:

> Somehow the present social science literature has failed to capture the essence of revolution. *Revolutions are desperate acts; they take unpredictable turns*, they can be reversed or arrested; but above all they aim at fundamental transformation of society and of man himself. They are fueled by ideologies which do not simply take advantage of discontent but point as well to a picture of the future. They are led by men, even when they seem most spontaneous. *Revolutions occur because men want them to occur* and not simply because of some general feeling of malaise which might be a necessary but not sufficient cause for action. Individual discontent must be translated into collective discontent and it is this translation process which raises questions about leadership, ideas and mobilization.[20]

The literature on modernization and political development has tended to depoliticize the process and, in almost a caricature of Marxism in its most determinist form, to reduce political development to a series of consequences flowing from given levels of economic and social development and group conflict. Dankwart Rustow, in an influential article, takes issue with this approach in a relevant and fruitful way:

> The denial of the primacy of politics and the attempt to explain it away accord well with the widespread acceptance of stability and equilibrium as the central ordering concepts of our social

19. Ibid.

20. Stanley A. Kochanek, "Perspectives on the Study of Revolution and Social Change," *Comparative Politics* 5, no. 3 (April 1973); italics added.

theory. A student of the sociology of knowledge might note that these tendencies have become prominent among American scholars in an era in which their country experiences unprecedented (if uneven) affluence at home and has undertaken unprecedented (if at times self-defeating) commitments to the status quo abroad.[21]

If any central unifying fact seems to emerge from the Yugoslav data, it is that the conscious political intervention of the league leadership appears to explain more about Yugoslavia and its specific path of development than any other single variable. Surely the traditional political cultures of Yugoslavia, varied as they were, and the historical past of the various Yugoslav lands would have argued against the successful development of a modernizing, one-party polity capable of imposing a singularly uniform economic and social system over areas with diverse histories and levels of development. Observers have noted the differences in the levels of development in the various Yugoslav republics, but it may be more relevant to stress the uniformities created by conscious political, social, and economic policies which constitute the underpinning of a new Yugoslav-wide political culture. To be sure, this "unified Yugoslav political culture" is primarily limited to the modern, urban, industrial sector and is most widespread among strata that have directly benefited from Yugoslav development. The multinationality and the varying levels of development of the country have certainly set objective limits on the rate of dissemination of this political culture. However, the three decades of development of the Yugoslav revolution have created similarities that will, in my opinion, only grow as time goes on.

Table 48 shows the 1971 distribution of income per employee in the Yugoslav republics, and the range of income differences between unskilled workers and university-educated experts. Given the history of the Yugoslav lands, the picture presented is remarkable for its uniformity. It applies, to be sure, to only the employed and not to the peasants and the population that is supported. But, if we look at that growing segment of the population, we find that the difference between the most developed and the least developed region in

21. Dankwart A. Rustow, "Modernization and Comparative Politics: Prospects for Research and Theory," *Comparative Politics* 1, no. 1 (October 1968).

Table 48

Income Distribution in Yugoslavia, by Republic, 1971

	Income per Employed Person (index: Yugoslavia = 100) [a]	Income Range: Unskilled Worker– College Educated [b]
Yugoslavia	100%	100–259
Bosnia-Herzegovina	95	100–294
Montenegro	88	100–254
Croatia	109	100–243
Macedonia	82	100–287
Slovenia	114	100–258
Serbia	94	100–258
Vojvodina	96	100–260
Kosovo	82	100–315

SOURCE: Adapted from *Statisticki godisnjak Yugoslavije, 1972.*

[a] The ratio of the lowest to the highest republic average is 1:1.4.
[b] If the average income of unskilled workers in the lowest-paid area is set at 100, the average income of the college educated in the highest-paid area is 380.

employee income was 32 percent in 1971, and the range of differences in income from 100–243 to 100–315. Such a range is clearly the result of conscious policies, which have produced this uniformity even without a central plan. Part of the difference is after all explained, not only by the varying levels of development of modern, industrial Slovenia and underdeveloped Kosovo, but also by the different composition of the work forces in the respective republics, with Slovenia having the higher percentage of skilled workers. Real differences in standard of living are greater, reflecting, as has been shown in chapter 6, the high natality rate of Kosovo. It is, however, a fact that the employed worker in Kosovo is increasingly more like a *worker* in the other republics than his relatives in the village in life style, expectations, and political norms.

The fundamentally successful development of the Yugoslav social and political system in the past two decades has won increasing acceptance of the new Yugoslav political culture among the young, the urban, and above all the workers. I follow Robert Tucker's usage of the term "political culture" which includes both the normative statements consonant with the ideology of the Yugoslav elite, and behavioral attitudes which may or may not be officially approved.[22] An example of this effect can be seen in table 49, which is based on research conducted in Croatia at a high point of pro-nationalist assertiveness in the local media and by the local leadership. The table summarizes responses to the question: "How should the younger generations be educated about nationality?"

Several things stand out in these results. To begin with, the politically approved response, that is, the concept of the Yugoslav socialist community within which national sentiment is legitimate, is second in frequency. It is significant, however, that a higher percentage of high school and trade school students, and young and old workers picked the "unitaristic" answer, that is, that there should be a trend toward developing a single Yugoslav nation; this was in sharp contrast to both the general control sample from the population and the official line at that time. The sentiment among these strategic groups was thus more unitarist than either the general sentiment among the populace or the "official" line. The pro-nationalist response (number 3) is significantly lower for all the specific groups sampled than for the control group. That is, both the young, who represent the future leadership of the society, and the industrial workers appear to be less nationalist than the general population. While one should not draw too many conclusions from this finding, it is consistent with my general thesis, which is that the Yugoslav system has strong followers among specific strata within a context of general acceptance by the population as a whole. Both responses 1 and 2 are basically prosystem, varying only in the degree of orthodoxy. Thus the response to a sensitive question about national identity, posed in Croatia at a time when national sentiment was riding high, was that shown in table 50.

The Yugoslav experience strongly suggests that political cultures and social structures are far more vulnerable to change over relatively short periods of time, at least in those matters important to regime legitimacy, than has been argued in the relevant sociological literature. A classic statement of the traditional attitude toward social change is Joseph Schumpeter's:

22. Robert Tucker, "Culture, Political Culture, Communism," paper presented at the Conference on Communism and Political Culture, Princeton, November 1971. I agree with Tucker's generally high opinion of Richard Fagen's *The Transformation of Political Culture in Cuba* (Stanford: Stanford University Press, 1969).

Table 49

How Should the Younger Generations Be Educated about Nationality? *

	University Students	High School Students	Trade School Students	Young Workers	Older Workers	Control
1. National differences should be overcome and there should be an effort to create a unitary Yugoslav nation.	35.8%	50.0%	47.1%	50.0%	45.3%	29.1%
2. Besides developing the feeling of belonging to a specific nation, we should develop the feeling of belonging to the Yugoslav socialist community.	46.3	36.5	39.5	29.1	37.9	39.9
3. We should develop the feeling of belonging to a specific nation as the most relevant expression of historical tradition, culture, and political freedom.	17.9	13.5	13.4	20.9	16.8	31.1

SOURCE: Siber, "Idejna orientacija mladih," p. 47.

* This question was posed in Zagreb in the spring of 1969 to groups of university students, high school and trade school pupils, young workers (under 30), and older workers. The control group was a general population sample.

Table 50

Summary of Responses to National Identity Question,
in Croatia

	University Students	High School Students	Trade School Students	Young Workers	Older Workers	Control
Pro-Yugoslav	82.1%	86.5%	86.6%	79.1%	83.2%	69.0%
Pro-Nationalist	17.9	13.5	13.4	20.9	16.0	31.0

Source: Adapted from Siber.

Note: This table was constructed by adding the two pro-Yugoslav responses in table 49.

Social structures, types and attitudes are coins that do not readily melt. Once they are formed they persist, possibly for centuries, and since different structures and types display different degrees of ability to survive, we almost always find that actual group and national behavior more or less departs from what we should expect it to be if we tried to infer it from the dominant forms of the productive process.[23]

The Yugoslav revolution buttresses the argument that social structures, types, and attitudes are coins that do indeed melt *when the proper degree of heat is applied.* What is perhaps the case is that a whole string of secondary attitudes deeply embedded in the cultural tradition of the country alters much more slowly, thus creating a situation where a string of potentially contradictory attitudes coexists. The norms of participation and development are very highly regarded in Yugoslavia by the same industrial workers who may have retained some very traditional attitudes toward the family, child rearing, and manual work. The point, however, is that there is sufficient leeway for the changes necessary for the legitimation of a revolutionary polity to occur within as short a span as a single generation. And here I should stress that revolutions and social processes are above all carried out by people: "*Ideas* can never lead beyond an old world system but only beyond the ideas of the old

23. Joseph Schumpeter, *Capitalism, Socialism, and Democracy*, cited in Reinhard Bendix, *Nation-Building and Citizenship* (New York: John Wiley, 1964).

world system. Ideas cannot *carry anything out* at all. In order to carry out ideas men are needed who dispose of a certain practical force." [24]

The Yugoslav revolution did not occur because it was based on an idea "whose time had come" but because men mustered the requisite amounts of practical force to shatter the old social order, lay the foundations for a new one, and carry out the complex processes of industrialization and modernization, at each point facing a number of options that coexisted within the limits of real possibilities. In modernizing polities it is this human factor that seems to make a crucial difference. To be sure, the ecological, historical, cultural, and economic factors all provide a framework and set the boundaries. But ultimately making something of them remains an intensely human endeavor, and the limits of change in developing societies have not yet been defined.

24. Marx and Engels, *Holy Family*, p. 160.

Appendix: Yugoslav Opinion Makers and Their Social Role

Through direct interviews carried out in 1968 and 1969, the Institute for Social Sciences of Belgrade and a team of Columbia University scholars undertook research on the strategic opinion-making leadership of Yugoslavia.[1] This research is part of a complex multinational study. However, for our purposes it provides insight into a key

1. Fuller results of the study are reported in Allen H. Barton, Bogdan Denitch, and Charles Kadushin, eds., *Opinion-Making Elites in Yugoslavia* (New York: Praeger Special Series, 1973); *Stvaraoci mnenja u Jugoslaviji*, ed. Firdus Dzinic (Belgrade: Institut Drustvenih Nauka, 1969); "Working Papers of the International Study of Opinion-Makers," ed. Bogdan Denitch, 3 vols. (New York, Bureau of Applied Social Research, Columbia University, mimeo., 1969–71); and Bogdan Denitch, "Elite Interviewing and Social Structure: An Example from Yugoslavia," *Public Opinion Quarterly* 36 (summer 1972).

The universe of Yugoslav opinion makers was initially defined in terms of a set of positions in six institutional sectors:

	Population	No. interviewed
Federal legislators (members of the Chamber of Nationalities and the Federal Representative Chamber, committee chairmen and officers of other chambers)	243	65
Federal administrators (higher civil servants at the federal level)	168	90
Mass organization leaders (officials of the League of Communists, Socialist Alliance, Trade Union Federation, Veterans' Association, and youth organizations at the federal level)	312	76
Economic administrators (directors of major enterprises, economic planners and advisers in government)	225	81
Mass communicators (directors, chief editors, and leading journalists of newspapers of largest national circulation, TV network, radio stations, and publishing houses)	179	101
Intellectuals (university professors of social science and philosophy, editors of intellectual journals, frequent contributors to intellectual journals, leading literary writers, theatrical and film directors and writers, artists)	286	104
Total positions	1,413	569
Total different individuals	1,290	517

The interviews were carried out from March 1968 to January 1969.

element of the Yugoslav social and political leadership at a time when functional differentiation, particularly through occupational roles, had been sufficiently developed so that the cementing role of this group could be examined.

Not the least significant aspect of this research was the simple fact that it could be carried out. That is, the Yugoslav political and intellectual leaders apparently were sufficiently confident of the legitimacy of their roles in society to be willing to collaborate with independent researchers who sought to examine them in a comparative context. I believe that it is the fact that most of the opinion makers perceived themselves as *legitimate* occupiers of positions holding *legitimate* authority in their society that made possible their participation in the project.

The group studied is composed of the leaders of six relatively arbitrarily defined sectors of Yugoslav political and public life.[2] A rather detailed examination of the six groups is necessary here since the designation of six groups of opinion makers, although of unequal weight and importance, already assumed a degree of institutional pluralism in Yugoslavia in 1968–69, and therefore the relevance of such a sample. The groups examined were federal legislators, federal administrators, mass organization leaders, economic administrators, mass communicators, and intellectuals. At the time of the study it had already become evident that taking a sample on only the federal level would mean leaving out a number of major figures because they operated primarily on the level of their republics. Nevertheless, since our concern was with the state opinion-making processes, with all the limitations that implies, the study turned out to be relevant as constructed. The time period chosen also appears to be critical, since evidence is accumulating that in the years since the study the process of pensioning off and retiring segments of the old leadership and replacing them with new cadres has accelerated. Thus we studied the Yugoslav leaders at an important crossroads for the old revolutionary leadership.

To return to the sample, two of the groups can be viewed as explicitly political—the legislators and the mass organization leaders. Two of the groups are primarily administrators—the federal

2. Charles Kadushin and Peter Abrams, "Social Structure of Yugoslav Opinion-Makers, Part 1, Informal Leadership," chapter 6 of Barton, Denitch, and Kadushin, *Opinion-Making Elites.*

administrators and the economic leaders. And two of the groups are basically communicators, operating on different levels—the mass communicators and intellectuals. This division is approximate since in a number of ways the federal administrators resemble the two explicitly political sectors more than the economic leaders.

Military personnel, as well as the top twenty political leaders, by a rough and arbitrary count, were excluded from the sample because of difficulty of access. However, the sociometric measures in the survey showed that our "head count" had been accurate: our interviews had begun with number twenty-one in the prestige hierachy as perceived by the sample itself. Two further qualifications need to be made. The explicitly political groups are subject to the process of rotation and therefore represent a shifting group; however, rotation occurs roughly at the same hierarchical level where they were interviewed. On the other hand, the permanent civil servants, intellectuals, and journalists are not subject to that process. Further, the federal character of the sample is explicit and formal in the case of the political groups but not in the case of the economic administrators, mass communicators, and intellectuals. There are exceptions to this last generalization; for example, some of the economic leaders are planners and advisers operating on a federal level, but by and large intellectuals, mass communicators, and economic leaders become federally important or are perceived as operating on a federal level because of achievement, whereas the legislators, administrators, and mass organization leaders were picked by virtue of their formal function. Thus there may be other equally important (or more important) figures in the latter categories who were not included in the sample, while in the case of the nonpolitical groups, because the formal and informal criteria are identical, this is not true. Finally, if the study were to be repeated today, a number of functions on the federal level would have to be redefined since they have been legislated out of existence by the increasing decentralization.

All these factors notwithstanding, the sample of opinion makers represents a good cross section of the politically and socially significant leaders of Yugoslavia operating on the statewide level, and an examination of it yields significant information about the working of that political system and its norms.

Social Background of the Opinion Makers

Although published findings from the study indicate that social and economic background was not the major factor determining the behavior and attitudes of the Yugoslav opinion leaders, that background is an indicator of the rapidity of social change and the type of political mobility that resulted from the Yugoslav revolution. It therefore merits at least cursory examination.

Table A-1 shows that the economic background of the top opinion leaders of Yugoslavia is predominantly manual labor, with the respondents' fathers being either workers or peasants in over half of the cases for all groups except the intellectuals and mass communicators. In the latter two groups a majority of respondents had parents in nonmanual occupations, and these groups show the greatest extent of social reproduction by previously educated strata. The only political group that shows a significant proportion of respondents with a nonmanual work background is the federal administrators, 40 percent of whose fathers had nonmanual occupations. They are also the oldest of the six groups. The case of the federal administrators is explained in part by the fact that a number of them appear to have been technical experts indispensable to the establishment of a complex governmental structure. The case of the journalists and intellectuals is clear since their particular role in society requires verbal skills and symbol manipulation, both of which correlate with intellectual background. Not surprisingly, the largest group of working-class origin is found among economic leaders, reflecting the fact that part of the economic elite of Yugoslavia was recruited from the class-conscious communist worker activists.

However, as is discussed also in chapter 5, the general socioeconomic background of these opinion makers should be viewed merely as a result of the fact that the victorious Yugoslav Communist Party, after taking power, had to promote cadres rapidly into positions previously occupied by the defeated ruling strata, and that quite naturally a substantial proportion of these new appointees came from peasant and working-class backgrounds. Incidentally, it has been remarked by historians of the Yugoslav revolution that large numbers of students were involved in the Partisan detachments and the prewar party. The figures in table A-1 suggest that a substantial proportion of the students who participated in the Partisan War

Table A-1

Occupations of Fathers of Public Opinion Makers

Father's Occupation	Legislators	Federal Administrators	Mass Organizers	Economic Leaders	Mass Communicators	Intellectuals	Total
Nonmanual work	26.1%	40.0%	26.3%	22.4%	50.4%	58.6%	39.2%
Worker	35.4 ⎫ 69.2	33.3 ⎫ 57.7	40.8 ⎫ 68.4	44.4 ⎫ 71.6	24.8 ⎫ 43.6	29.8 ⎫ 39.4	34.0 ⎫ 56.1
Peasant	33.8 ⎭	24.4 ⎭	27.6 ⎭	27.2 ⎭	18.8 ⎭	9.6 ⎭	22.1 ⎭
Other	4.6	2.2	5.2	6.0	8.0	2.0	4.7
	100.0%	100.0%	100.0%	100.0%	100.0%	100.0%	100.0%
N:	(65)	(90)	(76)	(81)	(101)	(104)	(517)

SOURCE: Vesna Popovic, "Social Structure and Mobility of Public Opinion-Makers" (mimeo., Belgrade: Institute of Social Science, 1970).

Table A-2

Educational Background of Opinion Makers
and Their Fathers

	Opinion Makers	Fathers
No schooling	1.1%	7.5%
Elementary school (4 yrs.)	4.2	55.6
Gymnasium	14.1	4.4
Other secondary school (trade, etc.)	5.6	16.2
University	75.0	16.3

SOURCE: Popovic.

went into intellectual professions after the victory, and that the party consciously recruited workers and peasants from its ranks for the top political positions.

Data on the educational background of the opinion makers permit two generalizations. First, table A-2 shows a dramatic rise in the educational level of the opinion makers over that of their fathers: the percentage of university-educated respondents is 75 percent compared to 16.3 percent of their fathers. These figures, when broken down by groups, as in table A-3, show a universal spread of university education among the opinion makers, which needs to be qualified in several ways. To begin with, the figures shown understate, if anything, the educational level of the opinion leaders since at least in the case of one group—the mass organization leaders—10 percent of the respondents were still completing their university education when the survey was conducted. Second, the figures show real university degrees and not the more general "acknowledged" university degree.[3] Only those respondents are included who have a degree from a specific faculty, and have done at least four years of university studies. Party schools and military academies are not included, since they do not have university status.

The picture is even clearer when we break down the university education by the type of degree, as is done in table A-4. The general conclusion based on an examination of the educational background, particularly if one controls for age, is that the path into the leading

3. Yugoslav legislation gave those who had participated in the war of liberation from the very beginning the right to claim a university education, even when they did not have one, for the purpose of getting a job.

Table A-3

Educational Background of Opinion Makers, by Group

Education	Legislators	Federal Administrators	Mass Organizers	Economic Leaders	Mass Communicators	Intellectuals	Total*
No schooling	1.5%	0.0%	0.0%	1.2%	2.0%	1.0%	1.0% (5)
Elementary school	9.3	2.2	10.5	3.7	1.0	1.9	4.2 (22)
Gymnasium	18.5	8.9	25.0	2.5	23.8	7.7	14.1 (73)
Other secondary school	4.6	5.6	7.9	6.2	6.9	2.9	5.6 (29)
University	66.2	83.3	56.6	86.4	66.3	86.5	75.0 (388)
	100.0%	100.0%	100.0%	100.0%	100.0%	100.0%	100.0%
N:	(65)	(90)	(76)	(81)	(10?)	(104)	(517)

SOURCE: Popovic.

NOTES: X^2 is significant on the level of 001; C = 35.

Table A-4

University Training Completed by Opinion Makers

	Legislators	Federal Administrators	Mass Organizers	Economic Leaders	Mass Communicators	Intellectuals	Total
Natural and technical sciences	9.1%	11.8%	4.3%	37.5%	2.8%	11.0%	13.5% (54)
Law	40.9	46.1	15.2	18.1	33.8	19.8	28.8 (115)
Economics	13.6	22.4	28.3	26.4	1.4	11.0	16.5 (66)
Administration and political schools	27.3	6.6	23.9	2.8	25.4	3.3	12.8 (51)
Humanities	2.3	7.9	23.9	2.8	28.2	51.6	21.8 (87)
Others and unknown	6.8	5.2	4.3	12.5	8.5	3.3	6.8 (27)
	100.0%	100.0%	100.0%	100.0%	100.0%	100.0%	100.0%
N:	(44)	(76)	(46)	(72)	(71)	(91)	(400)

SOURCE: Popovic.

NOTES: X^2 is significant at the level of 001; C = 56.

positions in Yugoslavia increasingly includes formal university training and that this training in the case of the existing leadership often took place after they had begun a political career. Perhaps even more significant is the finding that, even in the explicitly political groups, the political schools and schools of administration on the university level are a minor recruiter for leading positions, and that the major faculties producing political and social leaders in Yugoslavia are still the faculties of law, humanities, and economics—faculties that are firmly integrated into the university system and where the professional training is in the hands of relatively depoliticized experts. The political faculties and administrative schools within the universities seem to be producing secondary cadre and are apparently designed for the adult training of persons who need university degrees in local and regional administration. Incidentally, the Yugoslav social scientists working on this study were themselves taken aback by the extent of university education among the opinion leaders, particularly by the high (86.4) percentage of economic leaders who have university degrees. One of the most common stereotypes among Yugoslav intellectuals, which has persisted for years, is of a political and above all economic elite that is crude and half-literate, and basically occupies its position by virtue of wartime achievements.

Wartime achievements and the appropriate party career were a major factor in the recruitment of the Yugoslav opinion-making elite. Chapter 5 discussed the effect of party-league seniority and participation in the war of liberation on the political careers of Yugoslav opinion leaders. It only remains to underline two additional factors. First, as shown by table A-5, except for the intellectuals, a "mere" 70 percent of whom are in the League of Communists, membership in the league is all but universal on this level; furthermore, this membership dates from the earliest possible moment for most of the respondents. Therefore, the opinion makers are simultaneously the societal political elite of Yugoslavia and the league elite.

These data on the sample of Yugoslav opinion makers indicate that, although the backgrounds of the opinion makers were relatively heterogeneous, their political socialization was as homogeneous as could have been expected in a population representing several generations. The common league background should not obscure the

Table A-5

Membership in the League of Communists

	Legis-lators	Federal Adminis-trators	Mass Organizers	Economic Leaders	Mass Communi-cators	Intellec-tuals	Total
Members	100%	97.8%	98.7%	98.8%	94.1%	70.2%	92.0% (476)
Nonmembers	—	2.2	1.3	1.2	5.9	29.8	8.0 (41)
	100%	100.0%	100.0%	100.0%	100.0%	100.0%	100.0%
N:	(65)	(90)	(76)	(81)	(101)	(104)	(517)

SOURCE: "Codebook Yugoslav Opinion Makers" (mimeo, New York: Bureau of Applied Social Research, Columbia University, 1970).

fact that the sample represents a group of persons who have had vastly different experiences, ranging from membership in a hunted illegal party before the war to joining a ruling party. However, the findings of Allen Barton and Dragan Pantic are reasonably clear on the fact that the relevant socialization within the Yugoslav opinion-making elite takes place not on the age cohort line but rather on the basis of functional distribution and specialization, that is, occupation.[4] This generalization is qualified by one factor—the relatively large number of divergent functions held by those in the political sector of the opinion makers. The intellectuals have tended to specialize earlier and to enter fairly well-defined careers, whereas the political leaders have apparently been assigned to various tasks as the needs of society became more and more complex.

Table A-6 gives another part of the picture. Here all jobs held by the opinion makers throughout their careers have been grouped into categories and totaled up. Some degree of specialization appears to exist. The mass communicators show the highest level of specialization: 69.6 percent of the total jobs held by this group were in the field of mass communications. As for the intellectuals, 57.9 percent of the total of 408 jobs were in their specific field. The only similarly high figure for other groups is for the federal administrators, who show 58 percent of a total of 555 jobs in the field of administration; but one should add that these jobs varied in character and function and, above all, in level.

Further breakdowns by professional background show the highest degree of interchange to be among the explicitly political sectors, with legislators and mass organization leaders and some of the higher administrators shifting among these sectors roughly on the line legislature-political administration-league leadership. That is, the tops of those three pyramids appear to be occupied by persons whose careers have not jelled in any one specific area; absent from the picture is the phenomenon more familiar to East European specialists—a party career limited to posts within the party organization. This is the meaning, and it is a very limited meaning, of the Yugoslav emphasis on deprofessionalizing politics. On the higher

4. Allen H. Barton, "Determinants of Leadership Attitudes in a Socialist Society," Barton, Denitch, and Kadushin, *Opinion-Making Elites*; and Dragan Pantic, *Stavovi stvaraoca mnenja u Jugoslaviji* (Belgrade: Institut Drustvenih Nauka, 1970).

Table A-6

Employment Background of Opinion Makers

Type of Job	Legislators	Federal Administrators	Mass Organizers	Economic Leaders	Mass Communicators	Intellectuals	Total	
Economy	6.6%	4.7%	7.5%	45.8%	1.7%	3.2%	11.2%	(304)*
Social Services	5.6	10.6	1.4	11.3	1.9	2.9	5.9	(159)
Government administration (republic or federal)	42.4	58.0	31.6	27.2	8.3	7.7	30.4	(825)
Political organization	30.7	11.9	40.8	8.2	12.1	5.2	17.8	(483)
Art, culture, education	5.3	4.7	4.4	4.2	3.8	57.9	12.5	(340)
Mass communications	1.6	2.0	5.6	0.5	69.6	18.4	16.4	(445)
Security	7.3	6.1	7.8	2.3	1.5	2.0	4.5	(123)
Other	0.5	2.0	0.9	0.5	1.1	2.7	1.3	(35)
	100.0%	100.0%	100.0%	100.0%	100.0%	100.0%	100.0%	
N:	(427)	(555)	(425)	(430)	(469)	(408)		(2,714)

SOURCE: Vesna Popovic, "Svaraoci mnenja i njihove drustvene uloge," *Socioloski Pregled*, fall 1970.

levels a political career is apparently considered broadly, and one does not move up through regularized bureaucratic channels in well-defined hierarchies.

Since these social background and career lines probably represent an unrepeatable pattern unique to the generation that took and consolidated state power, the more interesting question about the Yugoslav opinion leaders concerns the interconnections among the functional sectors, or the linkages between the six hierarchical pyramids described. In order to get an approximation of these linkages, the study used the instrument designed by Charles Kadushin which has been employed in other elite studies since then. This was an application of sociometry to the study of elites, and, one must immediately add, an application the success of which surprised the entire working team conducting the study. Five sociometric questions were asked:[5]

Q.76. What three people do you consider most influential in the process of discussion of the most important political questions?

Q.77. Could you tell us the names of three people who have had the greatest influence on your opinions on the most essential problems in your field?

Q.78. With what three people in the past month have you most often had discussions about problems in your field?

Q.79. With what three people in the last month have you most often discussed important questions of general significance?

Q.80. Taking into consideration the aims of this investigation, could you suggest to us some person in your field whom we should interview?

The average response rate on the questions was 95.6 percent, a very high rate for this type of question in any study, and a surprisingly high rate for a politicized population aware of the fact that the study was an international one.

Kadushin and Peter Abrams have written in some detail about the responses to these questions, singling out certain facts of general significance. The sample of 517 persons interviewed named only 1,436 persons in their responses to all five questions. Of these 1,436,

5. Kadushin and Abrams, "Social Structure."

19 percent were already in the sample and another 21 percent were in the universe of opinion makers as defined by the study. That is, 40 percent of the persons named were in the universe, indicating reasonably close agreement between the opinion leaders and the study team on the relevant universe. The 60 percent not included in the universe defined by the study represent a relatively wide scatter, only 13 percent being mentioned by two or more respondents, whereas 52 percent of those in the universe were named by two or more people, showing that the list of persons in the universe was of an altogether different quality from the other names mentioned.[6]

Without going further into the highly technical data obtained by the sociometric questions, I will introduce some charts that give a general picture of the linkages present. Figure 1 graphically presents the responses to question 76, that is, the persons perceived as generally influential, and shows some rather surprising details. Three of the groups appear to think well of themselves: 54, 35, and 26 percent of the persons named by the mass organization leaders, legislators, and intellectuals, respectively, were in their own field. This can be taken as cold realism in the case of the first two, and a not unusual self-confidence in the case of the intellectuals. Neither the federal administrators nor the economic leaders appear to think of themselves as being generally influential, an opinion shared by the other four groups. This is, at the very least, a curious finding, in the light of the discussion current at the time of the interviews of the influence of technocracy, and, when one combines that with the general consensus by all groups on the centrality of the two political sectors, it appears to confirm Svetozar Stojanovic's description of Yugoslavia as being more like a politocracy than a technocracy on the top level.[7]

The centrality of the two political sectors should not obscure the fact that the mass organization leaders are more important than the legislators to the opinion leaders as a whole, with the exception of the federal administrators, for whom, for obvious professional reasons, figures in the legislature are often more directly influential.

6. Ibid.

7. Svetozar Stojanovic, "Jugoslovensi socijalizam na raskrscu," *Praxis* 9, nos. 3–4 (1972).

If the study were repeated today, the mass organizational group would appear, if anything, more powerful.

The other significant finding illustrated in figure 1 is the relatively high number of persons named by economic leaders who are outside the universe—32 percent. On closer examination many seem to be regional, i.e., republic or commune, leaders, who are apparently more important to the economic leaders than is the federal center, reflecting the high degree of decentralization already achieved in the economic field by 1968–69.

Figure 2 gives a description of influence in one's own field as perceived by the opinion leaders. Question 77 produced a greater scatter of responses, if for no other reason than the more specialized nature of the influence measured. Incidentally, this particular question acted as an important self-correcting feature in the sampling since it showed at least ten persons who should have been included in the sample by virtue of position and were therefore added by nomination. Again, we get a picture of the centrality of the mass organization leaders, although the spread is wider, and it becomes evident that the mass communicators and intellectuals are also primarily oriented toward their own professional grouping in terms of persons they perceive as influential.

A general point should be made concerning both charts: for the federal administrators, legislators, and organization leaders, "one's own field" should probably be defined as politics per se, rather than as the specific functional position of the respondent, since in all probability that field is not conceptualized by the respondent along strict organizational lines.

Sociometric questions have a number of uses, and for our purposes one of the more directly relevant results is the picture it allows the opinion leaders to give us of the nature and composition of the "top" of their own society. Questions 76–80 can be grouped into interactional and reputational questions, which naturally give somewhat different hierarchies. The reputational questions generated a list of 21 names, including 2 dead persons; the interactional questions produced a list of 19 persons, all living. The nationality makeup of the nineteen persons on the latter list was 7 Serbs, 6 Croats, 3 Slovenes, 2 Macedonians, and 1 Montenegrin; this breakdown is a convincing argument that, even without the use of a national "key"

Fig. 1 Percentage of Different Persons Mentioned by Each Group as Generally Influential According to the Sector of the Person Mentioned[*] (Question 76)

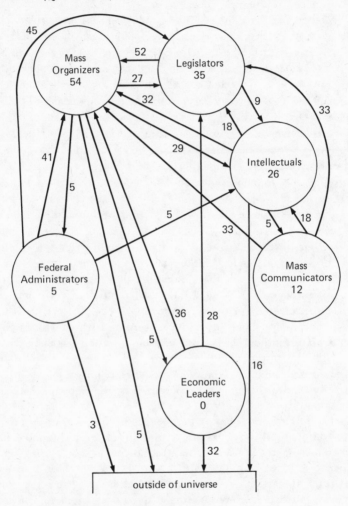

SOURCE: Kadushin and Abrams, p. 169.

[*]Figures under 5 percent omitted. Own sector within circle.

Fig. 2 Percentage of Different Persons Mentioned by Each Group as Generally Influential in Own Field According to the Sector of the Person Mentioned[*] (Question 77)

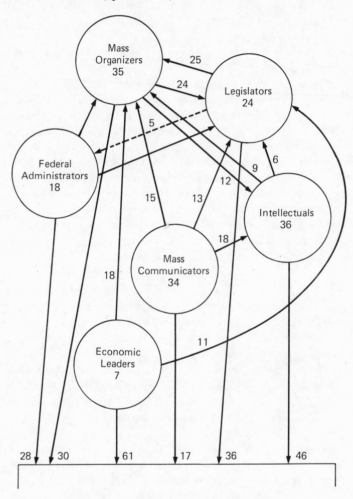

SOURCE: Kadushin and Abrams, p. 173.
[*]Figures under 5 percent omitted. Own sector within circle.

(discussed in chapter 6), the opinion leaders perceive the leadership of Yugoslavia as being multinational, although not necessarily balanced in proportion to the size of the nationalities making up the federation.

When the separate reputational and interactional lists are merged, the result is a "top 21" list of persons who can be examined from a variety of viewpoints in order to clarify the situation in Yugoslavia in 1968–69. With one exception, the group is composed exclusively of members of the League of Communists. One joined as "late" as 1945.[8] Most joined before the war and had been active throughout the war and the resistance. More remarkable in this rarefied height is the presence of three intellectuals who function as intellectuals—two authors and one university professor. The list is highly stratified in terms of the number of nominations, the steps going as follows: the person receiving the highest number of nominations (416) was a Croat; the second highest number (290) went to a Slovene. Next were four persons who had over 100 nominations each: a Croat, a Montenegrin, a Macedonian, and a Serb, all political leaders functioning primarily in league bodies at the federal level.

The third layer or step is composed of six persons: one, a league theoretician, had died recently; the others were leaders primarily in their own republics. This group includes one Macedonian, two Serbs, one Croat, and two Slovenes (one dead). They are generationally similar, younger than the top group, and represent that level of the league hierarchy which has had the heaviest number of casualties in the political shifts occurring since 1970. Specifically, out of the five living persons, three have been dropped[9] (or were pushed) from leading league bodies and moved out of a major role on either the federal or republic level.

The remainder, with fewer than 20 nominations each, represent a diverse group of nine persons, eight living, including the three intellectuals already mentioned, two persons who subsequently retired, and four who are still in the hierarchy.

It is my judgment that any list designed today would include the top six, more or less unchanged, and that the basic changes have occurred in the middle level via shifts on the level of the republics.

8. This was an intellectual who had been a party sympathizer since the late 1920s.

9. Some symmetry was maintained in that the three were one Serb, one Croat, and one Slovene.

That is, what was and is unique about the top six is that they basically operate on a suprarepublic level.

More interesting, and confirming the other findings from the sociometric material, is the total absence of any economic leaders, unless one were to include party theoreticians dealing with the problems of the economy on this "top 21" level. The top leadership thus seems to be explicitly political with a slight admixture of critical intellectuals, since all three intellectuals nominated are perceived as critics operating within the general consensus of the Yugoslav political system. On this top level differentiation and the development of independent republic bases has not yet occurred.

ATTITUDES OF YUGOSLAV OPINION MAKERS

Our survey of the opinion makers' attitudes revealed a surprising diversity or range of views among this group of Yugoslavs. The surprising character of this finding is emphasized by the similarity of their political backgrounds and the fact that they overwhelmingly belonged to the League of Communists. At the very least this shows that the opinion leaders were willing to discuss a range of differences they perceived as legitimate within the Yugoslav single-party system, and, one should add, a range that probably represents a semiofficial consensus on the boundaries of political discourse. I say this because it seems incredible that the opinion leaders, limited as they are in number, would trust assurances of the anonymity of any study of themselves. We were therefore getting semipublic views from the opinion leaders on important questions involving policy, attitudes, and definitions of their own role.[10] Allen Barton's paper on leadership attitudes in Yugoslavia goes into considerable detail on the views. Two things seem to stand out in Barton's findings. The first is his assertion that "value socialization for elite respondents is not parental or even based on early political experience but apparently takes place from working in a given field or institutional setting." [11] Second, Barton shows that the considerable variation in policy opinions expressed by opinion leaders follows the lines of institutional setting. He uses five basic scales, each of which is made

10. For a fuller discussion of the nature of the data obtained in this study, see my essay "Elite Interviewing and Social Structure: An Example from Yugoslavia," *Public Opinion Quarterly* 36 (summer 1972).

11. Barton, "Determinants of Leadership Attitudes."

up of a number of questions. The scales are: (1) a freedom of criticism index; (2) an economic development index; (3) a social criticism index; (4) a verbal egalitarianism index; and (5) a wage egalitarianism index.

Table A-7, a composite of these indices, shows that the intellectuals take their role as critics seriously, that economic administrators give the highest priority to economic goals, and that the three political groups are least critical and are the most optimistic in their perception of the level of criticism present in society. An interesting subfinding perhaps anticipated some of the more recent conflicts in Yugoslavia, specifically, the extremely important problem of egalitarianism; for it appeared that the two most explicitly political groups—the mass organization leaders and the legislators—like the intellectuals, favored a more egalitarian policy whereas the federal and economic administrators, those actually carrying out policies, did not.

Barton summarizes his findings in the following way. The positions taken by opinion leaders appear to correspond to the functional problems and goals of the institutions for which they work. Thus,

> intellectuals emphasize freedom to criticize; economic administrators give priority to economic growth; administrators generally favor substantial wage differentials; public officials don't want more press criticism of public officials; and political leaders generally see the public as more satisfied with their major policies than do intellectuals, communicators, and enterprise managers. The mass communicators may be reflecting in their rejection, particularly of the generalized verbal formulation of egalitarianism, their occupational commitment to selling the economic reform with its emphasis on incentives.[12]

This was the picture at the time the study was made. In all probability the spokesmen for the mass media would today be more explicitly egalitarian, as would the public servants, that is, the federal administrators. However, Barton's general point based on the opinion-maker data probably holds, with appropriate modifications; he concludes that there are

12. Ibid.

three basic poles of interest in the occupational structure of Yugoslav society: the economic administrators with their concern for economic growth, the political managers with a concern for maintaining control and avoiding excessive criticism and public discontent, and the intellectuals with their concern for freedom of expression and critical analysis. The mass communicators and the public administrators tend to be the servants of those in power rather than interest-groups in their own right, and do not express distinctive interests or values related to their positions.[13]

If anything, recent events have tended to stress the importance of the primary group in Yugoslav society—the political managers—in alliance with the social base of a growing working class, and to deemphasize those processes which had tended to increase the independence of service groups like the administrators and journalists. What may well be occurring, on the other hand, is a shift within the primary groups themselves, that is, a shift in the composition of the political leadership, reflecting both a generational factor and new and different organizational bases for political leaders, with growing importance attached to trade unions and local republican parties as the leadership formed and shaped as a Yugoslav-wide elite ages and retires.

The two decades of development of self-management have had a profound and long-range effect on the political culture of Yugoslavia. Findings from surveys of workers and the public at large confirm the fact that, although there is criticism of specific practices and abuses, self-management is the respected norm and the most characteristic feature of Yugoslav socialism.[14] This was also confirmed in the study of opinion leaders, who were asked, among many other things, what they thought were the major achievements of Yugoslav socialism. The question was broken down into three parts: What were the major achievements of Yugoslav socialism (1) for Yugoslavia proper, (2) as an example to developing countries, and (3) as a contribution to socialist theory? In all three cases, self-management, either in the economy or in the polity, was most

13. Ibid.
14. See the section in chapter 7 on survey data, particularly the Zvonarevic survey results.

Table A-7

Policy Opinions of Opinion Leaders

	Mass Organi-zers (76)	Legis-lators (65)	Federal Adminis-trators (90)	Economic Adminis-trators (81)	Mass Communi-cators (101)	Intellec-tuals (104)
Freedom of criticism:						
Press not critical enough of:						
Injustices to individuals by government agencies	54%	63%	51	56%	54%	77%
Bureaucratic attitude of government agencies	68	71	66	69	51	73
Mistakes by high officials	83	75	80	80	87	93
Abuses by enterprises	59	59	62	66	52	68
There should be no penalty for political attack on a prominent figure	22	22	48	25	39	52
Freedom of criticism index: high score	44	34	34	42	33	78
Priority of economic goals:						
Rank economic development first among list of 8 values and ideals	26%	31%	28%	53%	13%	12%
Rank economic development in first 3	45	51	47	76	39	25
Long-term economic development should be most important goal	82	78	83	93	77	64
High standard of living should be most important goal of society	71	72	72	85	60	38
Economic development index: high score	55	65	56	88	50	26

Perceived criticism:

	67%	77%	68%	64%	56%	38%

	67%	77%	68%	64%	56%	38%
Public is very satisfied with foreign policy	67%	77%	68%	64%	56%	38%
Public is satisfied with:						
Realization of economic reform	51	30	39	26	41	11
Standard of living	24	16	16	12	21	13
Present state of relations between nationalities	40	37	54	23	28	21
What two factors do majority of people consider most important for advancement: *Critical answers:**						
Luck	5	8	4	5	7	7
Personal relationships and acquaintances	55	57	61	52	63	73
Family connections	7	14	3	6	15	12
Social criticism index: high score	37	37	36	56	54	74
Verbal egalitarianism:						
Differences in income should be increased	65%	72%	60%	69%	42%	68%
Should be upper limit so no one can earn much more than others	47	47	51	62	27	59
Worker's son doesn't have chance to advance	30	43	49	32	43	56
Rank "refuse to accept differences based on social and economic inequalities"						
1st, 2d, or 3d	51	53	57	41	49	65
Verbal egalitarianism index: high score	53	60	47	52	32	65

Table A-7—Continued

	Mass Organizers (76)	Legislators (65)	Federal Administrators (90)	Economic Administrators (81)	Mass Communicators (101)	Intellectuals (104)
Wage egalitarianism:						
What should be salary of various professions:						
Ratio of factory director to unskilled worker: under 4.5 to 1	57%	66%	48%	54%	53%	59%
Ratio of professor to elementary school teacher: under 2.5 to 1	51	36	32	38	52	54
Ratio of cabinet member to white-collar worker: under 3.5 to 1	56	51	34	29	56	67
Ratio of precision machinist to unskilled worker: under 2.0 to 1	54	58	46	44	50	55
Wage egalitarianism index: high score	50	55	34	34	49	58

SOURCE: Barton, "Determinants."

NOTES: Underline: highest figure. Broken line: lowest figure.

* Favorable answers included personal ability (41%) and formal qualifications (27%).

often cited. For Yugoslavia proper, designation of self-management as the first choice ranged from a high of 72.3 percent for the legislators to 53.8 percent for intellectuals. Furthermore, the second and third choices, namely, freedom and socialist democracy, and the solution of the national question, were not unrelated.[15]

In contrast, the opinion leaders did not view self-management *in industry* as an exportable item for underdeveloped countries. There the answers ranged from 27.3 percent for economic leaders to 16.8 percent for journalists and mass communicators. For underdeveloped countries, *political* self-management and economic development were considered to be the Yugoslav models worth emulating.

In the field of theory, again self-management was regarded as the major Yugoslav contribution, 58.2 percent emphasizing industrial self-management and 27.1 percent communal self-management. Interestingly enough, intellectuals were again the least enthusiastic, although a substantial majority did pick self-management.

These findings should be considered in their proper context. There is in most societies a gap between normative descriptions of the system and its performance. However, the leaders of Yugoslav society clearly agreed in 1968–69 that the major innovation of Yugoslav socialism was self-management. All major economic, political, and social reforms since that period have basically concentrated on working out the kinks and details of a system to which they are generally committed.

The relative diversity found among the top Yugoslav opinion leadership may well provide a degree of flexibility in policy formulation within a general line. Thus one constant is that various detailed economic and social policies are open to a variety of approaches and emphases. This in turn means that the ruling position of the League of Communists within Yugoslav society is not that intimately and specifically linked to any given economic policy and thus shifts in economic policy are not necessarily accompanied by shifts in the party elite. Criticism of a given economic policy is therefore not automatically an attack on the league and its leadership. In other words, the political elite has delineated the area

15. Data from International Study of Opinion Makers, "Codebook for the Yugoslav Project" (mimeo., New York: Columbia University, Bureau of Applied Social Research, April 1969), question 12. Percentages are based on total responses to this question, excluding "Do not know," "no answer," etc.

of its exclusive competence far more narrowly than party organizations in other East European states. This means that it is less likely to clash with technical experts, economists, and intellectuals over matters where expertise is required. Tension continually exists between critics and the political leadership since the boundaries of criticism are not institutionally and explicitly identified, and therefore there is always the possibility that criticism which is called for and legitimate at one point may transgress the ill-defined boundary at another. This uncertainty, however, is a price Yugoslav society pays for its undoubted dynamism, and the resulting strains are felt not merely by intellectuals who see themselves as critics. They are also extended to groups more sheltered in East European one-party systems—the state officials and the political organization leaders, who in Yugoslavia are repeatedly reminded of the fact that simply serving time and implementing a line is exceedingly difficult in a society where the line is not explicitly and clearly defined. Simply stated, the element of uncertainty that so troubles intellectual critics in Yugoslavia also keeps much of the party and governmental bureaucracy on its toes, and the rules of the game of Yugoslav politics demand from aspirants to leading positions considerably more than bureaucratic routine.

Bibliography

Acimovic, J. *Bibliografija o radnickom samoupravljanju.* Belgrade: Institut Drustvenih Nauka, 1968.

Adizes, Ichak. *Industrial Democracy Yugoslav Style.* New York: Free Press, 1971.

Almond, Gabriel A., and Verba, Sidney. *The Civic Culture.* Princeton: Princeton University Press, 1963.

Apter, David E. *The Politics of Modernization.* Chicago: University of Chicago Press, 1965.

Arendt, Hannah. *On Revolution.* New York: Viking Press, 1970.

————. *The Origins of Totalitarianism.* Rev. ed. New York: Harcourt, Brace, 1966.

Autogestion (Paris).

Avakumovich, Ivan. *History of the Communist Party of Yugoslavia.* 2 vols. Aberdeen: Aberdeen University Press, 1964.

Azrael, Jeremy R. *Managerial Power and Soviet Politics.* Cambridge: Harvard University Press, 1966.

Bacevic, Ljiljana. *Jugoslovensko javno mnenje o omladini i religiji.* Belgrade: Institut Drustvenih Nauka, 1969.

Barber, Bernard, and Inkeles, Alex, eds. *Stability and Change.* New York: Harcourt, Brace & World, 1972.

Barnes, Samuel. *Party Democracy.* New Haven: Yale University Press, 1967.

Barringer, H. R., et al., eds. *Social Change in Developing Areas.* Cambridge, Mass.: Schenkman Publishing Co., 1965.

Barton, Allen H. "Determinants of Leadership Attitudes in a Socialist Society." In *Opinion-Making Elites in Yugoslavia,* ed. Allen H. Barton, Bogdan Denitch, and Charles Kadushin. New York: Praeger Special Series, 1973.

————; Denitch, Bogdan; and Kadushin, Charles, eds. *Opinion-Making Elites in Yugoslavia.* New York: Praeger Special Series, 1973.

Bendix, Reinhard. *Nation-Building and Citizenship.* New York: John Wiley, 1964.

Bienen, Henry. *Violence and Social Change.* Chicago: University of Chicago Press, 1968.

Bilandjic, Dusan. *Borba za samoupravni socijalizam u Jugoslaviji, 1945–1969.* Zagreb: RAD, 1969.

Black, Cyril E. *The Dynamics of Modernization: A Study in Comparative History.* New York: Harper & Row, 1966.

Blumberg, Paul. *Industrial Democracy.* New York: Schocken, 1969.

Borba. Special suppl. January 24, 1970.

Bosnjak, Branko, ed. *Religija i drustvo.* Zagreb: RAD, 1969.

Broekmeyer, M. J., ED. *Yugoslav Workers' Self-Management.* Dordrecht, Netherlands: D. Reidel, 1970.

Brzezinski, Zbigniew, and Huntington, Samuel P. *Political Power: USA/USSR.* New York: Viking Press, 1964.

Burks, R. V. *The Dynamics of Communism in Eastern Europe.* Princeton: Princeton University Press, 1961.

———. "The National Problem and the Future of Yugoslavia." Mimeographed. Santa Monica, Cal.: Rand Corporation, October 1971.

Cartwright, D., ed. *Studies in Social Power.* Ann Arbor: University of Michigan Press, 1959.

Clissold, Stephen. *A Short History of Yugoslavia.* Cambridge: Cambridge University Press, 1966.

———. *Whirlwind: The Rise of Marshal Tito to Power.* New York: Cresset, 1949. *Codebook for the Yugoslav Project.* International Study of Opinion-Makers. Belgrade: Institut Drustvenih Nauka, April 1969.

Cohen, Lenard. "Social Background and Recruitment of Yugoslav Political Elites, 1918–1949." In *Opinion-Making Elites in Yugoslavia,* ed. Allen H. Barton, Bogdan Denitch, and Charles Kadushin. New York: Praeger Special Series, 1973.

Coser, Lewis. *The Functions of Conflict.* New York: Free Press, 1956.

Cvijic, Jovan. *Balkansko poluostrvo.* Belgrade: Srpska Knjizjevna Zadruga, 1969.

Dahl, Robert. *After the Revolution.* New Haven: Yale University Press, 1972.

———. *A Preface to Democratic Theory.* Chicago: University of Chicago Press, 1956.

Dahrendorf, Rolf. *Class and Class Conflict in Industrial Society*. Stanford: Stanford University Press, 1959.

Dallin, Alexander, and Breslauer, George. *Political Terror in Communist Systems*. Stanford: Stanford University Press, 1970.

Daniel, Robert. *The Conscience of the Revolution*. New York: Simon & Schuster, 1960.

Dedijer, Vladimir. *The Battle Stalin Lost*. New York: Universal Library, 1972.

———. *Sarajevo*. New York: Random House, 1968.

———. *Tito*. New York: Simon & Schuster, 1953.

——— et al. *History of Yugoslavia*. New York: McGraw-Hill, 1974.

Denich, Bette. "Social Environment and Economic Niches." Mimeographed. Proceedings of the Sixty-Ninth Annual Meeting, American Anthropological Association, 1970.

———. "Social Mobility in a Yugoslav Town." Ph.D. diss., University of California, Berkeley, 1969.

Denitch, Bogdan. "Codebook: Comparative National Development." Mimeographed. University of California, Berkeley: Institute on International Affairs, 1966.

———. "Elite Interviewing and Social Structure: An Example from Yugoslavia." *Public Opinion Quarterly* 36 (summer 1972).

———. "Is There a New Working Class?" In *Workers' Control*, ed. Gerry Hunnius. New York: Random House, 1973.

———. "Mobility and Recruitment of Yugoslav Leadership." In *Proceedings of the World Congress of the International Political Science Association*. Munich, 1970.

———. "Political Cultures and Social Mobility." In "Proceedings of the World Congress of the International Sociological Association." Mimeographed. Varna, 1970.

———. "Religion and Social Change in Yugoslavia." In "The International Symposium on Religion and Atheism in Communist Societies." Mimeographed. Ottawa, 1971.

de Schweinitz, Karl, Jr. "Growth, Development and Political Modernization." *World Politics* 22, no. 4 (July 1970).

Diruković, Borislav. "Učeše seljaka komunista." *Sociologija Sela* 8, nos. 27–28 (1970).

Djilas, Milovan. *Conversations with Stalin*. New York: Praeger, 1958.

———. *The New Class*. New York: Praeger, 1957.

Djodan, Sime. "Gdje dr. Stripe Suvar 'pronalzai' nationalizam a gdje ga ne vide." *Kolo*, no. 7 (1969).

Djordjevic, Jovan. *Politicki sistem*. Belgrade: Savezna Admistracija, 1970.

———. *Ustavno pravo*. Belgrade: Savezna Admistracija, 1970.

Dokumentacija Savezne Skupstine. Belgrade: Savezna Admistracija, 1969.

Dumont, Rene, and Mazoyer, Marcel. *Development and Socialism*. New York: Praeger, 1972.

Durham, Mary Edith. *Through the Lands of the Serbs*. London: E. Arnold, 1904.

Durkheim, Emile. *Division of Labor in Society*. New York: Free Press, 1970.

Dzinic, Firdus, ed. *Stvaraoci mnenja u Jugoslaviji*. Belgrade: Institut Drustvenih Nauka, 1969.

Eckstein, Alexander. "Economic Development and Political Change in Communist Systems." *World Politics* 22, no. 4 (July 1970).

Eckstein, Harry, ed. *Internal War*. New York: Macmillan, 1964.

Eisenstadt, S. N. *Modernization: Protest and Change*. Englewood Cliffs, N.J.: Prentice-Hall, 1966.

Ekonomist. Special ed., Zagreb, 1969.

Etzioni, Amitai. *A Sociological Reader on Complex Organizations*. New York: Holt, Rinehart & Winston, 1969.

Farrell, R. Barry, ed. *Political Leadership in Eastern Europe and in the Soviet Union*. Chicago: Aldine, 1970.

Fisher, Jack. *Yugoslavia: A Multi-National State*. New York: Chandler, 1966.

Fleron, Frederick J., ed. *Communist Studies and the Social Sciences*. Chicago: Rand McNally, 1969.

Friedrich, Carl, and Brzezinski, Zbigniew. *Totalitarian Dictatorship and Autocracy*. Rev. ed. Cambridge: Harvard University Press, 1965.

———; Curtis, Michael; and Barber, Benjamin. *Totalitarianism in Perspective: Three Views*. New York: Praeger, 1969.

Gellner, Ernest. "The Pluralist Anti-Levelers of Prague." *Dissent*, summer 1972.

Gitelman, Zvi. "Beyond Leninism: Political Development in Eastern Europe." *Newsletter on Comparative Studies of Communism* 5, no. 3 (March 1972).

———. "Power and Authority in Eastern Europe." In *Change in*

Communist Systems, ed. Chalmers Johnson. Stanford: Stanford University Press, 1970.

Gouldner, Alvin. *The Coming Crisis in Western Sociology.* New York: Avon, 1971.

Gramsci, A. *The Modern Prince and Other Essays.* New York: International Publishers, 1970.

———. *Soviets in Italy.* London: Institute for Workers' Control, 1973.

Gurr, T. R. *Why Men Rebel.* Princeton: Princeton University Press, 1971.

Halpern, Joel. "Modernization." In *Contemporary Yugoslavia*, ed. Wayne S. Vucinich. Berkeley: University of California Press, 1969.

Hammel, Eugene A. *The Pink Yo-yo: Social Prestige and Occupations in Yugoslavia.* Institute on Eastern Europe. Berkeley: University of California Press, 1969.

Harrington, Michael. "The New Working Class." *Dissent*, summer 1970.

Historical Statistics of the U.S. Washington, D.C.: Bureau of Labor Statistics, 1970.

Hobsbawn, Eric. *Social Bandits and Primitive Rebels.* Glencoe, Ill.: Free Press, 1959.

Hoffman, George W., and Neal, Fred Warner. *Yugoslavia and the New Communism.* New York: Twentieth Century Fund, 1962.

Horvat, Branko. *An Essay on Yugoslav Society.* New York: International Arts & Sciences Press, 1970.

———. *Privredni sistem i ekonomska politika Jugoslavije.* Belgrade: Savezna Admistracija, 1969.

Huntington, Samuel. *Political Order in Changing Societies.* New Haven: Yale University Press, 1968.

———, and Moore, Clement H., eds. *Authoritarian Politics in Modern Society: The Dynamics of Established One-Party Systems.* New York: Basic Books, 1970.

Ilic, Pavle. *Sprski narod i njegov jezik.* Belgrade: Srpska Knjizevna Zadruga, 1971.

Inkeles, Alex, and Geiger, K., eds. *Soviet Society.* Cambridge: Cambridge University Press, 1960.

Innovation in Higher Education: Reforms in Yugoslavia. Zagreb: Organization for Economic Cooperation & Development, 1970.

"Intellectuals and Change," *Daedalus* 101, no. 2 (summer 1972).

"Intellectuals and Tradition," *Daedalus* 101, no. 1 (spring 1972).

Ionescu, Ghita. *The Politics of the European Communist States.* New York: Praeger, 1967.

Izborni sistem u uslovima samoupravlijanja. Belgrade: Institut Drustvenih Nauka, 1969.

Janina-Lagneau, Vera. *Education, egalité, et socialisme.* Paris: Anthropos, 1968.

Javno mnenje stanovnistva S.R. hrvatske, 1969. Zagreb: Institut za Drustvena Iztrazivanja, 1970.

Jelavic, Charles, ed. *The Balkans in Transition.* Berkeley: University of California Press, 1963.

Johnson, Chalmers, ed. *Change in Communist Systems.* Stanford: Stanford University Press, 1970.

———. "Civilian Loyalties and Guerrilla Conflicts." *World Politics* 14, no. 4 (July 1962).

———. *Peasant Nationalism and Communist Power: The Emergence of Communist China.* Stanford: Stanford University Press, 1962.

———. *Revolutions in the Social System.* Stanford: Stanford University Press, 1964.

Johnson, Ross. *Transformation of Communist Ideology: The Yugoslav Case, 1945–1953.* Cambridge: MIT Press, 1972.

Jovanov, Neca. "The Relationship between Strikes and Self-Management." In *Proceedings of the First International Conference on Participation and Self-Management,* vol. 1. Zagreb: Institut za Drustvena Iztrazivanja, 1972.

"Jubilarno izdanje drustveno politicke zajednice." In *Federacija,* vol. 1. Belgrade: Interpress, 1968.

Kadushin, Charles, and Abrams, Peter. "Social Structure of Yugoslav Opinion-Makers, Part 1, Informal Leadership." In *Opinion-Making Elites in Yugoslavia,* ed. Allen H. Barton, Bogdan Denitch, and Charles Kadushin. New York: Praeger Special Series, 1973.

Kanet, R., ed. *The Behavioral Revolution and Communist Studies.* New York: Free Press, 1971.

Kardelj, Edvard. *Slovenicko nacijonalno pitanje.* Ljubljana: Cancar, 1953.

Kautsky, K. *The Class Struggle.* Chicago: C. H. Kerr, 1910.

Kautsky, John H. *Communism and the Politics of Development.* New York: John Wiley, 1968.

———. "Patterns of Elite Succession in the Process of Development." *Journal of Politics* 31, no. 2 (May 1969).

Kerner, Robert J., ed. *Yugoslavia.* Berkeley: University of California Press, 1949.

Kochanek, Stanley A. "Perspectives on the Study of Revolution and Social Change." *Comparative Politics* 5, no. 3 (April 1973).

Kolic, Milije N. "Some Basic Features of Yugoslav External Migration." *Yugoslav Survey* 13, no. 1 (February 1972).

Korac, Miladin, et al., eds. *Politika dohotka.* Belgrade: RAD, 1972.

Korbonski, Andrzej. "Comparing Liberalization Processes in Eastern Europe: A Preliminary Analysis." *Comparative Politics* 4, no. 2 (January 1972).

Laird, R. D. "Some Characteristics of the Soviet Leadership System: A Maturing Totalitarian System." *Midwest Journal of Political Science* no. 10 (February 1966).

Lange, Oscar. *Papers in Economy and Sociology.* London: Pergamon, 1970.

LaPalombara, Joseph, ed. *Bureaucracy and Political Development.* Princeton: Princeton University Press, 1963.

————, and Weiner, Myron, eds. *Political Parties and Political Development.* Princeton: Princeton University Press, 1966.

Lenin, Vladimir Ilich. *State and Revolution.* New York: International Publishers, 1932.

————. *What Is to Be Done?* New York: International Publishers, 1933.

Lerner, Daniel, et al. *The Passing of a Traditional Society.* Glencoe: Free Press, 1958.

Linz, Juan J. "An Authoritarian Regime: Spain." In *Cleavages, Ideologies, and Party Systems*, ed. Erik Allard and Yrjo Littunan. Turku: Abo Tidnings och Tryckeri Aktiebolag, 1964.

Lipset, Seymour M. *Political Man.* New York: Doubleday, 1969.

————, and Denitch, Bogdan. "Codebook on Yugoslav Student Survey." Mimeographed. Berkeley: University of California Institute of International Affairs, 1965.

Lord, Albert, and Parry, Milman. *Serbo-Croatian Heroic Ballads.* Cambridge: Harvard University Press, 1953.

Lord, Robert. "The Polish Crisis of the Eighteenth Century." In *Man, State, and Society in East European History*, ed. Stephen Fischer-Galati. New York: Praeger, 1970.

Ludz, Peter. *The Changing Party Elite in East Germany.* Cambridge: MIT Press, 1972.

Lukacs, G. *Early Political Writings*. London: New Left Books, 1972.

―――. *History and Class Consciousness*. Cambridge: MIT Press, 1972.

McClelland, Woodford. "Post-war Political Evolution." In *Contemporary Yugoslavia*, ed. Wayne S. Vucinic. Berkeley: University of California Press, 1969.

Mallet, Serge. *La Nouvelle Classe ouvriere*. Paris: Seuil, 1963.

Marcuse, H. "On Authority." In *Studies in Critical Philosophy*. London: New Left Books, 1972.

―――. *Soviet Marxism*. New York: Vintage Books, 1970.

Marczali, Henry. "The Ruling Class of Hungary." In *Man, State, and Society in East European History*, ed. Stephen Fischer-Galati. New York: Praeger, 1970.

Marx, Karl. *Selected Writing in Sociology and Social Philosophy*, ed. Thomas Bottomore and Maximalien Rubel. Cambridge: Cambridge University Press, 1964.

―――, and Engels, Friedrich. *The Holy Family*. Moscow: Foreign Languages Publishing House, 1954.

Meiser, Albert. *Ou va l'autogestion yougoslave?* Paris: Anthropos, 1970.

―――. *Socialisme et autogestion: L'experience yougoslave*. Paris: Seuil, 1964.

Merton, Robert K. *Social Theory and Social Structure*. New York: Free Press, 1968.

Meyer, Alfred G. "Authority in Communist Political Systems." In *Political Leadership in Industrialized Societies*, ed. Lewis J. Edinger. New York: John Wiley, 1967.

Michels, R. *Political Parties*. Glencoe, Ill.: Free Press, 1948.

Milenkovic, Miodrag. "Razvoj visokoskolskog sistema u Jugoslaviji." *Ideje* 1, no. 2 (Belgrade, 1971).

Milenkovich, Deborah. *Plan and Market in Yugoslav Economic Thought*. New Haven: Yale University Press, 1971.

Montgomery, John D. "The Quest for Political Development." *Comparative Politics* 1, no. 2 (January 1969).

Moore, Barrington. *The Origins of Dictatorship and Democracy*. Boston: Beacon Press, 1970.

―――. *Political Power and Social Theory*. New York: Harper Torchbook, 1965.

―――. *Terror and Progress in the USSR*. Cambridge: Harvard University Press, 1954.

Moore, W. E. "A Reconsideration of Theories of Social Change." *American Sociological Review* 25, no. 6 (December 1960).

———. *Social Change*. Englewood Cliffs, N.J.: Prentice-Hall, 1963.

Moraca, Pero, et al., eds. *Istorija SKJ*. Belgrade: Prosveta, 1965.

Morse, Nancy C., and Weiss, Robert S. "The Function and Meaning of Work." *American Sociological Review* 20 (1955).

Mosca, G. *The Ruling Class*. New York: McGraw-Hill, 1948.

Nase Teme. Special ed., no. 12 (December 1972).

Novak, Grga. *Hrvatska povijest*. Belgrade: Nedeljne Informativne Novine, Jogoslovenska Akademija Nauka, 1908.

Nyrere, Julius. "One-Party Rule." In *The Ideologies of Developing Nations*, ed. Paul E. Sigmund, Jr. New York: Praeger, 1963.

Obradovic, Josip. *Participacija i motivacija u radnickom samoupravljanju*. Zagreb: Institut za Drustvena Iztrazivanja, 1968.

Oppenheimer, Martin. *The Urban Guerrilla*. Chicago: Quadrangle, 1969.

Pantic, Dragan. *Stavovi stvaraoca mnenja u Jugoslaviji*. Belgrade: Institut Drustvenih Nauka, 1970.

Parkin, Frank. *Class Inequality and Political Order*. New York: Praeger, 1971.

Parsons, Talcott. *The System of Modern Societies*. Englewood Cliffs, N.J.: Prentice-Hall, 1967.

Participation and Self-Management, vols. 1–6. Papers of the First International Conference on Participation and Self-Management. Dubrovnik, 1972.

Pecujlic, M. *Buducnost koja je pocela*. Belgrade: Institut za Politicke Studije, 1969.

Perovic, Radosav. "Religious Communities." *Yugoslav Survey* 11, no. 3 (August 1970).

Politika (Belgrade).

Popis Stanovnistva Jugoslavije. Belgrade: Savezni Zavod za Statistiku, 1971.

Popov, Z. "Zemlje najbrzim privrednim razvojom." *Ekonomska Analiza* 1–2 (1967).

Popovic, Vesna. "Social Structure and Mobility of Public Opinion-Makers." Mimeographed. Belgrade: Institute of Social Science, 1970.

———. "Svaraoci mnenja i nkihove drustvene uloge." *Socioloski Pregled*, fall 1970.

Portoroz. *Drustveni konflikti i socijalicki razvoj jugoslavije.* 3 vols. Belgrade: Prosveta, 1972.

Powell, Charles A. "Structural-Functionalism in the Study of Comparative Communist Systems: Some Caveats." *Studies in Comparative Communism* 4, nos. 3–4 (July–October 1971).

Racki, I. *Povijest hrvata.* Zagreb: Jugoslovenska Akademija Nauka, 1901.

Radio Free Europe Research. Washington, D.C.

Rankovic, Alexander. *Report to the Fifth Congress CPY.* Belgrade: Komunist, 1948.

Remak, Joachim. *Sarajevo: The Story of a Political Murder.* New York: Criterion, 1959.

"Report to Central Committee LCY." *NIN,* no. 1135 (October 1972).

"Report on Rumanian Party Leadership." *Scaitaia,* March 20, 1970.

Rhodes, Clifford. *Authority in a Changing Society.* London: Constable, 1969.

Rigby, T. H. " 'Totalitarianism' and Change in Communist Systems." *Comparative Politics* 4, no. 3 (April 1972).

Rose, Richard. "Dynamic Tendencies in Authority of Regimes." *World Politics* 21, no. 4 (July 1969).

Rothenberg, Gunther. *The Military Border in Croatia, 1522–1741.* Urbana: University of Illinois Press, 1960.

Rothschild, Joseph. *East Central Europe between the Two World Wars.* Seattle: University of Washington Press, 1974.

Rus, Vojin. "Kultura politika." *Nase Teme* 11 (November 1972).

Russett, Bruce M., et al. *World Handbook of Political and Social Indicators.* New Haven: Yale University Press, 1964.

Russinow, Dennison. *The Crisis in Croatia.* New York: American Universities Field Staff, 1972.

———. *Yugoslavia: 1969.* American Universities Field Staff Report, Southeast Europe Series, vol. 16, no. 8.

Rustow, Dankwart A. "Modernization and Comparative Politics: Prospects for Research and Theory." *Comparative Politics* 1, no. 1 (October 1968).

———. "The Study of Elites: Who's Who, When and How?" *World Politics* 18 (July 1966).

Sartori, Giovanni. "The Typology of Party Systems: Proposals for

Improvement." In *Mass Politics in Political Sociology*, ed. Stein Rokkan and Erik Allardt. New York: Free Press, 1970.

Schumpeter, Joseph. *Capitalism, Socialism, and Democracy*. New York: Harper Torchbook, 1967.

Sefer, Berislav. *Dohotak i primanja u Jugoslaviji*. Belgrade: Zavod za Iztrazivanja Trzista, 1972.

Segvic, Petar. "O Politickim tendencijama u Crkvi kod nas." *Nase Teme* 12 (December 1972).

"Selo i proljoprivreda u drustveno-ekonomskom razvoju Jugoslavije." *Sociologija Sela*, special ed., vol. 8, nos. 29–30 (1970).

Siber, Ivan. "Idejna orientacija mladih." *Politicka Misao* 6, no. 4 (1969).

Sisic, H. *Za ciste racune*. Zagreb: RAD, 1970.

Skilling, H. G. "Interest Groups and Communist Politics." *World Politics* 18 (April 1966).

SKJ u uslovima samoupravljanja. Belgrade: Kultura, 1969.

Smelser, Neil J. *The Sociology of Economic Life*. Englewood Cliffs, N.J.: Prentice-Hall, 1963.

Sociologija, special ed., no. 1 (Belgrade, 1972).

Sorel, G. *Reflections on Violence*. London: Collier Books, 1970.

Statistical Yearbook. Belgrade: Savezni Zavod za Statistiku, 1970.

Statisticki bilten: Predstavnicka tela drustveno-politickih zajednica; izbori i sastav. Belgrade: Savezni Zavod za Statistiku, 1964, 1965, 1967, 1969, nos. 266, 372, 491, 590.

Statisticki godisnjak Jugoslavije. Belgrade: Savezni Zavod za Statistiku.

Stinchcombe, A. *Constructing Social Theories*. New York: Harcourt, Brace & World, 1968.

Stojanovic, Svetozar. *Between Ideals and Reality*. Oxford: Oxford University Press, 1973.

———. "Jugoslovensi socijalizam na raskrscu," *Praxis* 9, nos. 3–4 (1972).

Strumthal, Adolf. *Workers' Councils*. Cambridge: Harvard University Press, 1964.

Supek, Rudi. *Humanisticka inteligencija i politika*. Zagreb: Razlog, 1971.

———. "Two Types of Self-Managing Organizations and Technological Process." In *Proceedings of First International Conference on Participation and Self-Management*, vol. 1. Zagreb: Institut za Drustvena Iztrazivanja, 1972.

Suvar, Stipe. "Da li je hrvatska eksploatirana," *Nase Teme* 12 (December 1969).

―――. *Nacije i medjunacijonalni odnosi.* Zagreb: *Nase Teme,* 1970.

Svitak, Ivan. *The Czechoslovak Experiment, 1968–1969.* New York: Columbia University Press, 1971.

Tadic, Dobrosav. "Changes in the Countryside, 1961–1969." *Yugoslav Survey* 10, no. 4 (November 1969).

Tanic, Zivan. *Workers' Councils in India.* Belgrade: Institut Drustvenih Nauka, 1965.

Tito, Yosip Broz. *Report to the Fifth Congress CPY.* Belgrade: Komunist, 1948.

Tomasevich, Jozo. *Peasants, Politics, and Economic Change in Yugoslavia.* Stanford: Stanford University Press, 1956.

―――. *War and Revolution in Yugoslavia: The Chetniks.* Stanford: Stanford University Press, 1975.

Tozi, D., and Petrovic, D. "Politicki odnosi i sastav skupstina drustveno-politickih zajednica." *Socijalizam* 11 (1969).

Trotsky, L. *The History of the Russian Revolution.* 3 vols. Ann Arbor: University of Michigan Press, 1960.

―――. *Revolution 1905.* New York: Pioneer Publisher, 1952.

Tucker, Robert. "Culture, Political Culture, Communism." Mimeographed. Paper presented at the Conference on Communism and Political Culture, Princeton, November 1971.

Vranicki, Predrag. "Socijalizam i nacijonalno pitanje." *Praxis* 5, no. 4 (1968).

Vrcan, Srdjan. "Vjera i politika." *Nase Teme* 12 (December 1972).

Vucinich, Wayne S. "Interwar Yugoslavia." In *Contemporary Yugoslavia,* ed. Wayne S. Vucinich. Berkeley: University of California Press, 1969.

―――. "Nationalism and Communism." In *Contemporary Yugoslavia.*

Ward, Benjamin. "Political Power and Economic Change in Yugoslavia." *American Economic Review* 58, no. 2 (May 1968).

Weber, Max. *Economy and Society.* New York: Bedminster Press, 1968.

Welsh, William A. "The Usefulness of the Apter, Easton, and Spiro Models in the Study of Communist Systems in Eastern Europe." *Newsletter on Comparative Studies of Communism* 5, no. 4 (August 1972).

Wesclowski, W., and Slomczynski, K. *Social Stratification in Polish Cities.* Belgrade: Institut Drustvenih Nauka, 1967.

Wolff, Robert Lee. *The Balkans in Our Time.* New York: Norton, 1956.

"Working Papers of the International Study of Opinion-Makers." 3

vols. Mimeographed. New York: Bureau of Applied Social Research, Columbia University, 1969–71.

Zaninovich, M. George. *The Development of Socialist Yugoslavia.* Baltimore: Johns Hopkins Press, 1968.

Zeitlin, Maurice. *Revolutionary Politics and the Cuban Working Class.* New York: Harper & Row, 1970.

Zvonarevic, Mladen. *Seoska omladina u S. R. Hrvatskoj.* Zagreb: Institut za Drustvena Iztrazivanja, 1971.

Index

Abrams, Peter, 219–20
Administration personnel: in LCY, 7, 88, 91, 92, 95; decrease in, 158
Africa, 54
Age factor: in leadership, 20 and *n*, 42, 47; and dissatisfaction, 26; generational cleavages, 27, 47; and industrialization, 64; and religion, 71; in LCY, 84, 89 and *n*, 121; in YPA, 119; of deputies, 135–36; in self-management, 163
Agriculture. *See* Cooperatives; Land holdings
Albania, 7 *n*, 38, 41; and government representation, 111; and YPA representation, 114–15; and LCY, 121–22
Alexander, King, 36
Algeria, 54, 151
Anti-Fascist Council of National Liberation of Yugoslavia. *See* AVNOJ
Arendt, Hannah, 186
Army: prewar nationalists' power in, 37, 55, 105; prewar status of, 48, 55. *See also* YPA
Asia Minor, 144
Atheism, 69, 70, 74
Austria, 36; social product growth in, 140, 141; rate of development in, 143
Austro-Hungarian Empire, 18, 32, 36, 60, 105, 153. *See also* Austria; Hungary
Authoritarianism, 186–89 passim
AVNOJ (Anti-Fascist Council of National Liberation of Yugoslavia), 124–25

Balkan wars, 35, 60
Banking, 131, 171–72, 179

Barnes, Samuel: *Party Democracy*, 138–39
Barton, Allen: on leadership, 217, 225–27
Belgium, 21
Belgrade: University of, 72; and LCY, 77 *n*, 90; housing problems in, 107, 110; fall of, 124
Bihac, 124
Black, Cyril, 197
Bolsheviks, 1, 102
Bor collective, 156
Bosnia-Herzegovina, 7 *n*, 18, 106; violence in, 35, 68; representation by women in, 44 *n;* early land holdings in, 60; religion in, 74; and government representation, 108–11; and YPA representation, 114; and LCY, 120 and *n;* established as republic, 124; social product growth in, 141; population growth in, 142; per capita income in, 143; illiteracy rates in, 144; and compulsory education, 144–45; employment structure in, 145; development potential in, 146; income distribution in, 202
Britain. *See* England
Broekmeyer, M. J., 150
Brzezinski, Zbigniew, 186
Bulgaria, 36, 38; social product growth in, 140
Bureaucracy, 13, 101 *n;* status of, 48, 55, 56; and LCY, 100; and institutionalization, 189, 190
Burks, R. V., 194

Canada, 21, 23
Castro, Fidel, 52 *n*

Center for Public Opinion: poll on church activities, 71

Centralists, 194

Chetniks, 37–39 passim

China, 41; communism in, 1–3 passim, 13–14

Churchill, Winston, 125

Civil Procedures Act of Serbia, 61

Civil service: prewar, 7, 8, 55; and Federal Assembly, 8; postwar, 56, 113, 136

Civil war, 2, 3, 29; opponents in, 39; losses in, 39; Proletarian Brigades, 42; consequences of, 45–47 passim, 49, 52–53, 57; and nationalism, 105

Cohen, Lenard, 90

Collectivization, 51, 62–63, 66, 95

Colombia, 187

Colonialism, 18

Cominform, 102, 103, 125

Commerce: prewar private sector of, 55

Commune assemblies, 157

Commune committees, 44 n

Commune councils: representation on, 19; and self-management, 153, 156, 158–60 passim, 189

Communist International, 152

Communist Party, later LCY (League of Communists of Yugoslavia): and legitimation, 1–2, 11–14 passim, 29, 36, 139–40, 185–206; variance of, 2–3, 10–16; consequences of break with Soviets, 2, 32, 125–30, 139–40, 198; compared to Chinese communism, 2, 3, 13–14; freedom allowed by, 3–4; membership of, 7, 20, 41–42, 82–83, 89–97, 103–04, 121, 215–17, 225; socioeconomic problems of, 18–28; prewar, 20, 30, 41, 84, 85, 101–02; in villages, 20, 66, 95–96; general programs and policies of, 25, 27, 53, 80, 96, 99–104, 121, 132, 186, 191, 195, 197; rebuilding of, 30; youth organization, 30, 90 and n, 101; consolidates power, 31–32, 41–54, 123–32; and terrorism, 36, 50–51 and n; resistance and civil war, 38–41 passim; peasantry

policy of, 51–52, 198–99; land policies of, 57, 62–68 passim; major contributions of, 73; and NOB, 87–88; development trends in, 97–101; becomes LCY, 103; Central Committee, 103; Sixth Congress, 103; prewar opposition to Serbia of, 105; Eighth and Ninth Congresses, 127; and Croatian dispute, 131–32; develops political and social system, 132–38; furthers economic and social development, 138–47; main characteristics of, 151; social orders of, 188–92; and campaign process, 190–92; norms of, 194; research of leadership of, 207–32. See also Collectivization; Decentralization; Education; Egalitarianism; Federal Assembly; Federal Presidency Industrialization; Institutionalization; Mobilization, social; Modernization; Multinationalism; Partisans; Religion; Self-management; YPA

Communist Youth League. See SKOJ

Consensus, factor of, 22–23 and n

Constituent National Assembly, 30

Cooperatives, agricultural: and self-management, 157

Coordinating Committee, 137

County Conference, 138

Croatia, 7 n, 18, 33, 74; organization of, 32 and n; ultranationalists in, 36 and n; and World War II, 38, 68–69; Croats vs. Serbs, 38 n; current ideology in, 64–66; nationalism in, 73, 171, 194–97 passim, 203–05; student strike in, 80; and prewar army representation, 105–06; and government representation, 108–11; and YPA representation, 114, 116–19 passim; established as republic, 124; disputes with federal authority, 129–32, 138, 147; social product growth in, 141, 142; population growth in, 142; per capita income in, 143; illiteracy rates in, 144; employment structure in, 145; and self-management, 162, 165–68; tourism in, 196; income distribution in, 202

Cuba, 41, 52 n
Cvijic, Jovan, 17 and n
Czechoslovakia, 21, 41, 44 n, 82, 95; and self-management, 175–76

Dahl, Robert, 150–51
Dallin, Alexander, 186
Decentralization: effect of, 21; war related to, 52–53; opposition to, 73, 128; stress on, 100, 126, 129, 131, 158, 188, 198–99; stages of, 158–59
Dedijer, Vladimir: The Battle Stalin Lost, 2 n
Democratization, 11
Development, social, 139–47
Djordjevic, Jovan, 123 n
Durham, Mary Edith, 34

East Germany, 10; social product growth in, 140
Economic and Social Reform, 127, 128, 136
Economic Reform, 126
Economy: institutions of, 8; private sector of, 10, 19, 57–58; development of, 18–19, 138–47; urban vs. rural, 19–20; and postwar middle classes, 58; and LCY, 58–59. See also Commerce; Enterprises; Industrialization; Trade unions; Workers' councils
Education, 19: expansion of universities, 6, 26, 47, 58, 59, 75–80, 127; decentralized, 21; emphasis on, 46; religion related to, 65, 71–72, 74; and urbanization, 66; prewar, 83; as criteria for politics, 83, 90–93 passim, 96, 97, 99, 134–35, 212–15; two-year colleges, 97; compulsory, 144–45; and self-management, 151, 157, 160; and fellowships, 156; workers' levels of, 164–65, 192; related to political protests, 193; as prerogative, 221 n
Egalitarianism: trend toward, 10, 100, 174, 175; and women, 45; reaction to, 172 and n
Engels, Friedrich, 10
England, 21, 22, 199

Enterprises: and self-management, 156–61 passim, 164, 189 n
Ethiopia, 187
Ethnography, prerevolutionary, 17–18

Farmers, private: and LCY, 91, 92; and self-management, 182
Federal Assembly: and representation, 8, 10–12; power of, 23 n, 132–38 passim, 147–48; women in, 44 n; statistics on deputies in, 134–36
Federal Executive Council. See SIV
Federal Presidency: latent power of, 23 n, 107–08, 137; age factor of, 135; policies of, 190, 191 and n
Ferdinand, Archduke, 35
Five-Year Plan, 130
Fourier, François, 152
France, 21, 22, 112–13; self-management in, 179
Freedom and Information Center: freedom of press study, 3–4
Friedrich, Carl J., 186, 187

Gavrilo, Patriarch, 68
Germany: and World War II relations with Yugoslavia, 29–30, 37–39, 48–49. See also East Germany; West Germany
Gramsci, Antonio: Soviets in Italy, 153 n
Greece: social product growth in, 140
Guerrilla warfare, 2, 14; areas of, 31, 32, 35; consequences of, 42

Hammel, Eugene E., 78
Hitler-Stalin Pact, 30
Horvat, Branko, 96–97, 170; An Essay on Yugoslav Society, 150
Hungary, 7 n, 38, 56, 69, 74, 186; and representation as minority group, 111, 114, 121–22; social product growth in, 140; self-management in, 175, 177
Huntington, Samuel, 197

IMRO (Internal Macedonian Revolutionary Organization), 36
India, 151, 187

Industrialization: as sociopolitical factor, 5, 7, 10–12 passim, 43, 192; private sector of, 23, 55; and conflicts, 24; affects rural areas, 57, 64, 67, 74; age factor in, 64; and urban problems, 67; and LCY, 83. *See also* Trade unions; Workers' councils

Institute of Social Science: self-management study, 160–63; research on leadership, 207–32

Institutionalization: of power factors, 7, 8, 12; of multinationality, 22, 105–48; legitimacy related to, 189, 190, 192

Intelligentsia: liberal, 3; technical, 5–6, 12, 77–80, 100, 131–32, 140; humanistic, 5–6; general, 7; in LCY, 7, 91–93, 99, 101, 215; prerevolutionary, 18, 29; and unemployment, 26; in early wars, 35; postwar, 56, 59, 73; traditional, 132; and self-management, 160, 175; and political protest, 193–95 passim

Interest groups, 8 and *n*

Internal Macedonian Revolutionary Organization. *See* IMRO

International Study of Opinion Makers: research on leadership, 135, 207–32

Islam, 18, 38 *n*

Italy, 21, 22, 32 *n*, 103, 124; relations with Yugoslavia, 36 and *n*, 38–39; communist party in, 53; officialdom in, 112–13; socialist party in, 139; rate of development in, 143; self-management in, 179

Jajce, 125

Japan, 187; officialdom in, 112–13; economic growth in, 126, 140, 141

Jews, 40, 69, 70

Johnson, Chalmers: *Peasant Nationalism and Communist Power*, 13–14

Johnson, Ross: *Transformation of Communist Ideology*, 13

Kadushin, Charles, 219–20

Kochanek, Stanley A.: on revolution, 200

Korac, Miladin, 159

Kosova, 7 *n*, 112; land holdings in, 60; religion in, 71; and government representation, 108–10; social product growth in, 141; population growth in, 142; per capita income in, 143; illiteracy rates in, 144; compulsory education in, 144–45; employment structure in, 145; unemployment in, 146; development potential in, 146; income distribution in, 202

Land holdings: limitations of, 10; of peasantry, 43 *n*, 51, 57, 60–63; communist policy for, 57, 62–68 passim; prewar, 60–63; private, 67

LCAF (League of Communists of the Armed Forces). *See* YPA, institutionalization

LCY (League of Communists of Yugoslavia). *See* Communist Party

Leadership: and localism, 20; age factor of, 20 and *n*, 42, 47; and egalitarianism, 172 and *n;* research on, 207–32

League of Communists of the Armed Forces. *See* YPA, institutionalization

League of Communists of Yugoslavia. *See* Communist Party

Legislature. *See* Federal Assembly

Legitimation: prerevolutionary concepts of, 17–18; and policy formation, 189–90; and campaign process, 190–91; and institutionalization of self-management, 192–93; challenges to, 193–97; and authority bases, 197–206. *See also* Communist Party, legitimation

Lenin, V. I., 10; *The State and the Revolution*, 152

Liberalism, 133, 189

Liberation: wars of, 2, 31, 37, 40–41; SUBNOR, 8; ideology of, 14; NOB war, 87, 88, 89 *n*

Linz, Juan: on authoritarianism, 187, 188

Lipset, Seymour Martin, 129

Ljubljana: LCY action in, 77 *n*

Localism, 20, 21, 25, 36

Macedonia, 7 *n*, 64; guerrilla warfare in, 35; revolutionaries in, 36; representation by women in, 44 *n;* early land holdings in, 60, 61; and government representation, 108–11; and YPA representation, 114, 116; and LCY, 121; social product growth, 141; per capita income in, 143; illiteracy rates in, 144; employment structure in, 145; unemployment in, 146; income distribution in, 202

Managers: in LCY, 91–93, 99; in workers' councils, 148 *n*, 155–56; and self-management, 160–61, 175

Marseilles, 36

Marx, Karl, 10, 152

Marxism, 6, 11, 73, 75, 132, 179, 186, 194, 200

Massacres, 38, 45, 46, 68

Mass media: freedom of, 3–4; postwar influences on, 6, 58; and urbanization, 19; and behavior patterns, 27; and egalitarianism, 172 and *n*

Matica Hrvatska, 8 *n*

Middle class: status of, 11, 13; as influencing factor, 26, 46–48 passim; in postwar economy, 58; and self-management, 183

Mihailovic, Draza, 38–39

Milenkovich, Deborah, 194

Military. *See* Army; YPA

Mobilization, social: strata in, 2, 4–9 passim, 13; self-management approach to, 14–15; assets and problems of, 14, 42–49, 55–80 passim; influences on, 15; present level of development in, 18–19; urban vs. rural, 19–20, 57–58, 64–66; effects of violence and war on, 29–52; and LCY, 82–104 passim

Modernization: assets and problems of, 4, 11–12, 55–59 passim, 192; and LCY, 58–59, 83, 96, 121, 127; opposition to, 144–45

Montenegro, 7 *n*, 17, 33, 34; guerrilla warfare in, 32, 36; and World War I, 35–36; and prewar army representation, 37, 105, 106; and World War II,

38; representation by women in, 44 *n;* early land holdings in, 60, 62; religion in, 70, 71; and government representation, 108–11; and YPA representation, 113–16, 118; and LCY, 120, 121; social product growth in, 141; population growth in, 142; per capita income in, 143; illiteracy rates in, 144; employment structure in, 145; income distribution in, 202

Moore, Barrington: *Terror and Progress in the USSR*, 15; *The Origins of Dictatorship and Democracy*, 15

Morse, Nancy C.: "The Function and Meaning of Work," 165–66

Moslem Slavs, 18, 33, 55, 61, 69, 74; collaboration by, 68; in postwar era, 70, 72; government representation by, 106, 111; YPA representation by, 114–16; and LCY, 121

Mufti, 68

Multinationalism, 21, 22; prewar representation problems of, 105–07; postwar institutionalization of, 107–48

Natality, 19

National Committees of Liberation (NOOs), 123–25, 153

Nationalism: ethnic, 3, 5, 6, 21–22, 45, 55, 73; linguistic, 6; traditional, 6, 48–49, 56, 58, 73; of peasantry, 14 and *n;* prerevolutionary, 17–18; romantic, 35; organized, 36 and *n*, 38–39; expansionists, 40; and republics, 73, 159, 171, 194–97 passim, 203–05; and civil war, 105; and LCY, 133; and modernization, 144; demands of, 147, 159; and workers, 197. *See also* Multinationalism

Nazism. *See* Germany

NOB. *See* Liberation

NOOs. *See* National Committees of Liberation

North Vietnam, 52 *n*

Orders, social-political: types of, 188–90

Organic Law, 126

Orthodox Church, 18, 33, 55, 68; Serbian, 7, 55, 69; Macedonian, 69; in postwar era, 69–70, 72

Pantic, Dragan, 217
Particularism, 21, 25, 36, 58, 189 and n, 190, 192
Partisans, 152; and peasantry, 4, 31–32, 40–41; and nationalism, 14 n; aims of, 31; and communism, 38–39, 49, 87–88, 90, 95, 102–03, 120, 134–35, 140, 210–11; role of women in, 44–45; veteran solidarity of, 47; and bureaucracy, 56; and YPA, 56–57, 113–16, 119; and religion, 68; and commune councils, 153. See also Civil war
Pavelic, Ante, 36 n
Peasantry: social status of, 4–5, 19; and nationalism, 13–14; and social mobility, 14, 42–43, 57, 59, 67; prerevolutionary, 29; and industry, 43; land holdings of, 43 n, 51, 57, 60–63; and communism, 51–52, 93–96, 152, 198–99; and religion, 55–56; and collectivization, 62–63; and modernization, 83–84; and self-management, 160. See also Partisans
Pensioners: and LCY, 84, 87, 91, 95, 122 and n; and self-management, 182
Poetry, epic: influence of, 33–34
Poland, 10, 38, 56, 69, 82, 186; social product growth in, 140; self-management in, 175, 177
Police: prerevolutionary, 7, 30; and terrorists, 36; status of, 48; punitive action for, 128–29
Praxis, 193
Press: freedom of, 3–4
Protestantism, 69
Provinces. See Kosova; Vojvodina
Purges, 50, 128

Radic, Stepan, 36
Rand Corporation, 100
Rankovic, Alexander, 115, 128–29
Religion: prewar policies of, 18, 55; in

postwar era, 55–56; education related to, 65, 71–72, 74; communist policies toward, 68–75; and urbanization, 70, 74; and age factor, 71; and modernization, 144. See also Atheism; Jews; Moslem Slavs; Orthodox Church; Protestantism; Roman Catholicism
Representation: and peasantry, 19; and commune councils, 19; multinationality of, 22, 107–23; by women, 44 and n; and trade unions, 133, 176; and workers' councils, 148 n; in self-managing institutions, 157; geographic, 192
Republics: education in, 21; legislatures in, 147–48; and decentralization, 158–59; and nationalism, 159, 195–97; workers' representation in, 160; interdependence of, 195–96; income distribution in, 201–02. See also Bosnia-Herzegovina; Croatia; Macedonia; Montenegro; Serbia; Slovenia
Resistance: veteran figures, 87. See also Civil war; Guerrilla warfare
Retirement. See Pensioners
Revolution, Serbian, 34
Roman Catholicism, 18, 33, 55, 60; in postwar era, 65, 69–70, 72–75; and collaboration, 68, 69; and Partisans, 68
Rose, Richard, 12; "Dynamic Tendencies in Authority of Regimes," 197–200 passim
Rumania: social product growth in, 140
Rustow, Dankwart: on modernization, 200–01

Sarajevo, 35; University of, 72
Saric, Archbishop, 68
Savez Kommunisticke Omladine Jugoslavije. See SKOJ
Savezno Izvrsno Vece. See SIV
Schumpeter, Joseph: on social change, 203, 205
Security personnel: and LCY, 91–93 passim
Sefer, Berislav, 159–60
Self-management: as factor, 14–15, 188,

192–93, 195, 198–99; components of, 151–52; background of, 152–56; norms of, 154 *n;* areas of, 156–60; and decentralization, 158; survey data on, 160–75; approaches to, 175–78; prospects for, 178–84; nonparticipants in, 182. *See also* Enterprise; Trade unions; Workers' councils

Serbia, 7 *n,* 17, 18, 32 *n;* and religion, 7; violence in, 32–36 passim; and World War I, 35–36; prewar domination by, 37, 55, 105–07; and World War II, 38; Serbs vs. Croats, 38 *n;* and Chetniks, 38–39; factories in, 48; early land holdings in, 60–62; nationalism in, 75 *n,* 195–97; and government representation, 107–12, 116–17, 119; and YPA, 113–14; and LCY, 121; established as republic, 124; social product growth in, 141; population growth, 142; per capita income in, 143; illiteracy rates in, 144; employment rates in, 145; self-management in, 159; income distribution in, 202

Serfs, 60–61

Services, social: and self-management, 156, 157

SIV (Federal Executive Council, Savezno Izrsno Vece), 108–10, 132–33, 137, 138

SKOJ (Communist Youth League, Kommunisticke Omladine Jugoslavije): prewar, 30, 90 and *n,* 101

Slavonia, 62

Slovakians, 7 *n*

Slovenia, 7 *n,* 37; representation by women in, 44 *n;* early land holdings in, 60; and new social order, 64; religion in, 68, 70, 71, 74; and prewar army representation, 105, 106; and government representation, 108–11; and YPA, 114, 116, 118; and LCY, 121; established as republic, 124; social product growth in, 141, 142; population growth in, 142; per capita income in, 143; illiteracy rates in, 144; em-

ployment structure in, 145; unemployment in, 146; income survey in, 172–75; nationalism in, 195, 196; income distribution in, 202

Socialist Alliance, 8, 98, 103, 160

South Slavs, 32, 33, 106

Soviet Union, 2, 4, 11, 38, 149, 187, 194

Spain, 21, 187

Stalin, Joseph, 153, 194; and Tito, 43, 50; *History of the Communist Party (Bolshevik) U.S.S.R.,* 152

State Secretariat for National Defense, 116–19

Stepinac, Archbishop, 68, 69

Stojanovic, Svetozar, 101 *n,* 220; *Between Ideals and Reality,* 150

SUBNOR (Veterans of the War of Liberation). *See* Liberation

Supek, Rudi, 101 *n,* 162

Sweden, 199

Sweezy, Paul, 10

Switzerland, 147, 199

Tadic, Ljubo, 101 *n*

Technology, 58, 76, 101 *n,* 194; and LCY, 12, 77, 100–01, 133

Terrorism, 36, 50–51

Tito, Josip Broz, 13, 107, 125; rebuilds communist party, 30; and Stalin, 43, 50; executive positions of, 116, 127; and Rankovic, 128–29; and Croatian dispute, 131; policies of, 132; charisma of, 189–91 passim

Totalitarianism, 186, 188

Tourism, 3, 196 and *n*

Trade unions, 19, 103; as institutions, 8, 12; activization of, 23, 25, 98, 146–47, 164, 172; influence of, 132; representation in, 133, 176, 177; and self-management, 160, 176–77

Tripalo, Mika: on LCY membership, 90, 92

Trotsky, Leon, 15

Tucker, Robert, 202–03

Tunisia, 54

Turkish Empire, 60, 153; and Balkan wars, 32–35 passim, 38 *n,* 48

Unemployed: and representation, 19; and intelligentsia, 26; and LCY, 91, 92

United States, 15, 177; social cleavages in, 23, 25; officialdom in, 112; job categories in, 161, 180 *n*

Urbanization: postwar, 19–20, 55–58, 63–67, 96; and religion, 70, 74

Ustasi, 36 and *n*, 38, 40

Uzice, 152

Veterans of the War of Liberation. *See* Liberation, SUBNOR

Vojvodina, 7 *n*, 112, 196; guerrilla warfare in, 32; land holdings in, 60, 62, 63; religion in, 69; and government representation, 108–10; social product growth in, 141; population growth in, 142; per capita income in, 143; illiteracy rates in, 144; employment structure in, 145; income distribution in, 202

Weiss, Robert S.: "The Function and Meaning of Work," 165–66

West Germany: social product growth in, 140, 141

White-collar employees: and LCY, 94–95, 97, 99; and workers' councils, 148 *n*, 160–61

Women: and representation, 19, 44 *n;* changing status of, 26–27, 44–45, 49–50, 56, 77–79; in rural areas, 57, 64; and LCY, 91, 92, 99; and illiteracy, 144; and self-management, 162, 182

Workers: and LCY, 7, 91–99 passim, 102, 132; prewar, 29; and religion, 56; in new social order, 59, 64; and age factor, 64; and modernization, 83;

from undeveloped areas, 147; educational level of, 164–65, 192; and nationalism, 197. *See also* Trade unions; White-collar employees; Workers' councils

Workers' councils: and self-management, 2, 6, 8, 10, 12, 13, 23–24, 96, 151, 154–84 passim, 189, 192; representation in, 133, 148 *n*, 160–61, 176

Workers' Opposition (Russia), 152–53, 178

World War I: and Yugoslavia, 35

World War II: and Yugoslavia, 37–41; affects religion, 55; affects party membership, 102

YPA (Yugoslav Peoples' Army): institutionalization of, 7, 8, 12, 57; and LCY, 91; multinationalism of, 113–20; aids in punitive political action, 128

Yugoslavia: establishment and reestablishment of, 18; between world wars, 29–37; and World War II, 30, 37–41; violence in, 32–37; and World War I, 35; government in exile, 39, 125; postrevolutionary problems in, 48–54; early land categories in, 60; social product growth in, 140–41; population growth in, 142; rate of development in, 143; illiteracy rate in, 144; unemployment in, 146; income distribution in, 202. *See also* Bosnia-Herzegovina; Croatia; Communist Party; Kosova; Macedonia; Montenegro; Serbia; Slovenia; Vojvodina

Zagreb, 8 *n*, 65, 102, 168; University of, 72, 73, 161

Zvouarevic, Mladen, 64